THE REVELS PLAYS

Former general editors
Clifford Leech
F. David Hoeniger
E. A. J. Honigmann
J. R. Mulryne
Eugene M. Waith

General editors
David Bevington, Richard Dutton, Alison Findlay,
Helen Ostovich, and Martin White

ALL FOOLS

Manchester University Press

THE REVELS PLAYS

ANON *Thomas of Woodstock
or King Richard the Second, Part One*

BEAUMONT *The Knight of the Burning Pestle*

BEAUMONT AND FLETCHER *A King and No King
The Maid's Tragedy   Philaster, or Love Lies a-Bleeding*

CHAPMAN *Bussy d'Ambois   An Humorous Day's Mirth*

CHAPMAN, JONSON, MARSTON *Eastward Ho*

DEKKER *The Shoemaker's Holiday*

FORD *Love's Sacrifice   The Lady's Trial*

HEYWOOD *The First and Second Parts of King Edward IV*

JONSON *The Alchemist   The Devil Is an Ass
Epicene, or The Silent Woman   Every Man In His Humour
Every Man Out of His Humour   The Magnetic Lady
The New Inn   Poetaster   Sejanus: His Fall
The Staple of News   Volpone*

LYLY *Campaspe* and *Sappho and Phao   Endymion
Galatea* and *Midas   Love's Metamorphosis
Mother Bombie   The Woman in the Moon*

MARLOWE *Doctor Faustus   Edward the Second
The Jew of Malta   Tamburlaine the Great*

MARSTON *Antonio and Mellida
Antonio's Revenge   The Malcontent*

MASSINGER *The Roman Actor*

MIDDLETON *A Game at Chess   Michaelmas Term*

MIDDLETON *A Trick to Catch the Old One*

MIDDLETON AND DEKKER *The Roaring Girl*

MUNDAY AND OTHERS *Sir Thomas More*

PEELE *The Troublesome Reign of John, King of England*

WEBSTER *The Duchess of Malfi*

THE REVELS PLAYS

ALL FOOLS

GEORGE CHAPMAN

edited by Charles Edelman

MANCHESTER
UNIVERSITY PRESS

Introduction, critical apparatus, etc.
© Charles Edelman 2018

The right of Charles Edelman to be identified as the editor of this work has been asserted by him in accordance with the Copyright, Designs and Patents Act 1988.

This edition published by Manchester University Press
Oxford Road, Manchester M13 9PL

www.manchesteruniversitypress.co.uk

British Library Cataloguing-in-Publication Data
A catalogue record for this book is available from the British Library

ISBN 978 0 7190 8925 1 hardback
ISBN 978 1 5261 6399 8 paperback

First published 2018
Paperback published 2022

The publisher has no responsibility for the persistence or accuracy of URLs for any external or third-party internet websites referred to in this book, and does not guarantee that any content on such websites is, or will remain, accurate or appropriate.

Typeset
by Toppan Best-set Premedia Limited

for Alison Findlay

Contents

LIST OF ILLUSTRATIONS	viii
GENERAL EDITORS' PREFACE	ix
ACKNOWLEDGEMENTS	xii
EDITIONS, REFERENCES, ABBREVIATIONS	xiii
Editions and textual studies collated, in chronological order	xiii
Editions of primary works cited in commentary	xiii
Secondary works cited in commentary	xviii
Abbreviations: notes and collation	xix
INTRODUCTION	1
Chapman at the Rose, 1598–99	1
From the Rose to Blackfriars	4
Terence goes to London: the sources of *All Fools*	5
The primary plot: Terence transmogrified	11
Love and marriage in Terence and Chapman	19
The secondary plot: adultery for fun and profit	21
Ovid and the art of adultery	25
Cuckoldry as a spectator sport	28
Divorce English style	36
''Tis at the Half Moon Tavern'	39
In praise of the horn	44
The text	48
ALL FOOLS	55
APPENDIX	
The Walsingham Sonnet	187
INDEX	197

Illustrations

1 Title page, 1605 Quarto, courtesy of the Folger
 Shakespeare Library 56
2 Sonnet addressed to Sir Thomas Walsingham, courtesy
 of the John Henry Wrenn Library, Harry Ransom Center,
 University of Texas at Austin 186

General Editors' Preface

Clifford Leech conceived of the Revels Plays as a series in the mid-1950s, modelling the project on the New Arden Shakespeare. The aim, as he wrote in 1958, was 'to apply to Shakespeare's predecessors, contemporaries, and successors the methods that are now used in Shakespeare's editing'. The plays chosen were to include well-known works from the early Tudor period to about 1700, as well as others less familiar but of literary and theatrical merit. 'The plays included', Leech wrote, 'should be such as to deserve and indeed demand performance'. We owe it to Clifford Leech that the idea became reality. He set the high standards of the series, ensuring that editors of individual volumes produced work of lasting merit, equally useful for teachers and students, theatre directors and actors. Clifford Leech remained General Editor until 1971, and was succeeded by F. David Hoeniger, who retired in 1985.

Ever since then, the Revels Plays have been under the direction of four or five general editors: initially David Bevington, E. A. J. Honigmann, J. R. Mulryne, and E. M. Waith. E. A. J. Honigmann retired in 2000 and was succeeded by Richard Dutton. E. M. Waith retired in 2003 and was succeeded by Alison Findlay and Helen Ostovich. J. R. Mulryne retired in 2010. Published originally by Methuen, the series is now published by the Manchester University Press, embodying essentially the same format, scholarly character, and high editorial standards of the series as first conceived. The series now concentrates on plays from the period 1558–1642. Some slight changes have been made: for example, starting in 1996 each index lists proper names and topics in the introduction and commentary, whereas earlier indexes focused only on words and phrases for which the commentary provided a gloss. Notes to the introduction are now placed together at the end, not at the foot of, the page. Collation and commentary notes continue, however, to appear on the relevant pages.

The introduction to each Revels play undertakes to offer, among other matters, a critical appraisal of the play's significant themes and images, its poetic and verbal fascinations, its historical context, its characteristics as a piece for the theatre, and its uses of the stage for which it was designed. Stage history is an important part of the story. In addition, the introduction presents as lucidly as possible the criteria for choice of copy-text and the editorial methods employed in presenting the play to a modern reader. The introduction also considers the play's date and, where relevant, its sources, together with its place in the work of the author and in the theatre of its time. If the play is by an author not previously represented in the series, a brief biography is provided.

The text of each Revels play, in accordance with established practice in the series, is edited afresh from the original text of best authority (in a few instances, texts), in modern spelling and punctuation and with speech headings that are consistent throughout. Elisions in the original are also silently regularised, except where metre would be affected by the change. Emendations, as distinguished from modernized spellings and punctuation, are introduced only in instances where error is patent or at least very probable, and where the corrected reading is persuasive. Act divisions are given only if they appear in the original, or if the structure of the play clearly points to them. Those act and scene divisions not in the original are provided in small type. Square brackets are also used for any other additions to, or changes in, the stage directions of the original.

Rather than provide a comprehensive and historical variorum collation, Revels Plays editions focus on those variants which require the critical attention of serious textual students. All departures of substance from the copy-text are listed, including any significant relineation and those changes in punctuation which involve to any degree a decision between alternative interpretations. The collation notes do not include such accidentals as turned letters or changes in the font. Additions to stage directions are not noted in the collations, since those additions are already made clear by the use of brackets. On the other hand, press corrections in the copy-text are duly collated, as based on a careful consultation of as many copies of the original edition or editions as are needed to ensure that the printing history of those originals is accurately reported. Of later emendations of the text by subsequent editors, only those are reported which still deserve attention as alternative readings.

One of the hallmarks of the Revels Plays is the thoroughness of their annotations. Besides explaining the meanings of difficult words and passages, the annotations provide commentary on customs or usage, on the text, on stage business—indeed, on anything that can be pertinent and helpful. On occasion, when long notes are required and are too lengthy to fit comfortably at the foot of the page below the text, they are printed at the end of the complete text.

Appendices are used to present any commendatory poems on the dramatist and play in question, documents about the play's reception and contemporary history, classical sources, casting analyses, music, and any other relevant material.

Each volume contains an index to the commentary, in which particular attention is drawn to meanings for words not listed in the *OED*, and (starting in 1996, as indicated above) an indexing of proper names and topics in the introduction and commentary.

Our hope is that plays edited in this fashion will promote further scholarly and theatrical investigation of one of the richest periods in theatrical history.

DAVID BEVINGTON
RICHARD DUTTON
ALISON FINDLAY
HELEN OSTOVICH
MARTIN WHITE

Acknowledgements

If readers enjoy this edition, much of the credit belongs with those who have offered their expert advice and friendly encouragement. Special thanks go to David Bevington, Alison Findlay, Andrew Gurr, Yasmin Haskell, Richard Oram, Helen Ostovich, and Andrew Wilson. As always, Lesley Edelman provided support in innumerable ways.

Editions, References, Abbreviations

EDITIONS AND TEXTUAL STUDIES COLLATED, IN CHRONOLOGICAL ORDER

Q	*All Fools, A Comedy, Presented at the Black Friars, and lately before his Majesty. Written by George Chapman*, London, Printed for Thomas Thorpe. 1605.
Reed	Isaac Reed, ed., *A Select Collection of Old Plays*, v. 4 (London: Dodsley, 1780).
Collier	John Payne Collier, ed., *A Select Collection of Old Plays*, new ed., v. 4 (London: Septimus Prowett, 1825).
Shepherd	R. H. Shepherd, ed., *The Works of George Chapman: Plays* (London: Chatto and Windus, 1874).
Deighton	K. Deighton, *The Old Dramatists: Conjectural Readings* (Westminster: A. Constable, 1896).
Parrott[1]	Thomas Marc Parrott, ed., *All Fooles and The Gentleman Usher* (Boston: D. C. Heath, 1907).
Parrott[2]	Thomas Marc Parrott, ed., *The Plays of George Chapman: The Comedies*, London, 1914, reprint ed., 2 v. sequentially paginated (New York: Russell & Russell, 1961). Unless otherwise noted, references to Parrott in the critical commentary are to this edition.
Loane	George G. Loane, 'More Notes on Chapman's Plays', *Modern Language Review* 38 (1943): 341–6.
Yamada	'Bibliographical Studies of Chapman's *All Fools*', *Shakespeare Studies* (Tokyo) 3 (1964): 73–99.
Manley	Frank Manley, ed., *All Fools*, Regents Renaissance Drama (London: Edward Arnold, 1968).
Evans	G. Blakemore Evans, ed., *All Fooles*, in *The Plays of George Chapman: The Comedies*, gen. ed. Allan Holaday (Urbana: University of Illinois, 1970).
Hudston	Jonathan Hudston, ed., *All Fooles*, in *George Chapman: Plays and Poems* (Harmondsworth: Penguin, 1998).

EDITIONS OF PRIMARY WORKS CITED IN COMMENTARY

The spelling of all early modern texts quoted in the Introduction and Commentary is silently modernised when no modern-spelling edition is available.

Alemán	Mateo Alemán, *The Rogue, or The Life of Guzman de Alfarache* (London, 1623).
Aesop	*Aesop's Fables* (London: Dent, 1913).
Arcaeus	*A Most Excellent and Compendious Method of Curing Wounds* (London, 1588).

xiv   EDITIONS, REFERENCES, ABBREVIATIONS

Aristophanes — *Acharnians*, tr. Douglass Parker (Ann Arbor: University of Michigan, 1961).
Aristotle — *Complete Works*, ed. Jonathan Barnes, 2 v., sequentially paginated (Princeton University Press, 1984).
The Problems of Aristotle with other Philosophers and Physicians (Edinburgh, 1595).
Baley — *Brief Discourse of Certain Baths or Medicinal Waters in the County of Warwick* (London, 1587).
Beaumont — *The Knight of the Burning Pestle*, ed. Sheldon P. Zitner (Manchester University Press, 1984).
The Woman Hater, Fredson Bowers, ed., *The Dramatic Works in the Beaumont and Fletcher Canon*, v. 1 (Cambridge University Press, 1966).
Bible — *The Geneva Bible* (Geneva, 1560).
Boorde — *The Breviary of Health* (London, 1552).
Bugbears — *Bugbears: A Modernized Edition*, ed. James D. Clark (New York: Garland, 1979).
Burton — *Anatomy of Melancholy*, ed. Holbrook Jackson (New York: New York Review Books, 2001).
Camden — *Britain* (London, 1610).
Remains (London, 1605).
Castiglione — *Il Cortegiano*, ed. Ettore Bonora (Milan: Mursia, 1976), see also Hoby.
Chapman — *Chapman's Homer: The Iliad, the Odyssey and the Lesser Homerica*, ed. Allardyce Nicoll (London: Routledge & Kegan Paul, 1957).
The Conspiracy and Tragedy of Charles Duke of Byron, ed. John Margeson (Manchester University Press, 1988).
The Divine Poem of Musaeus (London, 1616).
Eastward Ho, ed. R.W. Van Fossen (Manchester University Press, 1979).
The Widow's Tears, ed. Akihiro Yamada (Manchester University Press, 1975).
All other plays: Thomas Marc Parrott, ed., *The Plays of George Chapman: The Comedies* (reprint ed., 2 v. sequentially paginated (New York: Russell & Russell, 1961).
Chaucer — *The Riverside Chaucer*, 3rd ed., gen. ed. Larry D. Benson (Oxford University Press, 1987).
Cicero — *De Officiis*, tr. Walter Miller (London, 1913).
Tusculan Disputations, tr. J. E. King (London: Heinemann, 1927).
Clowes — *A Short and Profitable Treatise Touching the Cure of the Disease called Morbus Gallicus* (London, 1597).
Cooke — *Greene's Tu Quoque, or the City Gallant*, ed. Alan J. Berman (New York: Garland, 1984).
Cowell — *The Interpreter* (Cambridge, 1607).
Davies — *The Poems of Sir John Davies*, ed. Robert Krueger (Oxford: Clarendon, 1975).
Dekker — *Non-Dramatic Works*, ed. A. B. Grosart, 5 v. (New York: Russell & Russell, 1963).

EDITIONS, REFERENCES, ABBREVIATIONS　　　xv

	Dramatic Works of Thomas Dekker, ed. Fredson Bowers, 4 v. (Cambridge University Press, 1953–61).
Dodoens	*A New Herbal, or History of Plants* (Antwerp, 1578).
Donne	*The Elegies, the Songs and Sonnets*, ed. Helen Gardner (Oxford: Clarendon, 1965).
Erasmus	*Adages*, tr. R. A. B. Mynors, *Collected Works*, v. 33–4 (Toronto University Press, 1991–2).
	Colloquies, tr. Craig R. Thompson, *Collected Works*, v. 39 (Toronto University Press, 1997).
	Correspondence, tr. R. A. B. Mynors, *Collected Works*, v. 1 (Toronto University Press, 1988).
	The Praise of Folly, tr. Clarence H. Miller (New Haven: Yale University Press, 1979).
Estienne	*A World of Wonders* (London, 1607).
Famous History	*The Famous History of the Life and Death of Captain Thomas Stukeley*, ed. Charles Edelman, *The Stukeley Plays* (Manchester University Press, 2005).
Ficino	*Marsilio Ficino's Commentary on Plato's Symposium*, tr. Sears Reynolds Jayne (Columbia: University of Missouri, 1944).
Fitzherbert	*The Book of Husbandry* (London, 1540).
Fletcher & Massinger	*The Spanish Curate*, Fredson Bowers, ed., *Dramatic Works in the Beaumont and Fletcher Canon*, v. 10 (Cambridge University Press, 1996).
Florio	*Florio's Second Fruits* (London, 1591).
	A World of Words (London, 1598).
Foxe	*Acts and Monuments* (London, 1583).
Gale	*Enchiridion of Chirurgerie* (London, 1563).
Gerard	*The Herbal or General History of Plants* (London, 1633).
Grahame	*The Anatomy of Humours* (Edinburgh, 1609).
Greene	*The Life and Complete Works in Prose and Verse of Robert Greene*, ed. Alexander B. Grosart, 15 v. (New York: Russell & Russell, 1964).
Guicciardini	*The History*, tr. Geoffrey Fenton (London, 1579).
Harrison	*Harrison's Description of England in Shakspere's Youth*, ed. F. J. Furnivall (London, 1877).
Harvey	*Pierce's Supererogation* (London, 1593).
Heminge	*The Plays and Poems of William Heminge*, ed. Carol A. Morley (Madison: Fairleigh Dickinson University Press, 2006).
Heresbach	*Four Books of Husbandry* (London, 1577).
Herodotus	*The Histories*, tr. Aubrey De Sélincourt (London: Penguin, 1996).
Herrick	*Poetical Works*, ed. F. W. Moorman (Oxford University Press, 1921).
Hesiod	*The Homeric Hymns and Homerica*, tr. Hugh G. Evelyn-White (London: Heinemann, 1914).
Heylyn	*Cosmography* (London, 1652).
Heywood	*England's Elizabeth: Her Life and Troubles, During her Minority from the Cradle to the Crown* (London, 1631).
Hoby	*The Book of the Courtier*, *The Tudor Translations*, v. 23 (London: David Nutt, 1900).

Holland	*The Philosophy Commonly Called the Morals, written by the Learned Philosopher Plutarch of Chaeronea* (London, 1603)
Horace	*The Satires of Horace and Persius*, tr. Niall Rudd (Harmondsworth: Penguin, 1973).
Isidore of Seville	*Etymologies*, tr. Stephen A. Barney et al. (Cambridge University Press, 2006).
Jonson	*The Cambridge Edition of the Complete Works of Ben Jonson*, gen. ed. David Bevington, Martin Butler, Ian Donaldson, 7 v. (Cambridge University Press, 2012).
	Eastward Ho, see Chapman.
Juvenal	*The Sixteen Satires*, tr. Peter Green (Harmondsworth: Penguin, 1967).
Kyd	*The Spanish Tragedy*, ed. J. R. Mulryne (London: A & C Black, 1989).
La Primaudaye	*The French Academy* (London, 1618).
Lording	*Ram Alley*, ed. Peter Corbin & Douglas Sedge (Nottingham University Press, 1981).
Lucian	*Works*, 8 v., tr. A. M. Harmon et al. (London: Heinemann, 1913–67).
Lucretius	*The Nature of Things*, tr. A. E. Stallings (London: Penguin, 2007).
Lydgate	*The Minor Poems*, ed. H. B. McCracken, 2 v. (Oxford University Press, 1962).
Lyly	*Euphues: The Anatomy of Wit* and *Euphues and his England*, ed. Leah Scragg (Manchester University Press, 2003).
	Mother Bombie, ed. William Tydeman, *Four Tudor Comedies* (Harmondsworth: Penguin, 1984).
Machiavelli	*Florentine History* (London, 1595).
Manningham	*The Diary of John Manningham of the Middle Temple*, ed. Robert Parker Sorlien (Hanover, NH: University Press of New England, 1976).
Marbury	*The Marriage Between Wit and Wisdom*, ed. Trevor N. S. Lennam (London: Malone Society, 1971).
Marlowe	*Dido, Queen of Carthage*, ed. H. J. Oliver (Cambridge, MA: Harvard University Press, 1968).
	Edward II, ed. Charles R. Forker (Manchester University Press, 1994).
	The Jew of Malta, ed. N. W. Bawcutt (Manchester University Press, 1978).
	Poems, ed. Millar Maclure (London; Methuen, 1968).
Marston	*Antonio and Mellida*, ed. W. Reavley Gair (Manchester University Press, 2004).
	Antonio's Revenge, ed. W. Reavley Gair (Manchester University Press, 1978).
	Eastward Ho, see Chapman.
	The Malcontent, ed. George K. Hunter (Manchester University Press, 1975).
	Poems, ed. Arnold Davenport (Liverpool University Press, 1961).
Middleton	*Collected Works*, gen. ed. Gary Taylor and John Lavagnino (Oxford University Press, 2007).

	The Family of Love [attrib.], ed. Simon Shepherd (Nottingham University Press, 1979).
Morley	*A Plain and Easy Introduction to Practical Music* (London, 1597).
Munday	*John a Kent and John a Cumber*, ed. Muriel St. Clare Byrne (London: Malone Society, 1923).
Nashe	*The Works of Thomas Nashe*, ed. R. B. McKerrow, 5 v. (London: Sidgwick & Jackson, 1910).
Ovid	*The Erotic Poems*, tr. Peter Green (Harmondsworth: Penguin, 1982).
	Metamorphoses, tr. A. D. Melville (Oxford University Press, 1986).
Owl	*The Owl and the Nightingale*, tr. Brian Stone (Harmondsworth: Penguin, 1971).
Pasquil	*Pasquil's Jests* (London, 1609).
Peele	*The Battle of Alcazar*, ed. Charles Edelman, *The Stukeley Plays* (Manchester University Press, 2005).
	Edward I, ed. F. S. Hook, *The Life and Works of George Peele*, gen. ed. Charles Tyler Prouty, v. 2 (New Haven: Yale University Press, 1961).
Persius	*The Satires of Horace and Persius*, tr. Niall Rudd (Harmondsworth: Penguin, 1973).
Plato	*Complete Works*, ed. John M. Cooper (Indianapolis: Hackett, 1997).
Plautus	*Plautus*, ed. & tr. Wolfgang de Melo, 5 v. (Cambridge, MA: Harvard University Press, 2011–13), quotations from this edition, referenced by line number.
Plutarch	*Moralia*, ed. Frank Cole Babbitt et al., 15 v. (Cambridge MA, Harvard University Press, 1927–76).
	The Rise and Fall of Athens: Nine Greek Lives, tr. Ian Scott-Kilvert (Harmondsworth: Penguin, 1960).
Rich	*The Honesty of this Age* (London, 1614).
Rowley	*A Search for Money* (London, 1609).
Saviolo	*Vincentio Saviolo his Practise* (London, 1595).
Shakespeare	*The Riverside Shakespeare*, 2nd ed., gen. ed. G. Blakemore Evans (Boston: Houghton Mifflin, 1997).
Sidney	*Arcadia*, ed. Maurice Evans (Harmondsworth, Penguin, 1977).
	A Defence of Poetry, ed. J. A. Van Dorsten (Oxford University Press, 1966).
Sir John Oldcastle	*The Oldcastle Controversy: Sir John Oldcastle, Part I and The Famous Victories of Henry V*, ed. Peter Corbin and Douglas Sedge (Manchester University Press, 1991).
Smith	*De Republica Anglorum*, ed. Mary Dewar (Cambridge University Press, 1982).
Spenser	*The Faerie Queene*, ed. J. C. S. Smith, 2 v. (Oxford University Press, 1961).
	The Yale Edition of the Shorter Poems of Edmund Spenser, ed. William A. Oram et al. (New Haven: Yale University Press, 1989).
Stow	*The Survey of London* (London, 1633).
Stubbes	*The Anatomy of Abuses*, ed. Margaret Jane Kidnie (Tempe: Arizona Center for Medieval and Renaissance Studies, 2002).

	EDITIONS, REFERENCES, ABBREVIATIONS
Suckling	*The Works of Sir John Suckling*, v. 1, ed. Thomas Clayton (Oxford: Clarendon, 1971).
Swan	*Speculum Mundi* (Cambridge, 1635).
Swinburne	*A Treatise of Spousals* (London, 1686).
Terence	*The Comedies*, ed. & tr. Peter Brown (Oxford University Press, 2006), quotations from this edition, referenced by line number. *The Comedies*, ed. & tr. Betty Radice (Harmondsworth, Penguin 1976).
Udall	Nicholas Udall, *Apothegms* (London, 1542).
Walker	*A Manifest Detection of Dice Play*, in *Life in Shakespeare's England*, ed. John Dover Wilson (Harmondsworth: Penguin, 1968).
Webster	*The Duchess of Malfi*, ed. John Russell Brown (Manchester University Press, 1974). *Northward Ho*, see Dekker.

SECONDARY WORKS CITED IN COMMENTARY

Abbott	E. A. Abbott, *A Shakespearian Grammar* (London: Macmillan, 1884).
Anglin	Jay P. Anglin, 'The *Schools of Defence in Elizabethan* London', *Renaissance Quarterly* 37 (1984): 393–410.
Arikha	Nogo Arikha, *Passions and Tempers: A History of the Humours* (New York: Ecco, 2007).
Armour	Richard Armour, *It All Started with Europa* (London: Hammond, 1962).
Barsby	John Barsby, ed. & tr., *Terence*, 2 v. (Cambridge, MA: Harvard University Press, 2001).
Bennett	Fordyce Judson Bennett, *The Use of the Bible in the Dramatic Works of George Chapman, Thomas Dekker, John Marston, Cyril Tourneur and John Webster*, PhD thesis, University of Illinois, 1964.
Brewer	*Brewer's Dictionary of Phrase and Fable*, 14th ed. (London: Cassell, 1989).
Brissenden	Alan Brissenden, *Shakespeare and the Dance* (London: Macmillan, 1981).
Dent	R. W. Dent, *Proverbial Language in English Drama Exclusive of Shakespeare, 1495–1616* (Berkeley: University of California, 1984).
Edelman	Charles Edelman, *Shakespeare's Military Language* (London: Athlone, 2000).
Finkelpearl	Philip J. Finkelpearl, *John Marston of the Middle Temple: An Elizabethan Dramatist in His Social Setting* (Cambridge, MA: Harvard University Press, 1969).
Forrest	Richard D. Forrest, 'Development of Wound Therapy from the Dark Ages to the Present', *Journal of the Royal Society of Medicine* 75 (1982): 268–73.
Gabriel & Metz	Richard A. Gabriel and Karen S. Metz, *A History of Military Medicine*, 2 v. (New York: Greenwood, 1992).

EDITIONS, REFERENCES, ABBREVIATIONS xix

Greaves	Richard L. Greaves, *Society and Religion in Elizabethan England* (Minneapolis: Minnesota University Press, 1981).
Gurr	Andrew Gurr, *The Shakespearean Stage*, 4th ed. (Cambridge University Press, 2009).
Halliwell	James Orchard Halliwell, *Dictionary of Archaic and Provincial Words*, 7th ed. (London: J. R. Smith, 1872).
Hoeniger	F. David Hoeniger, *Medicine and Shakespeare in the English Renaissance* (Newark: Delaware University Press, 1992).
Hope	Jonathan Hope, *Shakespeare's Grammar* (London: Thomson, 2003).
Keevil	*Medicine and the Navy*, v. 1 (Edinburgh: E. & S. Livingstone, 1957).
Oreglia	Giacomo Oreglia, *The Commedia dell'Arte*, tr. Lovett F. Edwards (London: Methuen, 1968).
Pelling & Webster	Margaret Pelling and Charles Webster, 'Medical Practitioners', in *Health, Medicine, and Mortality in the Sixteenth Century*, ed. Charles Webster (Cambridge University Press, 1979).
Prest	Wilfrid Prest, *The Inns of Court under Elizabeth I and the Early Stuarts* (London: Longman, 1972).
Salingar	Leo Salingar, 'Jacobean Playwrights and Judicious Spectators', *Proceedings of the British Academy* 85 (1989): 1–23.
Shapiro	Michael Shapiro, *Children of the Revels: The Boy Companies of Shakespeare's Time and their Plays* (New York: Columbia University Press, 1977).
Smith	Irwin Smith, *Shakespeare's Blackfriars Playhouse* (New York University Press, 1964).
Sugden	Edward H. Sugden, *A Topographical Dictionary to the Works of Shakespeare and His Fellow Dramatists* (Manchester University Press), 1925.
Swinburne	A. C. Swinburne, 'Essay on the Poetical and Dramatic Works of George Chapman', *The Works of George Chapman: Poems and Minor Translations* (London: Chatto & Windus, 1904).
Tymms	Samuel Tymms, ed. *Wills and Inventories from the Registers of the Commissary of Bury St. Edmunds* (London: Camden Society, 1850).
Williams	Gordon Williams, *A Dictionary of Sexual Language and Imagery in Shakespearean and Stuart Literature* (London: Athlone, 1994).

ABBREVIATIONS: NOTES AND COLLATION

bk.	book
cf.	compare with, see also
conj.	conjectural reading
DNB	*Oxford Dictionary of National Biography* (2004)
ed.	edition, edited by
F	Folio version of Jonson's plays
fol.	folio number, identifying page in early texts.
l., ll.	line, lines
Metam.	*Metamorphoses*

NQ	*Notes and Queries*
OED	*Oxford English Dictionary*
Q	quarto
SD	stage direction
sig.	signature, identifying page in early texts
SP	speech prefix
subst.	substantially
This ed.	reading adopted for the first time in this edition.
tr.	translator, translated by
v.	volume, volumes

Introduction

CHAPMAN AT THE ROSE, 1598-99

The last years of the sixteenth century were a very productive time for George Chapman. His first translations of Homer, *The Seven Books of the Iliads* and *Achilles' Shield*, were accompanied by his completion of Marlowe's *Hero and Leander*. Financially, however, things were not going well. He was plagued by debt litigation that had been going on since 1585, when he agreed to a bond of £100 for a loan from a broker named John Wolfall, who claimed that the bond was forfeit, while Chapman insisted that he never received the loan. Claims and counter-claims would continue into the next century.

At least Chapman could count on a steady source of income by writing plays for the Admiral's Men at the Rose. Their need for new works was greater than usual, since Edward Alleyn, their leading actor, had retired from the stage to concentrate on his business interests. The most popular Admiral's plays, such as *The Spanish Tragedy* and *The Jew of Malta*, were Alleyn vehicles, and Rose audiences would be unlikely to accept anyone else in the starring role. Similarly, there was no point in reviving Chapman's comedy, *The Blind Beggar of Alexandria*, the Rose's biggest hit of 1596, since that play featured Alleyn parodying his own great tragic parts. Indeed, it could not be accidental that in 1601, shortly after Alleyn came out of retirement, Philip Henslowe, the owner of the Rose, manager of the Admiral's Men, and stepfather of Alleyn's wife, bought 'things', presumably costumes and properties, for the *Blind Beggar* and *The Jew of Malta*.[1]

One play the Admiral's Men would certainly have revived is Chapman's *An Humorous Day's Mirth*. Just as Henslowe's *Diary* has *The Blind Beggar* as the Rose's top attraction of 1596, this play held the honours for 1597.[2] Unfortunately, Henslowe's practice of noting the title of each play with the daily takings, which he began in February of 1592, stopped on 5 November 1597. From then on, he recorded only weekly receipts, so we know in general how well the company was doing, but not what plays they were performing. We have, however, something nearly as interesting: Henslowe's record of payments made to the writers. It should be noted that Henslowe himself was not purchasing the plays, but was acting as agent for the Admiral's Men, and most payments were actually loans to the actors who were sharers in the company; they would then pass the money on to the playwright.

Given Chapman's track record, it is hardly surprising that the Admiral's Men turned to him, and between 16 May 1598 and 8 January 1599 he received payments totalling £18 for four commissions. First, there was partial payment for an unnamed lost play; this was followed by *The Will of a Woman*, later changed to *The Fountain of New Fashions* (also lost).[3] Then, in one of Henslowe's more curious entries, Chapman received £4 for 'one his play book & 2 acts of a tragedy of Benjamin's plot'. Benjamin, of course, is Ben Jonson. Why his play should be turned over to Chapman for completion is a question impossible to answer; it may have had something to do with Jonson's imprisonment to await trial after killing the Admiral's actor Gabriel Spencer in a duel on 22 September 1598.[4]

The *Diary*'s next entry offers evidence of Chapman's continuing financial troubles. Henslowe was not only a theatre owner, company manager, and bear-beating promoter, he also ran a money-lending business on the side. The day after getting his £3 advance for Jonson's play, Chapman borrowed the very large sum of £10 10s 'of lawful money of England' from Henslowe. Then, on 8 January 1599, Henslowe records full payment to Chapman for another unnamed lost tragedy.[5]

It was only two weeks before the Admiral's Men put Chapman to work again: on 22 January 1599, Henslowe loaned Admiral's actor Thomas Downton 'to lend unto Mr Chapman in earnest of a book called *The World Runs on Wheels*, the sum of £3'. Chapman duly signed the receipt, and his colleague Thomas Dekker witnessed it.[6] After a second payment of £1 on 13 February, Chapman is absent from the *Diary* until 2 June, when he received £1, followed by another £2 on 21 June, bringing the total so far for *The World Runs on Wheels* (every entry gives the title) to £7, already more than the normal fee of £6.[7] Chapman was not quite done, however, for on 2 July 1599 Henslowe loaned another £1 10s to Thomas Downton 'to pay Mr Chapman in full payment for his book called *The World Runs on Wheels* and now *All Fools But The Fool*'.[8]

Some time between Henslowe's entry in July of 1599 and 1 January 1605, when the play was performed at Court, *All Fools But the Fool* was shortened to *All Fools*. The changes in title are of no importance whatsoever. They say nothing about the play's content, since they are all generic titles for a comedy. The working titles Henslowe recorded in the *Diary* border on the chaotic, and many bear only slight resemblance to the title of the published play. Indeed, some are so far off as to provoke scholarly debate about which play is which. In this era, the only time a play's title had any relevance was in submitting it to the Master of the Revels for approval, advertising a performance, or registering it for publication.

Chapman finished writing *All Fools* in July of 1599, but since, as noted, Henslowe no longer included titles in his financial accounts, it is impossible to say when the play was first presented. The *Diary* has no record of the Rose's takings from 3 June until 6 October 1599. On that day Henslowe notes, 'Here I begin to receive the galleries again'; weekly or fortnightly income is recorded from then until 30 December.[9] We can only guess as to why the Rose was apparently shut for the summer. One obvious possibility is closure due to plague; if so, the Admiral's Men would have gone on tour. They might have done so even if there was no plague, since they could not hope to compete in London, when all interest was on the new Globe, open by 21 September at the latest. On that day a visiting Swiss doctor named Thomas Platter wrote about having 'crossed the water, and there in the house with the thatched roof witnessed an excellent performance of the tragedy of the first emperor Julius Caesar'.[10]

It is often thought that companies toured only when they absolutely had to, but, as Roslyn Lander Knutson cogently argues, 'touring was neither an act of economic desperation nor the refuge of bad companies'.[11] The ever-increasing documentary evidence collected by *REED* (Records of Early English Drama) shows that touring was an important and profitable part of the theatre industry, and there is no reason to believe that the players found it particularly unpleasant. Inns could not hope to attract steady business if they offered bad accommodation, and companies also played the great estates of the aristocracy, where the lodging could have been sumptuous.

All Fools would be perfect for touring. The cast is small for an Admiral's play: depending on the amount of doubling, it requires about ten men, three women, and one boy, i.e., ten men and four boys in Elizabethan terms, plus a few supernumeraries. It can be presented on one level—neither a tiring house gallery nor a trap door is required—and there are no elaborate stage effects to manage or heavy properties to transport.

Whether or not such a tour took place, we can be quite certain that the Admiral's Men presented *All Fools* at the Rose soon after the theatre reopened in October of 1599. No company would pay £8 10s for a play and not perform it, especially when its author was working on another play for them; a receipt amongst Henslowe's papers reads 'received by me George Chapman for a pastoral ending in tragedy in part of payment the sum of forty shillings this 17th of July 1599'.[12] This lost pastoral tragedy was to be Chapman's last play for the Admiral's Men; when next we hear of him, he is working with the Chapel Children at Blackfriars.

FROM THE ROSE TO BLACKFRIARS

The first theatre at the Blackfriars monastery opened in 1577, and the Chapel Children performed there until 1584, when disputes over the lease brought about its demise. In 1596 Richard Burbage, always in search of an indoor venue to expand his operations, bought most of upper frater (refectory) block, and all the Duchy chamber building, for £600.[13] After having spent nearly as much on renovations, Burbage found that influential citizens of the area, who may have tolerated the boy companies with their one or two performances per week, did not want a commercial adult company in their neighbourhood. Desperate to get some return for his investment in order to finance construction of the Globe, Burbage leased out the premises on 2 September 1600 to Henry Evans, a scrivener and entrepreneur. Evans then engaged Nathaniel Giles, Master of the Chapel at Windsor, to assemble a new company of boy players, and, by the end of the year, the Children of the Chapel, or the 'little eyases', as Hamlet calls them, were back in business.[14]

Exactly why Henslowe and the Admiral's Men would have sold *All Fools* to the Blackfriars is impossible to determine. They certainly needed the money; in December of 1599 Henslowe signed a lease for the Shoreditch property where he would build the Fortune. This would require an enormous amount of capital, especially since his lease on the land where the Rose stood had another six years to run.[15]

The title page of the 1605 quarto reads '*All Fools*, A Comedy, Presented at the Black Friars, and lately before His Majesty'. The Court performance took place on 1 January 1605, the Revels accounts noting that the 'Boys of the Chapel' presented 'on newers night a play called *All Fools*'. The first Blackfriars performance cannot be dated with any certainty. All London theatres were closed in March 1603, when the Queen died, and did not reopen until April 1604,[16] eliminating one year, but we have no other external evidence except for an interesting entry in the *Diary* of law student John Manningham, who lived at the Middle Temple during the first few years of the seventeenth century.

The surviving manuscript of Manningham's *Diary* covers only sixteen months, from January 1602 to April 1603, but it is a rich source of information about life in Elizabethan London, especially at the Inns of Court. He describes the sermons he heard each Sunday (usually one in the morning followed by another in the afternoon), along with gossip and poems. There is a fascinating account of Queen Elizabeth's last days, and, in a passage well known to students of Shakespeare, an entry in February of 1602 records his attendance at the Middle Temple's Candlemas Feast, where he saw 'a play called "Twelve night, or what you will"'.[17]

INTRODUCTION 5

Manningham also enjoyed writing down the witticisms he heard, sometimes mentioning the source, but often not doing so; in November of 1602, he noted the aphorism, 'Women, because they cannot have their wills when they die, they will have their will while they live',[18] a close paraphrase of Curio's question to Cornelio: 'Why, then, sir, should you husbands cross your wives' wills thus, considering the law allows them no wills at all at their deaths, because it intended they should have their wills while they lived?' (3.1.222–5).

Throughout his *Diary*, Manningham shows enthusiasm for legal quibbles and proverbs about women. This one about women and wills is similar in both length and wit to 'one fee is too good for a bad lawyer, and two fees too little for a good one', and one he heard from his cousin's wife:

To furnish a ship requireth much trouble
But to furnish a woman the charges are double.[19]

Blackfriars was a short distance from the Inns of Court, and performances by the Chapel Children were very popular with the lawyers, law students, and other residents.[20] There is no way to tell for certain if Manningham heard the expression himself at a performance, from a friend who passed it on, or by some other, unrelated means, but the note in his *Diary* does at least suggest that *All Fools* was presented at Blackfriars, some time between late 1600, when the theatre opened, and November, 1602.

Previous editors have speculated how much of *All Fools* Chapman may have revised for the Blackfriars. The Prologue and Epilogue, directed to the fashionable wits who liked to sit on the Blackfriars stage, are definitely new, but the text of the play itself has no reference to events outside the theatre that were not current in 1599. In the absence of any evidence to the contrary, the safest assumption is that, Prologue and Epilogue excepted, the quarto text represents *All Fools* as it was performed at the Rose in 1599.

TERENCE GOES TO LONDON: THE SOURCES OF *ALL FOOLS*

There's nothing said today that has not been said before. (Terence, Prologue to *The Eunuch*)

In an address to the 'noble minds, flower of Spain' of the Academy of Madrid, the great playwright Lope de Vega spoke of his wish to create a new, contemporary style of comedy, unconstrained by classical precepts. He said, 'when I have to write a comedy ... I eject Plautus and Terence from my study, to prevent them from howling at me'.[21] Lope gave his lecture in about 1608; were there a British Academy at that time, one could easily imagine the Spaniard's contemporaries, Shakespeare, Jonson, and Chapman, saying precisely the same thing. They had, by then, created a type of comedy as uniquely English as Lope's is uniquely Spanish, yet they too owed a huge debt to Plautus and Terence, as did every comic dramatist of their era.

Many plays have been proposed as Shakespeare's first: even if *The Comedy of Errors* cannot claim that distinction, it is beyond doubt one of the earliest. As everyone knows, Plautus's *The Two Menaechmuses* provides the plot, except for the brilliant sequence of Antipholus of Ephesus being locked out of his own house, which comes from *Amphitryon*.[22] In 1597, Jonson did his version of Plautus with what is thought to be his very first play, *The Case Is Altered*. Like *The Comedy of Errors*, its plot combines two of Plautus's works, *The Captives* and *The Pot of Gold*, but the setting is updated to contemporary Milan.

Jonson's play seems to have been well received. In *Lenten Stuff* (1599), Thomas Nashe mentions 'the merry cobbler's cut, in the witty play of *The Case Is Altered*',[23] and in 1601, the poet and clergyman Charles Fitzgeoffrey published a book of Latin epigrams and epitaphs, including a clever poem addressed to Jonson. As we read in A. B. Grosart's translation, Fitzgeoffrey accuses him 'of stealing and of wicked thieving' from 'Plautus, most merry of the choir of poets', but then acquits him, saying it was actually Mercury who stole Jonson's play and gave it to Plautus, who then read it to the gods on Olympus,

> drawing smiles from Jupiter's grim visage,
> Each pole of heaven thundering with applauses.[24]

Jonson was working with the Earl of Pembroke's Men in 1597, and so *The Case Is Altered* was probably performed at the Swan.[25] At approximately the same time, Chapman's *An Humorous Day's Mirth*, the first-ever comedy of humours, was doing great business nearby at the Rose, prompting Jonson to try his hand at this new style of comedy for his next play, *Every Man In His Humour*, presented by the Lord Chamberlain's Men in 1598. Whether or not Chapman was somehow inspired to do some imitating in return is impossible to say, but it is oddly coincidental that the following year Chapman tried his hand at adapting Roman comedy, turning two of Terence's plays, *The Self-Tormenter* and *The Brothers*, into *All Fools*.

In basing *All Fools* on Roman comedy, Chapman was only following the example set by Plautus and Terence, who took most of their plots and characters from Menander, Apollodorus, and other masters of the New Comedy that flourished in Greece during the fourth century BC. Terence does not merely admit this, he virtually boasts of it. Although we think of him as a supremely Roman dramatist, his plays were known as *fabulae palliate* ('Greek cloak plays'), since they retained their Greek setting and Greek dress. In each of his prologues, Terence names the plays he has used, saying, in a sense, that the best playwright is not the most original one but the one most skilled at using Menander. The prologue to *The Eunuch* is a particularly interesting example, since Terence is responding to his rival Lucius's charge of plagiarism—not from Menander, which was expected, but from another Roman comedy. The speaker expresses contempt for those who turn 'good Greek plays into bad Latin ones' (9), and assures the audience that his author worked directly from Menander's *The Toady*, with no knowledge of some other Latin version. He then asks how one can write a comedy at all 'if he's not allowed to use the same characters as someone else has used' (33-4), naming running slaves, good wives, bad prostitutes, and boastful soldiers.[26] To this far from complete list we might add the miserly father, nagging wife, lovesick youth, kindly nurse, baby lost at birth whose real identity is discovered at just the right time, and a host of other 'stock characters' who made their way from New Comedy to Roman comedy, and from there to the Elizabethan stage, either directly, or via Italian Renaissance comedy.

Chapman and the other Elizabethan dramatists also drew ideas about how a comedy is to be structured from Terence. Giambattista Giraldi, always known by his pen name of Cinthio, is familiar to many as author of the principal source of *Othello*. In his critical study *On the Composition of Comedies and Tragedies* (1543), Cinthio praises Terence's invention of the double plot,

> which make his plays succeed wonderfully. I call that plot double which has in its action diverse kinds of persons in the same station of life, as two lovers of different character, two old men of varied nature, two servants of opposite morals, and other such things.[27]

Dryden makes a similar observation in the Preface to his version of *Troilus and Cressida* (1679):

> Terence made an innovation in the Roman [comedy]: all his plays have double actions; for it was his custom to translate two Greek comedies, and to weave them into one of his, yet so that both their actions were comical, and one was principal, the other but secondary or subservient. And this has obtained on the English stage, to give us the pleasure of variety.[28]

The boy actor in Jonson's *Magnetic Lady* who says 'I learned Terence i'the third form at Westminster' (Ind.33-4) speaks for his author, who did indeed attend Westminster, and his experience was not unique. Chapman would have begun his study of Terence when he was about nine years old.

School, be it Jonson's Westminster, Shakespeare's New King's School, or the Hertfordshire grammar school Chapman attended, was for learning Latin—not just any Latin, but an elegant Latin that was, as William Tydeman notes, 'felt to be the basis of a good education and the passport to a successful and effective life thereafter'. For this purpose, Terence was *sine qua non*, largely due to the influence of Erasmus, who knew all the plays by heart, and believed that 'of all authors, Terence is the best, as well as the most enjoyable, for learning clear and correct Latin style'.[29]

In *On the Method of Study* (*De rationi studii*), the brief treatise wherein he lays out his educational principles, Erasmus asks, 'among Latin writers who is more valuable as a standard of language than Terence? He is pure, concise, and close to everyday speech, and then, by the very nature of the subject-matter, is also congenial to the young'. This congeniality could have been largely due to Terence's racy language and uninhibited attitude toward sex. Augustine of Hippo, who studied Terence at his north African school in the fourth century, quotes Chaerea's triumphant account of his sexual conquest from *The Eunuch* verbatim, but then asks, 'could we not have learned those useful words elsewhere?'. Some early modern educators demanded that Terence be expurgated or banned from the classroom entirely; fortunately, most schoolmasters agreed with Erasmus, who once wrote to a friend, advising him to ignore 'these fools, these goats, who grasp only at wickedness'.[30]

Erasmus develops his ideas on the value of studying Terence in *Foundations of Abundant Style* (*Copia*), the textbook used for teaching rhetoric throughout England. *Foundations* is full of phrases from and about Terence for young scholars to copy; they also learned something about creating a character. The chapter on *evidentia* (enrichment, vividness) advises that, in describing people, one should strive to imitate Plautus and Terence. These playwrights did not simply produce types, such as 'an old man, a slave, the head of a house, or a pimp ... the comic poets aimed at variety in characters belonging to the same general type'. Terence comes in for special praise, with his two sets of dissimilar siblings in *The Brothers*; Erasmus also notes that 'Plautus's courtesans are very different from Terence's, who for the most part depicts good courtesans'.[31]

The boys did more than read and memorise Terence; they also translated him, and got valuable theatre training by performing Terence and Plautus for their school plays.[32] Given all this, we might expect Elizabethan dramatists to have borrowed Terence's plots frequently, but *All Fools* is the sole surviving example, perhaps owing to Terence having written only six plays before his death at the age of just thirty-five, a circumstance that the Puritan pamphleteer William Prynne credits to divine retribution for choosing the theatre as a career.[33] Even so, unless they are among the many lost plays of the age, surprisingly, no one adapted *The Mother-in-Law*, *The Girl from Andros*, or *The Eunuch*, and the world had to wait for Molière to turn *Phormio* into his glorious *Scapin*.

The main plot of *All Fools* comes from *The Self-Tormenter*, which is itself based on a lost Menander play of the same title. The Prologue announces, 'today I am going to perform a fresh comedy taken from a fresh Greek play' (3-4). Menedemus, the 'self-tormenter', is an Athenian nobleman, recently moved to the country. His torment arises from the way he had spoken to his son, Clinia, about the affair Clinia was having with Antiphila, a young girl of unknown parentage. As he tells his neighbour Chremes,

> I got all worked up, the way fathers usually do ... 'What! Do you hope to be allowed to carry on behaving like this while I'm alive—me, your father!—giving your girlfriend very nearly the status of a wife? ... When I was your age, I didn't devote myself to love affairs, but I went off to Asia because I was so poor, and there I found both wealth and glory by fighting in wars'. (99-112)

Unfortunately, Clinia, rather than displease his father, followed his father's example and went to Asia with the king's army. Menedemus, filled with remorse, bought a farm and now spends his days at hard labour.

Chremes is well-meaning but an incorrigible busybody. His famous line, *mihi sic est usus, tibi ut opus facto est face*, 'I'm a man, I don't regard any man's affairs as not concerning me' (80), crops up constantly in Renaissance texts as synonymous with Donne's 'no man is an island', but, in context, Chremes is simply describing his complete inability to mind his own business. He is especially free with advice on child-rearing, believing that his relationship with his son, Clitipho, could hardly be improved upon, when in fact Clitipho is nothing like the person his father thinks him to be. He is in love with Bacchis, a *meretrix* (usually translated as 'courtesan' or 'prostitute'), but can only enjoy her favours as long as he showers her with lavish gifts. He knows that, if he asks his father for money, he will get only a lecture in return.

It falls to Chremes's slave, Syrus, to devise a trick so that Clinia, who has just returned from Asia, is able to resume his relationship with Antiphila, and Clitipho can get the money to finance his affair with Bacchis. Syrus's plan is to have both women be guests at Chremes's house; Bacchis will pretend to be Clinia's, not Clitipho's, *meretrix*, and enjoy her host's sumptuous hospitality, while Antiphila will pretend to be Bacchis's maid. This way, both young men will have free access to their women, although they must not be seen with their true partners lest the stratagem fall apart.

Sostrata, Chremes's wife, solves Clinia's problems when she notices Antiphila's ring, and realises that she is their daughter who was supposed to have been exposed at birth, but was secretly sent away. Menedemus would be happy to have his son marry her, now that she is known to be from a good family, but the discovery makes Clitipho's dilemma even worse, especially after Chremes sees him paying more attention to Bacchis than Clinia does. He scolds his son: 'That's outrageous behaviour on your part, to take a friend into your house and feel up his girlfriend' (565).

Syrus's means of sorting everything out are too complicated to recount here, but one of his strategies is particularly relevant to *All Fools*. He tells Chremes the truth—that Bacchis is actually the mistress of his, not his neighbour's, son—knowing that the old man will not believe it. When Chremes finally realises he has been duped, he furiously threatens to disinherit Clitipho, and relents only if Clitipho promises to marry. Menedemus assures Clitipho that marriage is all right 'once you've got used to it' (1058), and, after rejecting his mother's suggestion of 'that red-haired girl with grey eyes, a spotty face, and a hooked nose' (1061), Clitipho declares himself 'happy enough' with a neighbour's daughter (1065). What the unnamed girl might have to say about the idea is not mentioned, nor do we hear what happens to Bacchis; presumably she is paid off and contentedly moves on to her next client.

Chapman also draws extensively on Terence's *The Brothers*, which provides a rich source of characterisation. Like *The Self-Tormenter*, it comes from a lost Menander play with the same title, although one scene is taken from Menander's contemporary, Diphilus.[34] Micio, a city-dwelling bachelor, begins by telling the audience about the contrasting lives he and his brother Demea lead:

> I have pursued the gentle life of leisure, and as for what some people think a blessing—a wife—I've never had one. *He* [Demea] has been the opposite in all the following respects: he's spent his life on the farm, he's always lived a frugal and hard existence. (42–4)

Micio explains that Demea has two sons, Ctesipho and Aeschinus. Unable or unwilling to look after them both, Demea gave Aeschinus to him to raise: 'I've brought him up from childhood; I've regarded him as my own, and loved him accordingly'. Micio believes that one should take a liberal and lenient approach to child-rearing: 'it's better to keep a hold on your children by inspiring respect and showing generosity than by means of fear' (54–7).

Demea is quite the opposite of his brother. He is tight-fisted with his money, and believes that children need a disciplined upbringing. The brothers' conflicting ideas of how strict or permissive a parent should be form the central question of the play. Demea thinks that his son Ctesipho 'devotes himself to work and stays on the farm, frugal and sober' (95), when of course the young man spends all his time trying to work out how to find the money in order to buy a *meretrix* from the pimp Sannio. Like her counterpart in *The Self-Tormenter*, she is named Bacchis, but here is called a 'lyre-girl', for such young ladies were expected to perform musically as well as sexually.[35] Aeschinus agrees to help his brother by pretending that he is Bacchis's suitor and breaking into the pimp's house to carry her off. Some very amusing bargaining follows, featuring Sannio's indignation over Aeschinus's expectation that he is to sell Bacchis at cost price (191-9). In the meantime, she is to be installed, in high style, in Micio's house, which bothers Micio not at all but has Demea apoplectic with rage.

In helping his brother, Aeschinus creates a major problem for himself. He is in love with Pamphila, daughter of a neighbour, the widow Sostrata. Indeed, Pamphila is about to give birth to his child, he having raped her nine months ago. In three of the four Terentian comedies taken directly from Menander, such rapes occur, and are seen as acceptable provided the young man marries the girl in the end—one of the few aspects of Terence that make him unpalatable to the modern reader.[36]

As usual, the person to solve the problem is Micio's slave. Like his counterpart in *The Self-Tormenter*, his name is Syrus, and his job is to trick Demea into providing the money for Ctesipho to purchase Bacchis, while making sure that Aeschinus's marriage to Pamphila goes ahead. Naturally, Demea ends up paying for everything, but Terence adds a real twist. In a long (by the standards of Latin comedy) soliloquy, Demea regrets having worked hard all his life for the benefit of his family, while his spendthrift brother is more popular with everyone (855-81). He decides to out-Micio Micio: first by demolishing the wall between his and Micio's garden so that they can dispense with the ceremonial passage of the bride, accompanied by musicians, from her old to her new house. He then bullies Micio into marrying the 'decrepit old woman' Sostrata (939); furthermore, Micio must give Sostrata's friend Hegio a valuable plot of land. Micio even has to reward Syrus by freeing both him and his wife. As for Ctesipho and Bacchis, Demea will 'let him keep her—but she'd better be the last!' (997).

THE PRIMARY PLOT: TERENCE TRANSMOGRIFIED

All Fools is set in contemporary Florence, although one hardly knows it, since the city is not named until we are well into the fourth act (4.1.297), and only once thereafter (5.2.186). A few other details have a Florentine, or at least Italian, flavour: we hear of a lawyer who 'crowds the senate', not the court, with his clients (2.1.344); the Notary's bill of divorce refers to the 'Duke' as head of state (4.1.294), and we hear the formal legal phrase 'courtesy of the city' rather than 'courtesy of England' (5.2.310). The characters may have Italian names, but in other respects this Florence, like the Florence of *Every Man In His Humour* (quarto version), and indeed the Paris of *An Humorous Day's Mirth*, is located in or near London, where English manners, customs, laws, and social institutions are the subject of some trenchant satire.

While the period is distinctly contemporary, Chapman makes good use of Roman comedy's physical setting, where everything occurs outdoors, during the day. Until he takes *All Fools* to the Half Moon tavern for the final scene, Chapman, like Terence, keeps the action outside, near the houses of Gostanzo, Marc Antonio, and Cornelio, with the exception of a brief sequence at the start of Act 3. In *All Fools*, as in Terence, life is lived in public, everyone knows everyone else's business, and sticking one's nose in it seems almost obligatory.

Chapman also exploits Roman comedy's social milieu, although how 'Roman' this milieu really is remains open to doubt. Terence is notably consistent in recreating Menander's Athenian world, and any local colour specific to Rome is difficult to find.[37] Plautus employs a different technique, John Barsby noting that 'the setting of a Plautine play is formally Greek, but the stage is peopled by characters who, though they wear Greek clothes and are careful to refer to the Romans as 'foreigners' (*barbari*), tend to lapse into Roman jokes or allude to Roman topography and laws and customs'. Nevertheless, Terence was often attacked by his contemporaries for not being faithful enough to his Greek originals, and, as Peter Brown writes, 'he does not remind his audience explicitly (as Plautus sometimes does) that they are Romans watching the antics of an alien world'.[38]

The families in *All Fools* are of the equivalent social and economic class to their counterparts in Terence. Chapman gives emphasis to this idea by having Marc Antonio and Gostanzo spoken of, and addressed, as 'knights', the most common translation of *equites* [equestrians]. Originally, *equites* were the elite cavalry, whose horses were paid for and maintained by the government; during the time of Plautus and Terence, they were evolving into a wealthy, land-owning aristocracy. Having little to do with the administration of government, a role reserved for members of the Senate, the *equites* concentrated mostly on accumulating wealth.[39] Terence, with his greater fidelity to the original Greek setting, never uses the word, but we do see it in Plautus: the prologue to *The Captives* tells us, *summo loco summoque genere captum esse equitem Aleum* ('an Elean

INTRODUCTION 13

knight of the highest rank and the highest family connections had been taken prisoner').[40]

Gostanzo and Marc Antonio are not your typical English knights, although the means of obtaining a knighthood in England are the subject of satire in the play (cf. below, pp. 33–4). Indeed, the only time either is addressed as 'Sir' occurs when Rinaldo indulges in some mock servility:

> What, Sir Gostanzo?
> How fares your knighthood, sir?
> (1.1.168–9)

Interestingly, *Signor*, the standard form of address for Italian gentlemen in early modern plays, is never used for the two knights; Chapman reserves it for the young courtiers, Dariotto and Cornelio, who inhabit the subplot.

Marc Antonio's and Gostanzo's different ideas about the proper way to raise a son come from Terence. Marc Antonio is even more lenient than his counterparts, Menedemus of *The Self-Tormenter* and Micio of *The Brothers*. As Gostanzo says, he is

> An honest knight, but much too much indulgent
> To his presuming children.
> (1.1.212–13)

Informed that Fortunio has married, Marc Antonio's initial reaction is only 'I love my son' (1.1.258), and he never offers so much as a mild rebuke, either for marrying Gratiana secretly, something Fortunio did not do, or for marrying Bellanora secretly, which Fortunio did do. Along with his 'gentle nature' (1.1.208), or perhaps because of it, Marc Antonio is easily gulled, something he admits:

> I, alas,
> Am no good politician. Plain believing,
> Simple honesty, is my policy still.
> (4.1.182–4)

The gullibility does not come from Terence, where Menedemus and Micio are often left in the dark or misinformed, but no one tries to trick them; all of the slave's machinations are directed at Gostanzo's counterparts, the nosy Chremes and the disciplinarian Demea. Similarly, all of Rinaldo's attentions lie with Gostanzo; he is the one to be gulled into blessing, and financing, his two children's marriages.

This 'old, politic, dissembling knight' Gostanzo (1.1.401), whose confidence that his son is 'a perfect pattern of sobriety' who 'dares not look a woman in the face' (1.1.221, 227) comes from Chremes of *The*

Self-Tormentor. To that we might add what Thomas Marc Parrott calls an 'overweening self-conceit',[41] taken mostly from Demea of *The Brothers*. A self-proclaimed expert on everything from parenting to poetry to the courtly art of kissing, Gostanzo promises Rinaldo that he will keep Fortunio's supposed marriage a secret, but immediately proceeds to tell Marc Antonio all about it, with advice on how to handle the situation. Openly scornful of his friend's trusting nature—

> You have a heart too open to embrace
> All that your ear receives,
>
> (4.1.33–4)

—Gostanzo has the self-satisfied attitude of the con-man or master salesman, who believes himself to be so good at manipulating others that he would instantly know if someone were trying to do the same to him.

Gostanzo remains clueless about Valerio's real life because his son behaves exactly as the old man tells him he should. Hounded for a gambling debt, Valerio says he needs money because he promised to help a friend in distress. Gostanzo replies:

> Promises are no fetters. With that tongue
> Thy promise passed, unpromise it again.
>
> (2.1.69–70)

Furthermore, Valerio should reject friendship, kindness, or honesty whenever it interferes with self-interest:

> Tush, friendship's but a term, boy. The fond world
> Like to a doting mother glazes over
> Her children's imperfections with fine terms.
> What she calls friendship and true humane kindness
> Is only want of true experience.
>
> (2.1.79–83)

It never occurs to Gostanzo that Valerio might act towards him as he has been instructed to act towards others; hence he repeatedly refuses to believe the truth no matter how forcefully it is presented. In 3.1, after he sees Valerio and Gratiana together and observes how he

> kissed her,
> Embraced and courted with as good a grace.
> As any courtier could,
>
> (3.1.55–7)

he cannot accept that Valerio may not be the shy husbandman he raised.

The younger generation, Fortunio, Valerio, and Rinaldo, offer no initial hint of their origins in Roman comedy. The play begins with their debate on the nature of beauty and love, a strange but effective mixture of neo-Platonic imagery and Juvenalian diatribe. Fortunio laments that he 'never can enjoy the sight' of Bellanora (1.1.19), leading Rinaldo to launch into a bitter account of his one love affair, denouncing all women and vowing 'eternal wars against their whole sex' (1.1.65). He draws on, and sometimes directly quotes, Juvenal's notoriously misogynistic sixth *Satire*.

Valerio responds with a neo-Platonic tribute to love's power, singled out for praise by some critics of the early twentieth century: A. H. Bullen calls it 'beautiful poetry', while William Archer, who finds little to admire in the play, sees this speech as 'a noble anticipation of Coleridge's "All thoughts, all passions, all delights"'.[42] It begins,

> I tell thee love is nature's second sun,
> Causing a spring of virtues where he shines,
>
> (1.1.97–8)

and goes on to honour love as the source of

> All virtues born in men ...
> ... valour, wit, virtue, and haughty thoughts,
> Brave resolution, and divine discourse.
>
> (1.1.103, 109–10)

Those in the original audience who had read Chapman's witty but famously obscure *Ovid's Banquet of Sense* (1595), or his continuation of Marlowe's *Hero and Leander* (1598), would have been familiar with their author's devotion to the neo-Platonist philosophy of Marsilio Ficino (1433–99), and so would not have been at all surprised to hear Valerio's discourse on love. The surprising thing is that, after little more than one hundred lines, matters of love disappear from the play, never to return. When Gostanzo enters and asks about the 'young gentlewoman' (1.1.181) he saw with Fortunio and Valerio, the tone of *All Fools* changes completely, and for the remainder Valerio bears no resemblance to the lovesick poet of the opening, neither is he the typical *adulescens* from Terence. In terms of plot structure, he is obviously based on Ctesipho of *The Brothers* and Clitipho of *The Self-Tormenter*, but in personality is quite different, an excellent demonstration of how Chapman transforms and transcends the Terentian model to create active, complex, and interesting characters.

Desperate for money to finance affairs with their mistresses, Terence's two young men leave nearly everything to their slaves, and lose their nerve at the first sign that something might go wrong.[43] Valerio, however, exudes total confidence that he can continue to lead a double life as a hard-working husbandman who studies

> how many loads of hay
> A meadow of so many acres yielded,
>
> (1.1.128–9)

and a city gallant,

> known in ordinaries and tobacco-shops,
> Trusted in taverns and in vaulting-houses.
>
> (1.1.156–7)

He eagerly goes along with Rinaldo's scheme so that he can be with Gratiana, never doubting its success. Such self-confidence is not always an asset: Valerio, as Parrott notes, is

> instinct with the Elizabethan charm of youth, high spirits, and poetry. Like his father, however, he is dominated by a master passion, that of parade. He is as vain of his accomplishments and gentlemanly vices as his father is of his worldly wisdom.[44]

A good example of what Parrott calls 'parade' is Valerio's extravagant account of how he avoided paying a debt and made a shambles of the senate's legal proceedings (2.1.310–35); we get the impression that he is embellishing the story to make sure others appreciate his cleverness. This desire to be centre of attention allows Cornelio and Dariotto to lead him into making himself look foolish rather easily (2.1.369–417), the first of the play's reversals, when someone who prides himself on gulling others is gulled himself.

Fortunio is rather bland when compared with his Terentian models, especially Aeschinus of *The Brothers*, who shows admirable spark and initiative in the way he abducts Bacchis on his brother's behalf, and carries off the confrontation with her pimp. Chapman does not give Fortunio much to do; he plays the penitent son very well when presenting his 'wife' Gratiana to Gostanzo (2.1.89–117), but, after a brief appearance in 3.1, he is not seen until he joins the drinking party at the Half Moon (5.2), wherein he has only a few lines. Overall, the main difference between him and Valerio is in their fathers, not their own personalities; as Marc Antonio's son, Fortunio never really risks anything. Knowing of his father's non-reaction to a fake secret wedding, Fortunio has no hesitation in carrying off a real one.

The cunning servant, ubiquitous in Italian Renaissance comedy and *Commedia dell'Arte*, rarely appears in English comedy, Musco (*Q*) / Brainworm (*F*) of *Every Man in His Humour* and Mosca of *Volpone* being notable exceptions. As the Elizabethan embodiment of Terence's clever slave, the young gallant Rinaldo of *All Fools* is cited by Madeleine Doran as a fine example of 'the typical English intriguer [who] is more apt to be a healthful exposer of men's follies than a malicious instigator of them ... a disinterested person merely exposing gullery for the fun of it'.[45] Despite the change from slave to member of the upper classes, one important element of the slave's *modus operandi* is taken up by Rinaldo wholeheartedly. In his short book *On Friendship*, Cicero observes how easy it is to dupe a 'comic geezer' through flattery, adding, 'even onstage the most ridiculous character is that of the witless and gullible old man'.[46] Syrus, in *The Brothers*, would agree, for flattery is the most potent weapon in his arsenal. When Demea says that his son Ctesipho could not possibly get up to any mischief secretly—'Wouldn't I have got a sniff of it six months before he began to do anything?'—Syrus immediately chimes in with 'You don't need to tell me how alert you are' (396–7). Similarly, Rinaldo is quick to tell Gostanzo that Valerio's fine character is due to the 'wisdom' he learned from his 'experient father' (1.1.205–6).

For all his cleverness, however, Rinaldo, like Syrus, depends on good fortune as much as his own wits. As noted by Doran, luck plays a key role in Roman comedy:

> In Plautus often, and in Terence always, solution is only possible with a recognition by tokens of one of the characters: the girl the young man wants to marry is happily discovered to be of free Athenian birth, usually the lost daughter of one of the older men in the play; she may be revealed as the hero's sister in time to prevent his union with her; or she may turn out to be the woman he himself has unwittingly wronged and her child to be his own.[47]

Chapman explicitly emphasises Dame Fortune's part in the proceedings, but handles it differently from Terence, where the chance discovery, for example that Antiphila is actually Chremes's daughter, occurs relatively late in the play. In *All Fools*, Fortune's task is to set the plot in motion, not to sort everything out at the last minute. Rinaldo's original lie to Gostanzo, that Fortunio is secretly married (1.1.182–3), seems a spur of the moment idea; he can hardly believe his luck when Gostanzo, with no prompting from anyone, suggests that the newlyweds live for a time at his house. When telling the young lovers about the stratagem they are to undertake, Rinaldo promises that they

> shall see to what a perfect shape
> I'll bring this rude plot, which blind chance—the ape
> Of counsel and advice—hath brought forth blind.
>   (1.2.122–4)

Rinaldo's ingenuity is put to its greatest test when Gostanzo sees Gratiana and Valerio embracing (3.1.18), and decides that she must leave his house. Improvising brilliantly, Rinaldo suggests that he and Gostanzo could have some 'princely sport' (3.1.98), Rinaldo will tell Marc Antonio that Valerio, not Fortunio, is the husband—the original story was only a practical joke—and ask that Gratiana stay with Marc Antonio in order to escape the ire of Gostanzo, who has just found out the 'truth'. At this point there is no suggestion that Gostanzo will somehow be tricked into publicly blessing Valerio's marriage, but once again luck takes over.

Gostanzo is primed to play the angry father when Valerio and Gratiana make their 'kind submission' (3.1.425), but, being Gostanzo, he enjoys his own chicanery too much, and overdoes it:

> No, no, live still, my son. Thou well shalt know
> I have a father's heart. Come, join your hands.
> Still keep thy vows, and live together still,
> Till cruel death set foot betwixt you both.
>
> (4.1.168–71)

Later, Rinaldo realises what has happened, and tells Valerio,

> Thou hast good plea against him to confess
> The honoured action, and to claim his pardon.
>
> (4.1.213–14)

To Rinaldo, the trickster's job is not one of planning and executing elaborate schemes, but waiting to see what Fortune gives him to work with, and then making the most of it. In a soliloquy at the start of Act 5, he gives her due credit:

> Fortune, the great commandress of the world,
> Hath divers ways to advance her followers.
> To some she gives honour without deserving.
> To other some, deserving without honour,
> Some wit, some wealth, and some wit without wealth,
> Some wealth without wit, some nor wit nor wealth.
>
> (5.1.1–6)

Yet his weakness is similar to Valerio's—it is one thing to be brilliant, another to want everyone to know it. Rinaldo reveals this himself in the same Act 5 soliloquy, boasting, 'My fortune is to win renown by gulling' (5.1.11). Gostanzo and Cornelio are such easy targets that he assumes they could not possibly turn the tables on him, and, when Cornelio does exactly that in Act 5, both his self-esteem and his ingenuity are put to the test.

LOVE AND MARRIAGE IN TERENCE AND CHAPMAN

Maybe money does not mean so much alongside of love at that, although personally I will take a chance on the money. (Damon Runyon, 'Princess O'Hara')

So far, we have seen how Chapman departs from Terence in some respects, while following him closely in others. Where he remains closest of all is in his exclusion of love and romance from *All Fools*.

Many readers will be familiar with Northrop Frye's profoundly influential analysis of comedy in his *Anatomy of Criticism*:

> The plot structure of Greek New Comedy, as transmitted by Plautus and Terence, in itself less a form than a formula, has become the basis for most comedy, especially in its more highly conventionalized dramatic form, down to our own day ... What normally happens is that a young man wants a young woman, that his desire is resisted by some opposition, usually paternal, and that near the end of the play some twist in the plot enables the hero to have his will.[48]

A delightful alternative version of Frye's clear and elegant 'formula' is offered by a couple of Hollywood screenwriters in Bella and Samuel Spewack's hilarious Broadway comedy of 1935, *Boy Meets Girl*:

> Listen, I've been writing stories for eleven years. Boy meets girl, boy loses girl, boy gets girl ... Or—girl meets boy, girl loses boy, girl gets boy. Love will find a way. Love never loses. Put your money on love.[49]

By including 'girl meets boy' and the word 'love', the Hollywood formula is closer to the great comedies of Shakespeare, with their female protagonists whose ultimate success is a wedding at the end of the play. Frye, in saying that 'a young man *wants* a young woman', is precisely correct about Terence, and also brings us closer to the structure of *All Fools*.

In an intriguing essay, Susanna Morton Braund notes that Frye's scheme contains a paradox when applied to Roman comedy, where marriage may be the objective, but 'already-established marriage is portrayed as a negative experience about which husbands and wives complain and from which husbands fantasize their escape'.[50] Ctesipho of *The Brothers* and Clitipho of *The Self-Tormenter* would agree—both 'want' their Bacchises, but neither has the slightest interest in marriage. Ctesipho never expresses any romantic feelings about Bacchis; with his brother's help, he has already stolen her, and now needs the money to keep her. Neither does Clitipho ever say a single word of love about, or to, his Bacchis. Instead, he informs the audience that she is 'overbearing, shameless, gives herself airs, extravagant, high and mighty' (226). She is completely forgotten when Clitipho is railroaded into getting married.

Obviously, Valerio does not have to keep a *meretrix* happy with lavish gifts, but his situation is similar to that of his Roman counterparts. He has married Gratiana—boy already 'has' girl—his fear is of being disinherited. As Fortunio says, the marriage 'would quite undo him, did his father know it' (1.1.162). Gostanzo, in advising Marc Antonio how to deal with Fortunio, shows what this undoing would mean:

> Cast him off,
> Receive him not. Let him endure the use
> Of their enforcèd kindness that must trust him
> For meat and money, for apparel, house,
> And everything ...
>
> (1.1.296–300)

Valerio may pay tribute to love in 1.1, but words of endearment to or about Gratiana are absent from his vocabulary. The first time they are together onstage (1.1.141–67), he does not say a word to her. In 1.2, Valerio merely jokes about their resemblance to a game of barley-break (1.2.65–7n.), and thinks about how wonderful everything would be if his father only had the good grace to drop dead (1.2.70–85). Indeed, the only times Valerio expresses his feelings are a six-line speech at the start of Act 3 (3.1.13–18), and when hamming it up in his pretended submission to Gostanzo (4.1.128–46).

If 'the course of true love' is of concern to anyone, it would be to Fortunio and Bellanora, and here the course runs so smoothly that it hardly merits consideration. Having exchanged vows, they are legally married before the play begins (3.1.7n.), and, since Fortunio knows that his always amenable father will approve the match, they have no hesitation in formalising the marriage secretly, an offstage event, some time before the start of Act 5.

All Fools ends with Gostanzo giving his blessing to his children's marriages, with the hope that all will 'live merrily together' (5.2.317). What married life will actually be like for the couples is, of course, unknown. It may be the 'joy and fresh days of love' Theseus promises the newlyweds of *A Midsummer Night's Dream* (5.1.29), or the 'many, many merry days' Mistress Page wishes upon her daughter and Master Fenton at the close of *The Merry Wives of Windsor* (5.5.240). On the other hand, marriage might be more like what Menedemus predicts for his son Clitipho in *The Self-Tormenter*: 'It's difficult to start with, when you're not familiar with it; once you've got used to it, it's easy' (1058). For a view of married life as one husband and wife experience it, we turn to the subplot.

THE SECONDARY PLOT: ADULTERY FOR FUN AND PROFIT

'Greater love than this', he said, 'no man hath, that a man lay down his wife for his friend. Go thou and do likewise'. (James Joyce, *Ulysses*)

In making the would-be courtier Cornelio's obsessive fear that his wife Gazetta is cuckolding him the driving action of the subplot, Chapman returns to a style of comedy that was successful for him in the past. He announces this, none too subtly, as Gazetta tells Bellanora and Gratiana,

Ye see, gentlewomen, what my happiness is.
These humours reign in marriage. Humours, humours.

(1.2.52–3)

Apart from Cornelio, Chapman introduces other characters, each with his individual humour: Curio, the precocious page who torments Cornelio with an elaborate speech in Gazetta's defence, Dariotto, the young courtier who wants everyone to think he is a great seducer, Pock, the surgeon who 'treats' the wound Cornelio gives him, and the loquacious Notary who prepares Cornelio's bill of divorce. As in *An Humorous Day's Mirth* and *Every Man In His Humour*, these 'humorous' characters provide both literary parody and social satire while displaying their eccentricities.

One only has to place *Othello* alongside *The Merry Wives of Windsor* to show that adultery can be the subject of both the darkest tragedy and the brightest comedy. As Martin Wiggins observes, during the Elizabethan theatre's earlier years, adultery, be it suspected or actual, was usually a serious matter: it 'is at the root of *Arden of Faversham* (1590), for example, in which the wife seeks to end her superseded marriage through murder; the play demonizes her not only as a response to her criminality but to her sexual infidelity too'.[51] To *Arden* we might add Shakespeare's *Henry VI* plays, with its doomed affair between Queen Margaret and the Duke of Suffolk.

A wealth of literature approaching adultery from a comic viewpoint was available to English playwrights, had they chosen to use it. The popular medieval tales known as *fabliaux* are, as Colin Wilcockson notes, preoccupied 'with comic, usually bawdy, situations, often involving old husband/young wife tensions, or the encounters of lascivious women with equally lascivious men, who were frequently priests or students'.[52] Boccaccio appropriated a number of them in writing the *Decameron*; more than twenty of its hundred stories are about adultery. A century and a half later, Italy's playwrights used the *Decameron* in creating such brilliant comedies as Machiavelli's *The Mandrake Root* (*Mandragola*), based on Boccaccio's tale of Ricciardo Mutolo, who has an extremely clever plan to seduce the young, beautiful, and married Catella (Day 3, Story 6).[53]

Plays such as Shakespeare's *Twelfth Night* and Chapman's *May Day* show that Italian comedies were partly or completely adapted into English versions, but those featuring a cuckold do not appear to have made the transition, with the possible exception of a lost Rose play, *The Dead Man's Fortune* (ca. 1590), which seems to come from a *Commedia dell'Arte* scenario. The surviving stage plot has exits and entrances for 'Panteloun', 'Aspida', who must be his wife, and 'Validore', who is disguised and is probably her lover.[54]

Chaucer's four comic tales of cuckoldry, told by the Miller, Reeve, Shipman, and Merchant, were also drawn from the *fabliaux*, and were widely known. They would make excellent plays, especially the Miller's and Reeve's tales, with all their local colour of Oxford and Cambridge. As far as we know from the extant corpus, however, no English dramatist took up the challenge.

While Chapman did not take the Cornelio–Gazetta plot from Boccaccio, Italian Renaissance comedy, or Chaucer, the earlier literature has some underlying patterns relevant to *All Fools*. First, little thought is given to whether or not the protagonists find true love—all interest is on the brilliant schemes they concoct in a never ending quest for sex. The most common word for such schemes in medieval and Renaissance Italian, ubiquitous in Boccaccio, is *beffa*, which Richard Andrews explains as

> an Italian term for 'mockery'. In literature and drama it refers to any narrative plot in which one character gets the upper hand over another—usually in the form of a practical joke, and almost always involving some kind of deception. There may be a practical advantage to be achieved (financial, or sexual), or the trick may be motivated by sheer love of the game.[55]

The plot of *All's Well that Ends Well*, with its 'bed trick', comes directly from Boccaccio's story of Giletta, the physician's daughter of Narbonne (Day 3, Story 9), and Giorgio Melchiori argues persuasively that *The Merry Wives of Windsor*, that most English of English comedies, is 'built on the basic scheme of the multiple *beffa* ... an Italian comedy in English dress'.[56]

Secondly, in considering English texts—*The Canterbury Tales* and *Merry Wives* are perfect examples—we find that cuckoldry, rather than adultery in general, is the focus, with an emphasis on the 'mockery' that is implicit in the *beffa*—*OED* defines 'cuckold' as 'a *derisive* name for the husband of an unfaithful wife' (n.[1] 1a). The standard view, that 'cuckold' derives from the European cuckoo being a brood parasite that lays its (usually one) egg in another bird's nest, is undoubtedly correct, although it is not a perfect fit—the male cuckoo, to the extent that it is involved at all, is the co-offender, not the victim. French historical dictionaries show that *cocu* or *coucou* was sometimes applied to the wife's lover, although the usual definition was, and is, *celui dont la femme est infidèle*.[57] For a husband to be a cuckold, or simply to show his fear of cuckoldry, automatically invites mockery, as it implies that he is sexually inadequate or unable to control his wife for some other reason. Just to say the word, regardless of the context, is a jibe, since 'cuckoo' is an onomatopoeic term in imitation of its familiar two-note song, traditionally the sound husbands most fear, as we hear at the end of *Love's Labour's Lost*:

> The cuckoo then on every tree
> Mocks married men, for thus sings he:
>   'Cuckoo,
> Cuckoo, cuckoo'—O word of fear,
> Unpleasing to a married ear.
>
> (5.2.907–11)

The third underlying pattern, whether dealing with unfaithful wives or philandering husbands, is that no moral opprobrium whatsoever is attached to adultery. As Joan Acocella notes, in the *Decameron* we see 'unfraught sex, of a kind that has probably not been wholly comprehensible to Western people since the Reformation'.[58] Similarly, no one could disapprove of the brazenness with which Alison of *The Miller's Tale* and May of *The Merchant's Tale* cuckold their husbands.

Chapman adopted these attitudes when he half-brought adultery into English comedy in 1596 with *The Blind Beggar of Alexandria*—'half' because there are two adulterous wives, but no deceived husband. Duke Cleanthes, the protagonist, has three other assumed identities: Irus the blind beggar, the 'mad-brain' Count Hermes, and 'Leon, the rich usurer'. As Hermes, he marries the 'bright nymph' Elimene, and, as Leon, he weds her sister Samathis. He then cuckolds Leon in the guise of Count Hermes, and vice versa, before having both husbands 'killed'. The outcome is satisfactory for the widows: they go on to marry kings.

An Humorous Day's Mirth has two ridiculously jealous wives, the Queen of France, married to a philandering King, and Countess Moren, whose husband is much younger than she, but the main interest is with Florilla, young wife of the old and impotent Count Labervele. Her air of holy Puritanism is either the cause of, or a reaction to, his debility—either way, it has nothing to do with her religious principles. The young gallant Lemot, purely for his own amusement and that of his friends, embarks on a scheme to approach Florilla, not secretly, but in Labervele's presence, 'which shall so heat his jealous humour till he be start mad' (2.94–5).[59] With Florilla's enthusiastic assistance, Lemot convinces Labervele that he should test her constancy by making advances to her, and, as a final proof, she 'must put on rich apparel, fare daintily, hear music, read sonnets, be continually courted, kiss, dance, feast, revel all night amongst gallants' (4.231–4). Florilla's response, 'O husband, this is perfect trial indeed!' (4.240), precedes her secret agreement to meet Lemot at a tavern where a private room has been reserved for an afternoon's pleasure.

For all her show of piety, Florilla appears not to have heard of the seventh commandment. She actively seeks every opportunity to cuckold her husband, but she fails, since her choice of lover, Lemot, has no real interest in having sex with her. He only wants to enjoy a 'humorous day' engaged in stripping away her veneer of purity. The brilliance of the comedy lies in Florilla's open defiance, denying everything and graciously forgiving her husband for suspecting her of doing what she actually did, 'For as men should ever love their wives, so should they ever trust them' (13.112–13), and in Lemot's refusal to expose her, leaving her free to try again.

In March of 1598, the Admiral's Men paid Thomas Dekker £5 for a play called *The Triplicity of Cuckolds*,[60] unfortunately lost; in September of the same year Jonson's *Every Man In His Humour* (quarto version) was acted at the Curtain.[61] The jealous husband Thorello, a rich merchant 'but lately married' (1.4.89) to Bianca, has both his sister Hesperida and Bianca's brother Prospero as house-guests.[62] His disquiet stems from Prospero's presumption in using his house to entertain friends, who 'swear, leap, and dance, and revel night by night' (1.4.54), but he cannot throw the unwanted visitors out:

> They would give out, because my wife is fair,
> Myself but lately married, and my sister
> Here sojourning a virgin in my house,
> That I were jealous.
>
> (1.4.88–91)

Determined to keep his fears to himself, Thorello saves his thoughts about Bianca for soliloquies. In a serious speech that could be delivered by Othello, Thorello reflects on his 'new disease': jealousy is a 'pestilence' (1.4.191) that infects the brain and then spreads through the body

> Till not a thought or motion in the mind
> Be free from the black poison of suspect.
>
> (1.4.202–3)

Thorello's jealous humour is never seen in public until the end, when there is a very funny confrontation with Bianca, each making wild accusations about the other (5.1.28–54). No one talks about his jealousy behind his back or teases him about it.

Things could not be more different in *All Fools*, where Cornelio's jealousy is no secret from anyone. Gazetta tells Gratiana and Bellanora all about it in their first scene (1.2.20–41), and soon afterwards we see that everyone else knows: having placed Gratiana in Gostanzo's house, Rinaldo needs a new source of amusement, so he proposes to Valerio that they visit

> the new-turned gentleman's fair wife,
> That keeps thy wife and sister company;
> With whom the amorous courtier Dariotto
> Is far in love, and of whom her sour husband
> Is passing jealous, puts on eagle's eyes
> To pry into her carriage.
>
> (2.1.215–20)

Chapman could not draw on Terence while thinking up the situations that follow. The woes of married life find their way into Roman comedy, but the plays of Plautus and Terence are without a deceived husband. The one exception, Plautus's *Amphitryon*, is a special case, since Jupiter takes on Amphitruo's form when seducing Alcumena (their child will be Hercules), and she is unaware that she is being unfaithful. The comic performances of the Roman mimes were different. These players worked without written scripts, so what we know about them is very limited, but judging by the number of times Roman poets describe it, the 'adultery mime', with husband at the door, wife in the bed, and wife's lover in the cupboard, was their most popular routine.[63] In any event, Chapman had no need of Plautus, Terence, or the mimes, for Rome's greatest poet was waiting in the wings, ready to take over.

OVID AND THE ART OF ADULTERY

> Virility feeds on sex, is boosted by practice. No girl's ever complained about *my* technique. (Ovid, *Amores*)

If we accept that a fundamental quality of the Renaissance is that its poets, painters, and other artists looked to antiquity in creating their own modes of expression, then no single work has had greater influence than the *Metamorphoses* of Ovid. One can hardly read a page of Shakespeare without finding an allusion to it, nor can anyone walk through the Uffizi or the Louvre without Ovid as a guide—the noted classical scholar Mary

Beard was only slightly overstating the case when she said, 'the whole of Renaissance art is really a commentary on Ovid's *Metamorphoses*'.[64]

Before Ovid even started the *Metamorphoses*, however, he was already Rome's most famous poet, his celebrity achieved on the success of the sensational (in every sense of the word) *Amores*, followed by *The Art of Love*. These works cannot be dated precisely, but we do know they were written when adultery was a major political issue in Rome. Starting in 18 BC, Emperor Augustus instituted strict legislation to regulate marriage and sexual morality; financial incentives were offered for having three or more children, and harsh penalties were put in place for adultery. Ironically, two of the law's victims were Augustus's daughter and granddaughter: 'Julia the elder', a serial adulteress, was exiled in 2 BC, and in AD 8 'Julia the younger', who took after her mother in every way, suffered the same fate.[65]

The real reason for Ovid's banishment to the Black Sea port of Tomis in the same year of AD 8 will never be fully known. In *Tristia*, written in exile, Ovid says it was because of a 'poem and an error' (2.207).[66] The poem was *The Art of Love*, which made Ovid 'a teacher of obscene adultery' (2.212), but the error is never specified, although Ovid implies that it was no secret at the time:

> The cause, too well known to all, of my ruin
> Is not to be revealed by any testimony of mine.
>
> (4.10.99–100)

It has long been thought that given the timing, and the fact that Augustus conducted the case personally without a public trial (*Tristia* 2.131-4), Ovid's error may have been an affair with the younger Julia. Eventually, this possibility gave rise to the historical tradition that Ovid's involvement was with the elder Julia, ignoring the fact that she was exiled ten years earlier, and that she was 'Corinna', the woman to whom Ovid addressed his wildly erotic *Amores* (in *Poetaster*, Jonson removes the story even further from history by making Augustus's daughter unmarried).

Marlowe was the first to translate the *Amores* into English, entitling the work *Elegies*, which is correct in that Ovid wrote in elegiac metre (alternating lines of hexameter and pentameter), in contra-distinction to the epic metre of the *Aeneid* (all hexameter). It is also misleading: in early modern English, an 'elegy' could be any love poem, as we know from Orlando's habit of hanging 'odes upon hawthorns and elegies on brambles' (3.2.361–2), but then, as now, the most common English definition was 'a song of lamentation, especially a funeral song' (*OED* n. 1). Latin elegies are indeed usually songs of lamentation, but the lament is not for a recently departed loved one—most often, the poet is lamenting the state of his own love life. The *Amores* is the story of Ovid's on-again off-again affair with Corinna, just as the poems of Ovid's two most admired predecessors in the genre, Catullus and Propertius, are agonised reports of their affairs with Lesbia and Cynthia. A major, if not the only, cause of all three poets' problem is that the ladies in question are already married.

Corinna, the name Ovid gives to the woman he so ardently desires, is first spoken of in the fifth poem, a very explicit description of a hot afternoon's sex. She is a fictional construct, not one particular person, but that did stop some women from claiming to be the 'real Corinna'. Ovid later boasts,

> many women aspire to fame
> Through my art. I know one girl who goes round
>   saying she's Corinna:
> What wouldn't the poor thing give for her dream
> To be true?
>
> (2.17.28–31)

By the end of the *Amores*, Ovid has seduced Corinna, her maid, and two other women, explaining,

> There's nothing to choose between them for looks.
>   They both dress smartly.
> On performance they're just about neck and neck.
>
> (2.10.5–6)

On the basis of these achievements Ovid declares himself a qualified instructor. No longer the desperate lover of the *Amores*, who implores the eunuch guarding the door of his latest flame's house to look the other way and let him in (2.2.15–23), he begins *The Art of Love* with

> Should anyone here in Rome lack finesse at love-making, let him
> Try me—read my book, and results are guaranteed!
> Technique is the secret.
>
> (1.1–3)

Books 1 and 2 have our hero giving detailed instructions on where to find girls, how to woo them, and how to keep them. Book 3 is addressed to women—how to attract men, and, importantly for Chapman, how to cheat on your husband. If any one particular part of the *Art of Love* offended Augustus the most, this was probably it, since the Emperor and his adultery laws get a mention:

> I was going to omit the ways of eluding a crafty husband
> Or vigilant guard—let the bride
> Respect her husband, let brides be guarded securely. That's proper:
> Modesty, law, and our Leader so prescribe.
> But watch *you*? A woman still scarcely used to her freedom?
> Intolerable! Let me instruct you in all
> The ways of deceit.
>
> (3.611–17)

Ovid's presence is felt right away in *All Fools*, albeit somewhat obscurely, when Gratiana uses the story of Pasiphaë from *The Art of Love* to describe Gazetta's marriage problems (cf. 1.2.57n.). No obscurity accompanies the first private conversation between Cornelio and Gazetta, however. Convinced that she is passing secret messages to Dariotto, Cornelio assures her,

> Yet do I understand your darkest language,
> Your treads o'th' toe, your secret jogs and wrings,
> Your intercourse of glances.
>
> (2.1.254–6)

If Gazetta did indulge in such 'secret jogs and wrings' (nudges and squeezes) or 'intercourse of glances' with Dariotto, she would only be following Ovid's instructions to Corinna. A brilliant passage in the *Amores* has Ovid learning that he, Corinna, and her husband are all to attend the same dinner party. After stating his fervent hope that the husband 'drops down dead before the dessert' (1.4.2), Ovid gives her detailed directions on what to do:

> When he pats the couch, put on your Respectable Wife expression,
> And take your place beside him—but nudge my foot
> As you're passing by. Watch out for my nods and eye-talk,
> Pick up my stealthy messages, send replies.
> I shall speak whole silent volumes with one raised eyebrow,
> Words will spring from my finger, words traced in wine.
>
> (1.4.15–20)

As for Gazetta's 'treads o'th' toe'. they are something that Ovid gives a special warning against:

> Don't start rubbing your thigh against his, don't go playing
> Footsy under the table.
>
> (1.4.43–4)

The many spectators at the Rose or Blackfriars who recognised passages from Terence in *All Fools* would have been equally adept at recognising the many quotations from and allusions to Ovid, whenever the subject turned to adultery. Indeed, Chapman might be adding another level of enjoyment to the performance by challenging the audience to spot as many quotations as it can, just as Marc Norman and Tom Stoppard do in their screenplay for *Shakespeare in Love*.

CUCKOLDRY AS A SPECTATOR SPORT

Ovid is all about the seducer and his women. Corinna's husband may get a mention, but he takes no active part in the proceedings, even though

INTRODUCTION 29

at one point Ovid wishes that he would show some resistance (cf. 3.1.284–8n.). Chapman approaches the subject from the opposite direction, and supplies what Ovid leaves out by making Cornelio, the husband, the leading player in this part of his comedy.

Cornelio's response of 'Well, no time past' (2.1.270) to Gazetta's strong denial of any impropriety with Dariotto is elliptical but clear—nothing may have happened so far, but tomorrow might be different. Like Thorello, who is also concerned with the potential for future disasters, Cornelio follows with a soliloquy, but he offers no introspection about the causes or symptoms of jealousy. He deals only with practicalities: others may 'inveigh against this mood of jealousy', but Cornelio knows no other way 'to check the ranging appetites' of women (2.1.274, 276). His choices are limited: one is to surrender, and allow Gazetta to go 'to feasts and revels and invite home gallants' (2.1.280); the other is to

> be pointed at, and thought
> A jealous ass.
> (2.1.286–7)

One might ask why Cornelio does not keep Gazetta at home, if he can, and deny entry to the gallants. The answer lies in his social ambition:

> I have a show of courtiers haunt my house.
> In show my friends, and for my profit too.
> (2.1.288–9)

As a 'start-up gentleman' (Actors.8), the 'profit' Cornelio seeks is acceptance among the fashionable courtiers of the city. Hence he must be

> content to ride abroad with them,
> To revel, dice, and fit their other sports.
> (2.1.292–3)

He even has to be outwardly friendly towards Dariotto, the man he thinks is out to cuckold him.

The delicate balancing act does not last long. When Cornelio happens upon his 'brave comrades' (2.1.295), everything they say is pointedly about Gazetta. Claudio asks, 'how does thy wife', Valerio 'where is she', and the answer, 'abroad, about her business', brings some unwanted advice. Valerio tells Cornelio to sell his farm in the country and attach himself to a powerful man at court, or even better, 'bring thy wife there, and she'll make thee great' (2.1.357). Cornelio's rejoinder, 'What, to the court? Then take me for a gull' (2.1.358), sets Valerio off on a display of what rhetoricians call *epistrophe*:

> Nay, never shun it to be called a gull,
> For I see all the world is but a gull,
> One man gull to another in all kinds.
> A merchant to a courtier is a gull,
> A client to a lawyer is a gull,
> A married man to a bachelor a gull,
> A bachelor to a cuckold is a gull,
> All to a poet, or a poet to himself.
>
> (2.1.359–66)

We might read this as an early statement of the play's central idea, that those who consider themselves masters at fooling others are bound to be fooled themselves, but the immediate dramatic context is the issue here. How a bachelor gulls a married man is obvious, especially to Cornelio, but the next line requires some unpacking. Saying the word 'cuckold' is bad enough, but the way a cuckold gulls a bachelor is to gain money or other advantage from him by being a 'wittol', i.e., a complaisant cuckold who knows about, and even encourages, his wife's infidelity.[67] Middleton plays on the word in naming John Allwit of *A Chaste Maid in Cheapside*, who is content to live off Sir Walter Whorehound, his wife's lover and father of her seven children.[68]

This is all too much for Cornelio. He turns to Dariotto and asks, in an aside, the question that sets the subplot in motion: 'shall we gull this guller?' (2.1.367). Cornelio's decision to praise Valerio as the possessor of courtly qualities, then to mock his demonstration of them, is more than an irritated reaction to Valerio's pointed remarks about his married life. What he wants most is to show Dariotto and the others that he is courtier material. He has already tried his hand at 'all games and recreations' (1.2.38); now he has an opportunity to show himself the master of another of another courtly skill, what Castiglione calls the 'merry prank'.

It would be difficult to overstate the influence of Castiglione's *Book of the Courtier* (1528), first in Italy, and then in England with Sir Thomas Hoby's translation of 1561. In four evenings of conversation, the distinguished guests of the Duke and Duchess of Urbino discuss topics including the attributes and behaviour of the true Renaissance courtier, neo-Platonism, the nature of virtue and beauty, the proper use of languages, and much more.

For the second evening's entertainment, Lady Elisabetta Gonzaga, the hostess, asks her guests to offer their views on the qualities of the courtier in the social sphere. The first half of the debate covers matters such as speaking and acting without affectation, physical exercises, dancing, music, proper dress, tact, and modesty. Lady Elisabetta then turns to

Bernardo Dovizi da Bibbiena with a request to share his thoughts on the art of *facezie* (jests). She asks him to describe how they are derived and how to use them, along with anything else he might know on the subject.[69]

Lady Elisabetta could not have chosen a better person to speak on *facezie*. The 'real-life' Bernardo Dovizi da Bibbiena (1470–1520), a nobleman, politician, and eventually papal officer, was the author of one of the liveliest comedies of the Italian Renaissance, *The Comedy of Calandro* (*La Calandra*), first performed in 1513.[70] The gullible old man Calandro comes from the *Decameron*; the plot involves multiple deceptions involving his wife and a young man, and his own desperate attempts to bed a young girl. Bibbiena's response takes up all the second half of Book 2. After a long discourse on amusing stories, quick witticisms, and other verbal *facezie*, he turns to his special area of expertise, which Castiglione calls the *burla*, a word given precisely the same definition as *beffa* in Florio's Italian–English dictionary of 1598: 'flout, scoff, jibe, frump, jest, mock'.[71] These words are all consistent with the idea, as noted above, of the *beffa* as a type of practical joke, which is accurate but somewhat clumsy, especially in our time when the term is more likely to mean Bart and Lisa Simpson telephoning Moe's tavern and asking to speak to Ivana Hugankiss. I believe that Hoby's expression, 'merry prank', hits the mark perfectly, although the victim would delete 'merry'.

If Cornelio consulted his copy of the *Courtier*, he would have read that one type of prank is accomplished 'when a man layeth (as it were) a net, and showeth a piece of a bait so, that a man runneth to be deceived of himself'.[72] In a display of quick-wittedness not seen until this moment, Cornelio casts the net, praising Valerio's knowledge of languages, dancing, singing, and 'playing on choice instruments' (2.1.379), knowing that after a brief attempt at false modesty, Valerio will happily demonstrate his talents. Chapman skilfully shows Cornelio's satisfaction at having succeeded by having him refrain from mocking Valerio directly; instead he rebukes Dariotto for his uncourtly behaviour:

> Go to, Signor Courtier.
> You deal not courtly now to be so plain,
> Nor nobly, to discourage a young gentleman
> In virtuous qualities, that has but stol'n 'em.
>
> (2.1.413–16)

Cornelio's great mistake was not reading another passage in the *Courtier*, Bibbiena's warning that a prank should be a 'friendly deceit in matters that offend not at all or very little', but 'he that will work a merry prank without respect, doth many times offend, and then arise debates and sore hatred'.[73] Valerio, the first of the play's proud gullers to be openly gulled himself, vows retribution:

> 'Tis very well, Master Courtier
> And Dan Cornuto, I'll cry quit with them both.
>
> (2.1.421-2)

Making Cornelio believe Gazetta is having an affair with Dariotto, something he is disposed to do anyway, is not the real point of Valerio's plan. We never see him, Iago-like, planting evil thoughts in Cornelio's ear—all that is done offstage. Valerio will get even by 'firing the poor cuckold's jealousy' enough to 'make him mad' (2.1.424-5), and making sure that everyone is present to enjoy the spectacle and admire Valerio's cleverness in setting him up. As Jill Levenson notes, it is the secondary plot that 'emphasizes the ubiquity of fools',[74] and, from here to the end of the play, we see pranks and counter-pranks, with the superior wits gulling the supposedly witless, only to be gulled in return. The agent of Valerio's revenge is Curio the page, assigned to give a formal speech in defence of womanhood. In itself, this would do nothing to make Cornelio believe Dariotto is cuckolding him, but being subjected to marriage counselling from a child would send anyone over the edge.

A page can be any boy or youth, but *OED*'s second definition of one 'employed as the personal attendant and messenger of a person of high rank' (n.[1] 2a) seems appropriate here. Chapman never makes it completely clear who the person of high rank is, but Gostanzo is the most likely candidate. Curio first enters at 2.1.37 with Valerio, who immediately sends him off with a message to a creditor—Valerio would not have such a retainer on the farm, but there is no illogicality in his giving orders to one from his father's household. Cornelio's wild accusation that Curio is Dariotto's bastard son (3.1.245-9) does make some sense in that illegitimate sons of the nobility were often sent to another household for employment and education.

Keeping with the Roman model of everything happening outdoors, Cornelio and the others enter in mid-argument, with Claudio and Marc Antonio trying to dissuade him from jumping to conclusions, and Valerio pretending to offer helpful advice before asking the boy to speak. Curio shares some qualities with another notable boy, Don Armado's Moth in *Love's Labour's Lost*, although there are distinct differences. As William C. Carroll notes, Moth's wit lies in his quick rejoinders, replies of one or two lines; his longest speech, 'No, my complete master ... snip and away' (3.1.9-20) is only eleven lines.[75] Curio defends 'that absent and honourable lady' Gazetta (3.1.168) with an elaborate discourse of seventy lines, interrupted only three times by short interjections. Moth might well be, as Don Armado admiringly says, a 'well-educated infant' (1.2.94), but not half as educated as Chapman's young orator, who draws arguments from Hesiod and Aristotle before launching into a parody of John Lyly's prose style.

Just having a precocious page, regardless of the way he speaks, is already a parody of Lyly, whose plays often include those whom David Bevington describes as 'pert boy-servants'. Some prominent examples are Epiton, Sir Tophas's 'long-suffering page' in *Endymion*, 'always there to point up by his diminutive size and ready wit the grossness and fatuity of his master', and Criticus and Molus of *Sappho and Phao*, who follow up the debate between their masters, the scholar Pandion and the courtier Trachinus, with a parodic debate of their own. Taken together, they confirm what Erasmus says in *The Praise of Folly*: 'a child wise beyond his years is a pest'.[76]

Chapman engages in some pointed political satire when Curio presumes 'to undertake the defence of the 'honourable lady' Gazetta, 'and in her of all that name—for lady is grown a common name to their whole sex' (3.1.168, 169–70). By the spring of 1599 Chapman must have given up all hope of receiving anything in return for the dedication of his two *Iliad* volumes to 'the most honoured now living instance of Achilleian virtues eternised by divine Homer, the Earl of Essex', for Essex had other things on his mind. On 12 March he received orders to take command of the expedition to put down the Earl of Tyrone's rebellion in Ireland. He sailed on 27 March,[77] and, soon after disembarking at Dublin he took up his old habit of knighting everyone in sight.

The 'Essex knights' had been a national joke since 1591, when the Earl took his first company of soldiers to France. Normally, a knighthood is granted for valour in the field, but the French holding Rouen would not be drawn into battle, so Essex thought it only fair that his men be knighted for what they would have done if given the chance. As we read in *The Journal of the Siege of Rouen*, on 8 October, 'not far from St. Catherine's castle', Essex 'commanded all the gentlemen to light, and said he was very sorry that no opportunity was offered him to have led them into a place where they might have gained honour; but the fault was not his, neither yet in them, for he had received a great goodwill in all, and thereof was determined to give notes of honour to some, and there made twenty-four knights'.[78] A letter found in the *State Papers Domestic* comments that 'great mockery was made', and, on 22 October, Lord Burghley sent Essex a reprimand: 'Your Lordship so liberal bestowing of knighthoods is here commonly evil censured, and when Her Majesty shall know it, which yet she doth not, I fear she will be highly offended, considering she would have had that authority left out of your commission'. In concluding, Burghley ruefully admits that what's done is done, and then makes the very same joke Chapman does eight years later in *All Fools*: '*quod factum est infectum esse non potest*, and hereby you have increased the state of ladies, present and future'.[79]

In 1599, Elizabeth gave Essex clear instruction that in Ireland he must refrain from knighting anyone who was not 'of ancient blood, good livelihood, or had done some especial service'. Essex's response was to knight thirty-eight more men.[80]

Later in the play, when Cornelio demands to know why Dariotto, if he is such an expert in courtly affairs, is not a knight, Dariotto's clever response is

> Tush, 'tis more honour still to make a knight
> Than 'tis to be a knight, to make a cuckold
> Than 'tis to be a cuckold,
>
> (3.1.330–2)

and swords are drawn. The fight does not last long, but at least Dariotto can say that he used his weapon for its intended purpose, which is more than Essex ever did. After a disastrous campaign he was back in England by the end of September, and Sir Robert Napper, Chief Baron of the Exchequer in Ireland, wrote from Dublin that even the rebels were saying that Essex 'never drew sword but to make knights'.[81]

Curio goes on to suggest that Cornelio consider his own imperfections before condemning Gazetta's, and asks,

> If she be wanton abroad, are not you wanting at home? If she be amorous, are not you jealous? If she be high set, are not you taken down? If she be a courtesan, are not you a cuckold?
>
> (3.1.187–90)

The pattern of rhetorical questions, all of the same length, is an identifying feature of euphuism, a word taken from the titles of Lyly's best-known works, *Euphues: The Anatomy of Wit*, and *Euphues and His England*. At the beginning of *The Anatomy of Wit*, Lyly introduces his main character, 'a young gentleman of Athens', and goes on to say how his virtues are placed in sharper relief by his defects, 'as therefore the sweetest rose hath his prickle, the finest velvet his brack, the fairest flour his bran'. Indeed, these comparisons are the first-ever examples of euphuism, and Curio parodies them nicely in his next statement—'Let us endure their bad qualities for their good, allow the prickle for the rose, the brack for the velvet'—although he drops the flour–bran comparison and substitutes the equally mundane 'the paring for the cheese' (3.1.199).

Curio's conclusion, 'that there are no cuckolds in the world but those that have wives' (3.1.243–4), has the desired effect. Cornelio runs off, rapier drawn, in search of Dariotto, who naturally enters moments later. The courtier's greeting,

> How now, my hearts, what, not a wench amongst you?
> 'Tis a sign y'are not in the grace of wenches
> That they will let you be thus long alone,
> (3.1.257–9)

shows that manœuvring him into puncturing his own pretensions will be easy. Consistent with the theme that anyone will fool himself if given the opportunity, Valerio uses the same weapon of flattery that Dariotto and Cornelio used against him. Knowing that the 'amorous courtier' (2.1.217) considers himself a great lover, Valerio and the others praise him for never boasting about his affairs, which prods Dariotto into claiming that he lives only for the challenge:

> I love to court and win, and the consent,
> Without the act obtained, is all I seek.
> (3.1.271–2)

When told that everyone knows things have often gone farther than that, he dismisses the danger of being caught by a jealous husband:

> The way to draw my custom to his house
> Is to be mad and jealous; 'tis the sauce
> That whets my appetite.
> (3.1.286–8)

Dariotto is talking about husbands in general, not Cornelio. Whether or not he really is as good as he claims is left delightfully unclear, but his befuddlement after his five-second swordfight with Cornelio (3.1.345–6) indicates that he has never been near Gazetta's bed. While waiting for the surgeon, Valerio reminds Dariotto that a true courtier is always modest:

> when you prove
> Victorious over fair Gazetta's fort,
> Do not, for pity, sound your trump for joy,
> But keep your valour close, and 'tis your honour.
> (3.1.359–62)

The only possible reason for Dariotto's wound (which apparently disappears by the time he arrives at the Half Moon in 5.2) is to bring on Pock the surgeon, adding the quack to the list of humorous characters that Chapman brings to the English stage for the first time. Chapman also provides an instructive look at the 'science' of medicine as it was practised in Elizabethan England. After examining Dariotto, Pock assures him that 'the incision is not deep, nor the orifice exorbitant. The pericranion is not dislocated.' Therefore, Pock guarantees a complete recovery 'without perishing of any joint' within ten days, all for a modest fee of forty crowns (3.1.381–3).

Pock's manner may seem a trifle weird, but hardly so alongside real surgeons practising in London at the time. William Clowes, an English surgeon who claims in his 1579 treatise to have cured more than a thousand men of syphilis during his five-year tenure at the Hospital of St Bartholomew, warns his readers against paying attention to fakes who 'disorderly and unadvisedly intrude themselves into other men's possessions, that is to say, take upon them the practice in that art wherein they have never been trained'. He then advises, 'I urge it very dangerous to touch any part of a man's body with lancet or knife, when as the moon hath motion in that sign which governeth the part that should be stricken'.[83]

Whether or not the moon and stars are in the most advantageous alignment for Dariotto's treatment, Valerio can claim success. The courtier and self-proclaimed seducer has been repaid in a most embarrassing way for ridiculing him, and Cornelio has made a complete ass of himself, all as a result of the *beffa* that Valerio set in motion. But the prank has now taken on a life of its own, for Cornelio has told all present that he is finished with Gazetta: 'I will presently be divorced, and then take her amongst ye' (3.1.347–8).

DIVORCE ENGLISH STYLE

Divorces are made in heaven. (Oscar Wilde, *The Importance of Being Earnest*)

For Valerio to 'have a tale' to make Cornelio 'mad' (2.1.425) is one thing, but for Cornelio to divorce Gazetta takes matters well beyond a joke. Rinaldo never expresses any approval of the idea. While waiting to see

>   what black ball of debate
> Valerio's wit hath cast betwixt Cornelio
> And the enamoured courtier,
>
> (3.1.123–5)

he says that Cornelio

> Hath ever watched occasion of divorce.
> And now Valerio's villainy will present it.
>
> (3.1.127–8)

INTRODUCTION 37

Rinaldo's use of the word 'villainy' is interesting. Later, Valerio dismisses the prospect of divorce as unlikely, 'I think it be not so; the ass dotes on her' (4.1.223), but Rinaldo warns him things may have gone too far:

> It is too true, and thou shalt answer it
> For setting such debate 'twixt man and wife.
>
> (4.1.224–5)

For all his dislike of women expressed in 1.1, we can believe Rinaldo when he promises Claudio that he will do his best to 'pacify' Cornelio's 'yellow fury' (3.1.138), assuring him,

> With all my heart, I consecrate my wit
> To the wished comfort of distressèd ladies.
>
> (3.1.139–40)

Nor should we doubt Claudio's assurance, after he tells Cornelio he has been duped, 'if this accident of your nose had not fallen out, I would have told you this before you set to your hand' (4.1.358–60). Nevertheless, none of this prevents Valerio, Rinaldo, Claudio, or the audience from enjoying the antics of the Notary whom Cornelio has engaged to prepare his bill of divorce.

Notaries were an integral part of the legal community in early modern Europe, and while precise duties varied from country to country, generally they were not very different from their modern-day counterparts. In England, a notary's usual tasks were to administer oaths and to draw up and certify contracts, deeds, and other legal agreements. The notary who seals the 'single bond' between Shylock and Antonio in *The Merchant of Venice* does not appear on stage, but it is fair to assume that he would bear little resemblance to the 'learned notary' (4.1.295) of *All Fools*, who reads out the document he has prepared to all assembled—a document seemingly filled with every arcane legal term in existence, never using one word when three or four are available.

No legal officer like this had appeared in English comedy before, but an Italian visitor to London would have recognised the *Notare* of the *Commedia dell'Arte*. This popular form of theatre was never as influential in England as in France, but Italian companies often toured abroad during the 1590s, and English writers offer scattered allusions to the *Commedia*, along with some appearances of their stock characters in their plays, such as the 'old Pantaloon' Gremio (3.1.36–7) of *The Taming of the Shrew*.[84]

The *Notare* was not nearly as important as *Pantalone*, but surviving scenarios show that he appeared frequently. The Correr collection at the

Museum of Venice has two scenarios with a notary, but with no description of what he does.[85] The Casamarciano collection of Neapolitan scenarios is more forthcoming, and, while details are maddeningly few, we do get some idea of the *lazzi* associated with his character. In *Rosalba the Shrew*, he draws up a marriage contract, and Rosalba beats him up for his trouble; *Pulcinella Duped* has a notary named Piombino ('leaden one') who has a 'usual scene with the usual lazzi, and after the usual prank the notary departs'. *The Basilisk of Barnagasso*, which exists in two versions, has some information about these *lazzi*: in one, a 'talkative notary' (*notare chiacciarone*) fights with an 'ailing notary' (*notare infermo*) for the job of drawing up a deed of gift, the winner then reading the deed aloud. The second version is similar to what we see in *All Fools*: the notary, once again given the name Piombino, enters, and 'with his usual lazzi he does not let Pulcinella say a word, and with the usual jokes, and their scene, the second act ends'.[86]

We get the impression that all Cornelio has to do to get a divorce is sign the document the Notary has prepared, but in Elizabethan England things were more complicated than that. Divorce proceedings were controlled by the church courts, which could grant one of two decrees. The first, rarely seen, was divorce *a vinculo matrimonii* (from the bond of marriage), essentially an annulment. The grounds might be affinity (family relationship of the couple), a pre-existing marriage contract made by one of the parties, bigamy, or impotence. Since the marriage was deemed never to have existed, the parties were free to remarry, and any children of the annulled marriage would be declared illegitimate.[87]

Cornelio wants the other type of divorce, as the Notary shows by saying that he will 'eftsoons divide, disjoin, separate, remove, and finally eloign, sequester, and divorce' Gazetta, from 'bed and your board' (4.1.309–11). This is divorce *a mensa et thoro* (literally, from table and bed). A decree might be granted because of sodomy, religious apostasy, heresy, or cruelty, but most often adultery. The catch was that it was not a divorce at all, as we think of it, but a formal separation—the husband and wife could not remarry during each other's lifetime.[88] From the time of Edward VI, more radical Protestant groups objected to the no-remarriage rule, but occasional attempts at reform came to nothing, since the Anglican establishment feared that adultery would increase if it could be used as a pretext for the dissolution of a marriage.[89]

If Cornelio ever did sign the bill, the matter would have gone to a church court. Rinaldo asks him, 'what are the presumptions' (4.1.265), i.e., presumptive evidence, he would offer, and Cornelio's answer does not inspire confidence. It amounts to the 'commerce of glances' between Gazetta and Dariotto 'last Sunday night at supper' (4.1.268–9), and his having caught them playing footsy (4.1.270–1). A husband suing for divorce *a mensa et thoro* also needed to provide eye-witnesses to his wife's adultery. For this requirement, Cornelio asserts that later the same night, when Gazetta was supposed to be alone, 'her dog barked', and asks, 'Did you not hear him, Valerio?'. Valerio assures him that he did, and is prepared to testify: 'And understand him too, I'll be sworn of a book' (4.1.273–4).

We may assume that no matter how 'strong in law' (4.1.279) the Notary's bill might be, a case with a dog as the only witness means the divorce is unlikely to happen. Yet, even after Claudio tells him he has been gulled, Cornelio insists,

> It may well be, yet have I cause enough
> To perfect my divorce.
>
> (4.1.361–2)

Claudio's revelation does have the effect of calming Cornelio down. For the first time since Curio's declamation, Cornelio speaks rationally. He promises to conclude things 'with a counterbuff' (4.1.363), and believes he understands the society he has aspired to join:

> Now I perceive well where the wild wind sits,
> Here's gull for gull, and wits at war with wits.
>
> (4.1.368–9)

' 'TIS AT THE HALF MOON TAVERN'

How Cornelio knows that Valerio will be spending the afternoon drinking and gambling at the Half Moon is not explicit, but is not improbable. His tall story to Rinaldo (5.1.26–56), designed to bring Gostanzo to the tavern, where he will

> at full discover
> His own gross folly and his son's distempers,
>
> (5.1.71–2)

injects some genuine suspense into the proceedings—no one knows how Gostanzo will react or what he will do once he witnesses Valerio's true behaviour.

Chapman creates some confusion by having Claudio say to Cornelio, 'I cannot but in kindness tell you that Valerio, by counsel of Rinaldo, hath whispered all this jealousy into your ears' (4.1.352–6), which is inconsistent with what happens at the end of 2.1. Claudio is not present to see that the idea is Valerio's own; Rinaldo does not object, but he offers no 'counsel' at all, and, as noted, he then does what he can to mitigate the damage. Having no reason to doubt Claudio's account, Cornelio expresses particular satisfaction in having fooled Rinaldo:

> Go, shallow scholar, you that make all gulls,
> You that can out-see clear-eyed jealousy,
> Yet make this sleight a millstone, where your brain
> Sticks in the midst amazed. This gull to him
> And to his fellow guller shall become
> More bitter than their baiting of my humour.
>
> (5.1.58–63)

Rinaldo gives himself credit for having gulled 'Gostanzo, Dariotto, and Cornelio' (5.1.12), even though all the gulling of Cornelio we actually see is done by Valerio, and Rinaldo does not take part. The inconsistency has led some commentators to assume that the main action of the final scene is Rinaldo receiving his comeuppance. Gordon Braden notes that the play 'rounds itself off ... when Rinaldo himself is gulled by, of all people, the comic husband in a humours subplot, who tricks him into a misstep that exposes everything'; to Frank Manley, 'Rinaldo's pride and brilliance carry him too far, and shortly afterward everything is laid open by Cornelio, the greatest fool of all'.[90]

As things play out, Rinaldo suffers only a minor setback, which he handles with good grace. When he realises Cornelio's story of Valerio's arrest was a fiction, and that he is therefore responsible for Gostanzo learning the truth, Rinaldo makes no excuse to himself: 'What a dull slave was I to be thus gulled!' (5.2.80). When Cornelio gloats,

> Why, Rinald, what meant you to entrap your friend
> And bring his father to this spectacle?
> You are a friend indeed,
>
> (5.2.81–3)

Rinaldo responds with a compliment, and hints that the game is not over:

> 'Tis very good, sir.
> Perhaps my friend, or I, before we part,
> May make even with you.
>
> (5.2.83–5)

The real interest in the scene is with Gostanzo. First he sees Valerio drinking and gambling, and when Marc Antonio tells him he observed

Valerio in bed with Gratiana while Fortunio 'sat laughing' (5.2.130) beside them, he is forced to face the truth. His initial reaction is a promise of retribution, saying he will leave everything to Bellanora (5.2.135–45); only when Fortunio reveals that he has married Bellanora, making him Gostanzo's heir, does the old man give up the game:

> Marc Antonio,
> Give me your hand, there is no remedy.
> Marriage is ever made by destiny.
>
> (5.2.155–7)

Some critics argue that the transformation is too sudden to be credible. Swinburne, who greatly admires the play, writes, 'I find but one slight and characteristic blemish worth noting in a comedy in which the proudest among his great compeers might have permissibly taken fresh pride: it is that the final scene of discovery which winds up the main thread and reconciles the chief agents of the intrigue is somewhat hurriedly dispatched, with too rapid a change of character and readjustment of relation'. Chapman did this, Swinburne believes, because he needed to make room for Valerio's long encomium in praise of cuckoldry, with which the play ends.[91]

Swinburne may be correct in saying that the resolution is 'hurriedly dispatched', but the cause derives more from the manner in which Chapman chose to adapt the corresponding situations in Terence's two plays, rather than undue haste to get to the end. On the surface, Gostanzo's reaction to learning the truth is similar to that of Chremes in *The Self-Tormenter*. His self-proclaimed expertise in fatherhood having been exposed as a sham, Chremes tries to pledge all his property to his daughter Pamphila as a dowry, but is dissuaded by Menedemus. In fact, things work out quite well for Chremes. Although he has been made to look foolish, a father's eternal problem—finding a suitable husband for his daughter—is solved within a day of knowing he has a daughter at all. Furthermore, he has reformed Clitipho, to an extent, by forcing him to marry. Therefore the only real penalty Chremes suffers, apart from embarrassment, is having to pay off Bacchis.

Demea, in *The Brothers*, is different from Gostanzo in one important way. While Gostanzo goes through the play with smug complacency, Demea is always angry—not over the behaviour of Ctesipho, the son he raised—but over the supposed behaviour of Aeschinus, which he puts down to Micio's lax upbringing. The play's ending, where, in W. Geoffrey Arnott's description, 'the austere martinet is transformed into a wise, kind adviser',[92] is a development Terence prepares us for by giving Demea some speeches wherein he justifies his parenting methods as well-meant and still available to both his sons, but only if they ask for it:

> Because you're young, there are some things you don't see too clearly, some things you're much too keen on; your judgement isn't what it might he. If you want me to control you in these respects, and correct you, and help you where appropriate, here I am to do that for you.
>
> (992–4)

He is even willing to pay the pimp Sannio for Bacchis and let his son keep her. Demea may be seriously out of pocket, but by the time the play ends with the traditional 'Give us your applause' (999), he has gained the respect of the other characters, and the audience.

Gostanzo's change of heart does seem abrupt as we read the play, although it need not be overly sudden in performance—a good actor can sustain a very long pause, mulling over the situation, before saying

> Now all my choler fly out in your wits.
> Good tricks of youth, i'faith, no indecorum.
>
> (5.2.153–4)

Pause or not, both his children have married secretly, a more serious offence than the purely financial swindles in Terence. Yet, while Gratiana's 'unnourishing dowry' (1.1.185) may be a lost cause, Bellanora's marriage is 'Knight's son, knight's daughter' (5.2.155). Like Chremes and Demea, Gostanzo has had an expensive day, but the more important issue, as with Terence's fathers, is that the man who fatuously told Marc Antonio he was

> simple, not acquainted
> With the fine sleights and policies of the world,
>
> (3.1.95–6)

was describing himself.

It is easy to see Gostanzo's discovery of the truth as the crisis point of the play, which quickly moves towards the traditional happy ending of welcoming his new daughter-in-law and son-in-law into the family. But this seemingly happy change in Gostanzo may actually be the real crisis. Many critics have observed that the 'happy ending' associated with comedy is not really an ending at all, but a promise of the characters' future contentment. However, if Rinaldo has lost his confidence as a trickster, and Gostanzo is never again to be the world's greatest authority on everything, then life will be very dull for everyone. Jonson closes *Every Man In* and *Every Man Out* with the humorous characters being forced to see the light and change their ways, but here, as in *An Humorous Day's Mirth*, Chapman makes sure that nobody changes at all.

INTRODUCTION 43

Rinaldo, having warned Cornelio that he has yet to concede defeat, begins his countermove by taking charge:

> Silence, my masters! Now here all are pleased,
> Only but Cornelio, who lacks but persuasion
> To reconcile himself to his fair wife.
>
> (5.2.158–60)

Knowing that a chastened Gostanzo would never do, Rinaldo employs his reliable weapon, flattery, and asks that Gostanzo, 'of all men our best speaker', to persuade Cornelio to 'reconcile himself to his fair wife' (5.2.161–2). He has no idea what Gostanzo will say, but as usual Fortune takes over, and Gostanzo has hardly begun before showing that he is back to his old self.

Gostanzo's idea of 'reconcile' is not to convince Cornelio that Gazetta is chaste, and therefore he must rid himself of his jealous humour. On the contrary, Gostanzo asks, 'would you desire to have such a wife as no man could love but yourself?' (5.2.169–70), then proceeds to assure Cornelio that there is nothing wrong with Dariotto having kissed Gazetta, 'or performed other offices of that nature, whereby they did converse together at bed and at board, as friends may seem to do' (5.2.172–4). The argument comes directly from the *Amores*, when Ovid advises Corinna's husband,

> It's so provincial
> To object to adulterous wives—a deplorable lack
> Of that *ton* for which Rome is famous ...
> ... If all you wanted was virtue, why pick a beauty?
> The two things just *never* coincide.
> If you're wise, you'll play up to her. Stop pulling damnable faces,
> Don't stand on your marital rights,
> She'll bring you scads of good friends: take care to cultivate them—
> A minimal effort, a substantial return:
> Freedom for you to drink with the boys, while endless
> Presents—from others—greet your eye at home.
>
> (3.4.37–9, 41–8)

The old knight knows this to be true because he knew Cornelio's parents. His mother was a clever woman with a sparkling personality, 'honest enough', but nonetheless ready to 'tickle Dob now and then'. Cornelio's father, 'knowing 'twas but her humour, for his own quietness' sake', rigged a special doorbell to his house so that his wife's lover would be warned and escape out the back door (5.2.187–93).

Having been informed that wittolry is a family tradition and the only proper attitude for a man to have, Cornelio has no hesitation in telling everyone that to be a wittol was what he intended all along: 'I did train the woodcock Dariotto into the net, drew him to my house, gave him opportunity with my wife—as you say my father dealt with his wife's friends—only to train him in' (5.2.209–12). As for seeing Dariotto in bed with his wife: 'I winked at it, and drew on the fool more and more, only to bring him within my compass ... and now shall the world see I am as wise as my father' (5.2.219–20).

IN PRAISE OF THE HORN

Now, you take my wife. Please! (Henny Youngman)

Valerio's encomium to the horn is probably a direct parody of Jonson's ending to the first version of *Every Man In His Humour*. Thorello, now claiming to have 'the faithfull'st wife in Italy' (5.3.351–2), recites a poem celebrating his cure from the terrible disease of jealousy:[93]

> For this I find: where jealousy is fed,
> Horns in the mind, are worse than on the head.
> See what a drove of horns fly in the air,
> Winged with my cleansèd and my credulous breath!
> Watch them, suspicious eyes, watch where they fall:
> See, see, on heads that think they have none at all!
> Oh, what a plen'uous world of this will come!
> When air rains horns, all men be sure of some.
>
> (5.3.353–60)

Obviously, Cornelio has not arrived at the same conclusion, so Valerio decides that a different type of speech would fit the occasion: 'Is't come to this? Then will I make a speech in praise of this reconcilement, including therein the praise and honour of the most fashionable and authentical horn!' (5.2.223–5).

Numerous theories have been offered to explain how most of Europe adopted horns as the symbol of cuckoldry.[94] Some cultural historians believe it is a sarcastic reference to the horns of the sexually potent bull or billy-goat, but the more compelling explanation is that the tradition derives from the raising of capons, i.e., cocks that are castrated in order to produce tender and flavourful meat. An old and widely practised custom was to remove the cock's spurs and comb along with its testicles, and then graft a spur on to its head where the comb was, so that it resembled a horn. The naturalist Ulisse Aldrovandi (1522–1605) describes the procedure as he observed it in his native Italy:

> Our farm wives pull out the testicles through the posterior parts after making a small incision with a knife. The wound is large enough to admit

a finger above the genitals under the septum where the testicles adhere and it is sufficient to draw them out one by one. When the testicles are removed they sew up the wound with thread and scatter ashes over it. They also cut off the rooster's crest in order to remove all of its virility. Some people insert a spur cut off from the leg in the place of the excised crest and this they say, grows back when the wound heals.[95]

The poor capon's new horn provided visual proof that he was no longer the bird he once was. Aldrovandi does not say if the other barnyard animals made fun of him, but there is no question that human animals had little hesitation in that regard.

Although, as Valerio says, 'their substance is incorporeal ... a spiritual essence, invisible' (5.2.252–5), the cuckold's horns were an invitation to mockery. Its most innocuous form was (and in some places, still is) the two-finger salute, with index and little finger. More seriously, a victim in early modern England could find horns or antlers affixed to his door; cases are also recorded of someone making horns out of branches and attaching then to the cuckold's pew in church, or tying them to the necks of his geese.[96] A man was not even immune on his wedding day, if people suspected that his bride was of questionable character. Martin Ingram quotes the record of a court action that arose out of an incident at Catacombe, Wiltshire, in 1616: one Richard Tomes went 'with a great company of young fellows in his company' to fetch his bride from a neighbouring parish. On the way back, the party was greeted by a buck's horn and 'a picture of a woman's privities' set up by the side of the road.[97]

Valerio sees only good in 'the use, the virtue, the honour, and the very royalty of the horn', and those 'already in possession of it may bear their heads aloft as being proud of such lofty accoutrements' (5.2.239–43). The speech concluded, Gostanzo urges Valerio to shake hands with the man 'in whose high honour' (5.2.312) he delivered it, and the ever-genial Marc Antonio congratulates Cornelio for finally being accepted amongst the gallants of the city, 'And you sir, join hands, you're one amongst them' (5.2.314).

The play seems to end happily, if unconventionally. Gratiana and Bellanora are welcomed into their new families, Gostanzo's authority is restored, and Rinaldo, as he promised, has won the last round of this day's bout with Cornelio. We may be certain that, however Cornelio copes with his new status as wittol, much entertainment will be had in witnessing it. Yet there is one more very important thing to consider: Gazetta and Gratiana have been present for the entire scene, silently watching and listening to everything.

Some may attribute Chapman's including the women in the final scene, only to have them remain mute, to haste in composition or inattention to detail; I see it as a fine example of how expertly he exploits the comic potential of a situation. In her study of feminine silence in early modern culture, Christina Luckyj presents an interesting counterpoint to the traditional view of silence as part of a woman's duty to be chaste and submissive, and argues that it can serve equally as a site of resistance to male authority.[98] This is particularly true of drama, since a character who might be expected to speak, yet remains silent, is physically present in a manner that cannot be achieved on the printed page. Although chiefly concerned with tragedy, Luckyj points out how Jonson exploits the comic possibilities of this idea in *Epicene*, where Morose, having realised his dream of a silent wife, is driven to distraction when, upon meeting her, he cannot get 'her' to say anything.[99]

In having Gazetta keep silent as Cornelio proudly tells everyone she has been unfaithful to him, Chapman offers a new twist to the comic depiction of cuckoldry. From Boccaccio to Chaucer, from Chapman's *An Humorous Day's Mirth* to Jonson's *Every Man In His Humour*, wives who hear their husbands accuse them of adultery, or describe their adulterous deeds to others, have offered a variety of responses, from outraged denial, even when caught in the act, to cheerfully admitting everything and asking their husbands what they plan to do about it. In *All Fools*, Gazetta's silence is an eloquent pointer to the realm of delightful possibilities now awaiting her. A bad actor would make all sorts of nods and winks to tell the audience what Gazetta is thinking; a good actor would leave the audience wondering if she meekly accepts the situation, or if she believes that this could be the greatest thing that has ever happened to her. Valerio thought that his plan might turn Gazetta 'divorced loose' (2.1.426) amongst himself and the other gallants. It now appears that, if she wishes, Gazetta can live the high life, enjoying the company of other men, and say she is merely following her husband's wishes. We have no idea what will occur, and that is precisely the point. I have argued that restoring Gostanzo to his position of authority is the real happy ending of the play. To that we can add the possibility, all the more delicious because it is not explicit, that life for Gazetta will soon be a very interesting.

One also wonders how Gratiana, having just received Gostanzo's blessing to her marriage, is to react when her new husband gives a speech extolling the virtues of cuckoldry. Again, the actor has any number of choices, reflecting the wonderful array of possibilities available to Gratiana about how she is to enjoy life in the future.

In some respects, Rinaldo would be the more appropriate character to deliver the horn speech. Having no wife, he is a neutral observer, and his cynicism about marriage is established in the first scene, when he compares the lovelorn Fortunio with the married Valerio by saying

> What different stars reigned when your loves were born.
> He, forced to wear the willow, you the horn.
> (1.1.39–40)

But Chapman has Valerio, just when he is feeling most triumphant, decide to speak. He then delivers an impassioned discourse, informing an enthusiastic audience, including his wife, that the best thing that can happen to a man is to be cuckolded.

Valerio might accompany the close of his grand declamation—an assurance that the cuckold's proud right to wear the horn is irrevocable—with a look of great satisfaction on his face. But should he then exchange glances with Gratiana, that expression could slowly change, as he realises, too late, what he has done. It is only fitting that Chapman ends *All Fools* with one last demonstration of the great guller gulling himself, while leaving the audience to imagine what delightful future may be in store for Gazetta and Gratiana—an apt demonstration of the old show-business maxim, 'Always leave 'em wanting more'.

It would be interesting to see how well *All Fools* might fare in a modern production. The only recorded performance I have found was done by the drama club of the Delta Epsilon Fraternity at Harvard on 22 April 1909, which Parrott attended and reviewed in the *Nation*:

> To my delight, I found that tried by the standard of actual representation, by intelligent amateur actors, the play gave distinct pleasure to a mixed and highly critical audience, which followed the story with unbroken interest, and burst out from time to time in hearty and spontaneous applause … Whether every member of the audience could have passed a rigid examination in the reconstruction of the plot is, I think, doubtful, but I am sure that the play as it unrolled carried along every spectator, with no trace of the feeling of hesitation and bewilderment which is so fatal to the enjoyment of a comedy of intrigue. As a measure of Chapman's originality it was interesting to note that the most effective scene, the mock repentance of Valerio and his father's feigned forgiveness, was one for which Chapman found no hint in his sources.

Parrott concludes by saying, 'the performance as a whole revealed in Chapman's play a vitality and breadth of comic power unrealised before even by one who has long loved and dutifully studied the work of this noble old poet and playwright'.[100] Perhaps, given the opportunity, many theatregoers, both those who have studied Chapman extensively and those coming to him for the first time, would respond in the same fashion.

THE TEXT

The 1605 quarto of *All Fools* was published by Thomas Thorpe. The printer's name does not appear, but ornaments on the title page are those of George Eld, one of London's busiest printers of dramatic texts in the first quarter of the seventeenth century.[101] Since the play was not registered with the Stationers' Company, how soon after the Court performance of 1 January 1605 the printing took place cannot be determined with any certainty, although events in which Chapman was deeply involved make it very likely that it was not long afterwards.

The Earl of Essex's abortive coup, followed swiftly by his trial and execution, took place in February of 1600; by 1605, Chapman's making fun of the great proliferation of knights was still topical, but in a new way. In *The Crisis of the Aristocracy: 1558–1641*, Lawrence Stone describes the 'reckless prodigality' of the first few months of the reign of King James, when 'he dubbed no fewer than 906 knights; by December 1604, England could boast of 1161 new knights, which means that the order had suddenly increased three fold'. This developed into a Court industry: Scottish courtiers would recommend to the King that someone be knighted for prices ranging from £7 10s to £50.[102] Meanwhile, Chapman was collaborating with Jonson and Marston on *Eastward Ho*, performed for the first time at Blackfriars in July or August of 1605. James himself was not in London at the time, but two powerful Scottish courtiers, Sir James Murray and his brother Sir John, were. They were less than amused by the play's jokes about buying knighthoods (Sir Petronel Flash paid £30, probably a swindle), and about life at the Jacobean Court, where the only way to get ahead was to please 'every groom that by indulgence and intelligence crept into his [King James's] favour, and by panderism into his chamber' (2.2.89–91). Singled out for special mention was 'my worshipful rascal, the groom of his close-stool' (2.1.92–3), who happened to be Sir John Murray himself.[103]

The Murrays complained to the King, Chapman and Jonson were arrested, and they remained in prison for at least several weeks during August and September of 1605. Jonson may have been embellishing the story when he later told William Drummond that they were under threat of having their 'ears cut and noses', a punishment for sedition, but there is no doubt that he and Chapman were in serious trouble. This is evident in the letters they wrote from prison, including one from Chapman to the King, asking the 'most excellent sovereign to take merciful notice of the submissive and amendful sorrows of your two most humble and prostrated subjects'.[104]

Eastward Ho was registered for printing on 4 September. The quarto, also printed by George Eld, has several gaps where offending passages were hurriedly removed; some other (rather mild) anti-Scot lines were deleted for a second print run, and exist in only a few surviving copies.[105] If King James was in the audience at the new-year Court performance of *All Fools*, he would not have been troubled by talk of selling knighthoods; as David Riggs notes, James 'thrived on debate, prided himself on his tolerance, and liked irreverent jokes'.[106] Nevertheless, it is hard to imagine that Chapman, after time in jail, would allow even the innocuous and good-natured knighthood jokes in *All Fools* to be published, and so it is more likely that the play was printed in the first half of the year, before the *Eastward Ho* scandal occurred.

Twenty-two copies of the 1605 quarto of *All Fools* are known to exist. Many corrections were made during the press run, resulting in a great number of variants. They are recorded by Akihiro Yamada in a brilliantly comprehensive article published in 1964; Yamada also provides a detailed analysis of the work of the three compositors who set the type.[107] Nearly all variants are accidentals; the few substantive ones that affect meaning are noted in the collation and commentary. *All Fools* is the first Chapman play to be well printed, both *The Blind Beggar of Alexandra* and *An Humorous Day's Mirth* being very poor productions. Inevitably, there are a few misplaced stage directions and incorrect or missing speech prefixes, but overall the copy-text appears to have been carefully prepared, and the compositors have done well with it. Given Chapman's love of inventing new and obscure words, we must be extra wary of accusing them of misreading the copy-text.

G. Blakemore Evans notes that the text has a few unusual spelling forms that appear in Chapman plays set by other printers, and therefore 'the likelihood is great that such a text was printed from Chapman's autograph (or at least, a transcript directly from his autograph)'.[108] The many Latin stage directions, admittedly not unique to Chapman, are consistent with Evans's view.

The quarto has many parentheses, often helpful in parsing Chapman's long sentences with their multiple subordinate clauses, but inappropriate to spoken dialogue, where everything relies on the actor's delivery. While not wanting to direct from the page, I have replaced them with other punctuation marks, usually dashes, in an attempt to show where a pause or change in tone is needed to make sense of the passage.

NOTES

1 R. A. Foakes, ed., *Henslowe's* Diary, 2nd ed. (Cambridge University Press, 2002), pp. 169–70; S. P. Ceresano, 'Edward Alleyn's "Retirement"', *Medieval and Renaissance Drama in England* 10 (1998): 99–100.
2 Andrew Gurr, *The Shakespeare Company, 1594–1612* (Cambridge University Press, 2004), p. 134; Gurr, *The Shakespearian Playing Companies* (Oxford: Clarendon, 1996), p. 240.

50 INTRODUCTION

3 Henslowe's chaotic spelling is 'the ylle of A womon'. Whether this was meant to be *The Ill* or *The Will* is unclear; I believe *Will* is more likely, first on syntactical grounds, and second because Chapman quips on the inability of married women to make wills in *All Fools*.
4 Foakes, p. 100; Ian Donaldson, *Ben Jonson: A Life* (Oxford University Press, 2011), pp. 132–3; Carol Chillington Rutter, *Docments of the Rose Playhouse*, rev. ed. (Manchester University Press, 1999), p. 153.
5 Foakes, pp. 174, 103.
6 Foakes, pp. 103, 268.
7 Foakes, pp. 105, 122.
8 Foakes, p. 122. Henslowe's spelling is 'the world rones A Whelles'.
9 Rutter, pp. 168–9.
10 Peter Razzell, ed., *The Journals of Two Travellers in Elizabethan and Early Stuart England* (London: Caliban, 1995), pp. 26–7.
11 Roslyn Lander Knutson, *Playing Companies and Commerce in Shakespeare's Time* (Cambridge University Press, 2001), p. 13.
12 Foakes, p. 266.
13 Irwin Smith, *Shakespeare's Blackfriars Playhouse: Its History and Design* (New York University Press, 1964), pp. 148–52, 164; Michael Shapiro, *Children of the Revels* (New York: Columbia University Press, 1977), pp. 14–18.
14 Andrew Gurr, 'Take Interest: Shylock Was No Venetian Jew but a London Loan Shark', *Times Literary Supplement* (10 August 2012): 12; Gurr, *Shakespearian Playing*, pp. 347–8.
15 Gurr, *The Shakespearean Stage*, 4th ed. (Cambridge University Press, 2009), pp. 64–5; Ceresano, p. 106.
16 E. K. Chambers, *The Elizabethan Stage*, 4 v. (Oxford: Clarendon, 1923) 4: 171, 3: 367; Gurr, *Shakespearian Playing*, p. 246.
17 Robert Parker Sorlien, ed., *The Diary of John Manningham of the Middle Temple* (Hanover, NH: University Press of New England, 1976), p. 48. The original text says 1603, because the Elizabethan year started in March; see also Edelman, 'John Manningham at the Blackfriars Theatre', *NQ* 60 (2013): 245–7.
18 Sorlien, p. 140.
19 Sorlien, pp. 193, 42.
20 William A. Armstrong, 'The Audience of the Elizabethan Private Theatres', *Review of English Studies*, n.s. 10 (1959): 234–49.
21 Felix Lope de Vega, in Michael J. Sidnell, ed., *Sources of Dramatic Theory I: Plato to Congreve* (Cambridge University Press, 1991), p. 184.
22 English titles of Plautus's plays are from Wolfgang de Melo, tr. and ed., *Plautus*, 5 v. (Cambridge, MA: Harvard University Press, 2011–13).
23 R. B. McKerrow, ed., *The Works of Thomas Nashe*, v. 3 (London: Sidgwick & Jackson, 1910), p. 220; W. David Kay. 'The Shaping of Ben Jonson's Career: A Re-examination of Facts and Problems', *Modern Philology* 67 (1970): 226.
24 A. B. Grosart, ed., *Poems of the Rev. Charles Fitzgeoffrey* (Blackburn: Privately Printed for Subscribers, 1881), pp. xxi–xxiii.
25 Robert S. Miola, intro., *The Case Is Altered*, in *The Cambridge Edition of the Works of Ben Jonson*, 7 v. (Cambridge University Press, 2012), 1: 7. All Jonson quotations are from this edition.
26 Terence quotations are from Peter Brown, ed., *Terence: The Comedies* (Oxford University Press, 2006), citing line numbers. English titles are taken from this edition.

27 Marvin T. Herrick, *Comic Theory in the Sixteenth Century* (Urbana: University of Illinois Press, 1950), p. 113.
28 Barrett H. Clark, ed., *European Theories of the Drama*, rev. ed. (New York: Crown, 1965), p. 148.
29 William Tydeman, *Four Tudor Comedies* (Harmondsworth: Penguin, 1984), p. 17; Erasmus, *On the Method of Study*, tr. Brian McGregor, in *Collected Works*, v. 24 (Toronto University Press, 1978), p. 668.
30 Brown, p. 178; Augustine of Hippo, *Confessions*, tr. Maria Boulding (Hyde Park, NY: New City Press, 1997), p. 56; Erasmus, *Method of Study*, p. 668; *Correspondence*, tr. R. A. B. Mynors, *Collected Works*, v. 1 (Toronto University Press, 1974), p. 59.
31 Erasmus, *Foundations of the Abundant Style*, tr. Betty I. Knott, *Collected Works*, v. 24, p. 584.
32 T. W. Baldwin, *William Shakespeare's Small Latine & Lesse Greeke*, 2 v. (Urbana: University of Illinois Press, 1944), 1: 328–9.
33 William Prynne, *Histrio-mastix: the Players Scourge, or, Actors Tragedy* (London, 1633), p. 553.
34 John Barsby, ed. and tr., *Terence*, 2 v. (Cambridge, MA: Harvard University Press, 2001), 2: 246.
35 Brown, p. 103.
36 W. S. Anderson, 'Love Plots in Menander and his Roman Adapters', *Ramus: Critical Studies in Greek and Roman Literature* 13 (1984): 125, 129.
37 Brown, p. xv; cf. A. S. Gratwick, ed. and tr., *The Brothers* (Warminster: Aris & Phillips, 1987), p. 19.
38 Barsby, 1: 13; Brown, p. xvi.
39 Ernst Badian, 'Equites', *The Oxford Companion to Classical Civilization*, ed. Simon Hornblower and Antony Spawforth (Oxford University Press, 1998).
40 De Melo, 1: 513.
41 Thomas Marc Parrott, ed., *The Plays of George Chapman: The Comedies*, 2 v. sequentially paginated (New York: Russell & Russell, 1961), p. 708.
42 A. H. Bullen, *Elizabethans* (London: Chapman & Hall, 1924), p. 52; William Archer, *The Old Drama and the New* (London: Heinemann, 1923), pp. 91–2.
43 A. J. Brothers, ed. and tr., *The Eunuch* (Warminster: Aris & Phillips, 2000), pp. 21–2.
44 Parrott, pp. 707–8.
45 Madeleine Doran, *Endeavors of Art: A Study of Form in Elizabethan Drama* (Madison: University of Wisconsin Press, 1954), p. 155.
46 Cicero, *On Living and Dying Well*, tr. Thomas Habinek (London: Penguin, 2012), p. 106.
47 Doran, p. 153.
48 Northrop Frye, *The Anatomy of Criticism* (Princeton University Press, 1957), p. 163.
49 Bella and Samuel Spewack, *Boy Meets Girl*, in Bennett A. Cerf and Van H. Cartmell, ed., *Sixteen Famous American Plays* (New York: Modern Library, 1941), p. 539.
50 Susanna Morton Braund, 'Marriage, Adultery, and Divorce in Roman Comic Drama', in Warren S. Smith, ed., *Satiric Advice on Women and Marriage* (Ann Arbor: University of Michigan Press, 2005), p. 40.
51 Martin Wiggins, *Shakespeare and the Drama of His Time* (Oxford University Press, 2000), p. 68.

52 Colin Wilcockson, intro., *The Canterbury Tales: A Selection* (London: Penguin, 2008), p. xiv.
53 See Salvatore Di Maria, 'From Prose to Stage: Machiavelli's Mandragola', *Modern Language Notes* 121 (2006): 130–51.
54 David Bradley, *From Text to Performance in the Elizabethan Theatre: Preparing the Play for the Stage* (Cambridge University Press, 1992), pp. 92–3; Kathleen Marguerite Lea, *Italian Popular Comedy: A Study in the Commedia dell'arte 1560–1620*, 2 v. (New York: Russell & Russell, 1962), 2: 388.
55 Richard Andrews, 'Beffa', *The Oxford Companion to Italian Literature*, ed. Peter Hainsworth and David Robey (Oxford University Press), 2002.
56 Giorgio Melchiori, *Shakespeare's Garter Plays* (Newark: Delaware University Press, 1994), p. 90.
57 Paul-Emile Littré, *Dictionnaire de la langue française* (Chicago: Encyclopaedia Britannica, 1994).
58 Joan Acocella, 'Renaissance Man', *New Yorker* (11 November 2013): 79.
59 Quotes are from Edelman, ed., *An Humorous Day's Mirth* (Manchester University Press, 2010).
60 Foakes, ed., p. 87.
61 David Bevington, intro., *Every Man In His Humour*, Cambridge Edition of the Works of Ben Jonson, 1: 113.
62 Thorello, Bianca, Hesperida, and Prospero are Kitely, Dame Kitely, Bridget, and Wellbred in the Folio version.
63 R. W. Reynolds, 'The Adultery Mime', *Classical Quarterly* 40 (1946): 77–84.
64 Beard was speaking on the BBC radio programme *In Our Time*, 'The Augustan Age'.
65 J. P. V. D. Balsdon, *Roman Women: Their History and Habits* (London: Bodley Head, 1962), pp. 76–89; Karl Galinsky, *Augustus: Introduction to the Life of an Emperor* (Cambridge University Press, 2012), pp. 96–137.
66 *Tristia*, tr. A. S. Kline, http://poetryintranslation.com/PITBR/Latin/Ovidexilehome.htm.
67 Frank Manley offers an excellent analysis of this speech in his edition (London: Edward Arnold, 1968), p. xiii.
68 Alan Brissenden, ed., *A Chaste Maid in Cheapside*, 2nd ed. (London: A & C Black, 2002), p. xvii.
69 Castiglione, *Il Cortegiano*, ed. Ettore Bonora (Milan: Mursia, 1976), p. 153. The Italian reads *e tutto quello che sopra questa materia voi conoscete*.
70 See Laura Gianetti and Guido Ruggiero, ed., *Five Comedies from the Italian Renaissance* (Baltimore: Johns Hopkins University Press, 2003), p. xiii; Richard Andrews, 'Dovizi', *Oxford Companion to Italian Literature* (Oxford University Press, 2002).
71 John Florio, *A World of Words* (London, 1598).
72 Sir Thomas Hoby, *The Book of the Courtier*, Tudor Translations, v. 23 (London: David Nutt, 1900), p. 191.
73 Hoby, p. 191.
74 Jill Levenson, 'Comedy', in A. R. Braunmuller and Michael Hattaway, ed., *The Cambridge Companion to Renaissance Drama* (Cambridge University Press, 2003), p. 266.
75 William C. Carroll, *The Great Feast of Language in Love's Labour's Lost* (Princeton University Press, 1976), pp. 53–5.
76 David Bevington, intro., *Endymion* (Manchester University Press, 1996), pp. 90, 42; Bevington, intro., *Sappho and Phao* (Manchester University Press, 1991),

INTRODUCTION 53

p. 163; Erasmus, *The Praise of Folly*, tr. Clarence H. Miller (New Haven: Yale University Press, 1979), p. 21.
77 G. B. Harrison, *The Elizabethan Journals*, 3 v. (London: Constable, 1938) 3: 12, 13.
78 J. G. Nichols, ed., *Journal of the Siege of Rouen, Camden Miscellany* 1 (1847): 27.
79 *Calendar of State Papers, Domestic Series, of the Reign of Elizabeth, 1591–1594* (Nendeln: Kraus Reprint, 1967), p. 118; *Calendar of the Manuscripts of the Most Hon. the Marquis of Salisbury ... Preserved at Hatfield House, Hertfordshire*, v. 4 (London: Her Majesty's Stationery Office, 1892), p. 151.
80 *Calendar of State Papers Relating to Ireland of the Reign of Elizabeth*, 1599 April–1600 February (Nendeln: Kraus Reprints, 1974), p. 218.
81 *Calendar of State Papers Relating to Ireland*, p. 260.
82 Leah Scragg, ed., *Euphues: The Anatomy of Wit and Euphues and His England* (Manchester University Press, 2003), p. 32.
83 William Clowes, *A Short and Profitable Treatise Touching the Cure of the Disease called Morbus Gallicus* (London, 1579), sig. B2r, C1v, C3r–v.
84 Kenneth Richards, 'Elizabethan Perceptions of the *Commedia dell'Arte*', in Gunnar Sorelius and Michael Srigley, ed., *Cultural Exchange between European Nations during the Renaissance* (Uppsala University Press, 1994), p. 216.
85 Carmelo Alberto, ed., *Gli Scenari Correr: La Commedia dell'Arte a Venezia* (Rome: Bulzoni, 1996), pp. 31, 130.
86 Francesco Cotticelli, Anne Goodrich Heck, and Thomas F. Heck, ed., *The Commedia dell'Arte in Naples: A Bilingual Edition of the 176 Casamarciano Scenarios*, 2 v. (Lanham, MD: Scarecrow Press, 2001) 1: 115–17, 174–6, 132–4, 87–90, 9–3; 2: 105.
87 B. J. Sokol and Mary Sokol, *Shakespeare, Law, and Marriage* (Cambridge University Press, 2003), p. 140; Martin Ingram, *Church Courts, Sex and Marriage in England, 1570–1640* (Cambridge University Press, 1987), pp. 145–6.
88 Sokol, p. 142; Ingram, pp. 146–7.
89 Richard L. Greaves, *Society and Religion in Elizabethan* England (Minneapolis: University of Minnesota Press, 1981), pp. 267–73.
90 Levenson, p. 266; Gordon Braden, 'George Chapman', in Fredson Bowers, ed., 'Elizabethan Dramatists', *Dictionary of Literary Biography*, v. 62 (Detroit: Gale, 1987), p. 16; Manley, p. xvi.
91 Algernon Charles Swinburne, 'Essay on the Poetical and Dramatic Works of George Chapman', *The Works of George Chapman: Poems and Minor Translations* (London: Chatto & Windus, 1904), p. xxv.
92 W. Geoffrey Arnott, *Menander, Plautus, Terence* (Oxford: Clarendon, 1975), p. 54.
93 Q has the passage in italics, indicating that Jonson might be quoting another poet, although no source has been found. In F, Kitely says 'I ha' learned so much verse out of a jealous man's part in a play' (5.5.70).
94 Anton Blok, 'Rams and Billy-Goats: A Key to the Mediterranean Code of Honour', *Man* 16, n.s. (1981): 427–40; Robert Bates Graber and Gregory C. Richter, 'The Capon Theory of the Cuckold's Horns: Confirmation or Conjecture?', *Journal of American Folklore* 100 (1987): 58–63.
95 L. R. Lind., tr., *Aldrovandi on Chickens: The Ornithology of Ulisse Aldrovandi* (Norman: University of Oklahoma Press, 1963), pp. 410–11.
96 David Underdown, 'The Taming of the Scold: The Enforcement of Patriarchal Authority in Early Modern England', in Anthony Fletcher and John Stevenson, ed., *Order and Disorder in Early Modern England* (Cambridge University Press, 1985), p. 128.

97 Ingram, p. 164.
98 Christina Luckyj, *'A Moving Rhetoricke' Gender and Silence in Early Modern England* (Manchester University Press, 2002).
99 Luckyj, p. 61.
100 Parrott, 'Elizabethan Revivals in College', *Nation* 88 (22 April 1909): 406-7.
101 G. Blakemore Evans, ed., *All Fooles*, in Allan Holaday, gen. ed., *The Plays of George Chapman: The Comedies* (Urbana: University of Illinois Press, 1970), p. 227.
102 Lawrence Stone, *The Crisis of the Aristocracy 1558–1641* (Oxford University Press, 1965), pp. 74-5; see also Edelman, 'Knights, Pigeons, and Chapman's *All Fools*', *NQ* 59 (2012): 553-7.
103 R. W. Van Fossen, ed., *Eastward Ho* (Manchester University Press, 1999), p. 6; Donaldson, pp. 209, 212.
104 *Informations to William Drummond*, in *Cambridge Edition of the Works of Ben Jonson*, v. 5, p. 373; Van Fossen, p. 218.
105 Donaldson, pp. 208-9; Van Fossen, pp. 45-6.
106 David Riggs, *Ben Jonson: A Life* (Cambridge, MA: Harvard University Press, 1989), p. 124.
107 Akihiro Yamada, 'Bibliographical Studies of George Chapman's *All Fools*, Printed by George Eld', *Shakespeare Studies* (Tokyo) 3 (1964): 73-99.
108 Evans, p. 229.

ALL FOOLS

AL FOOLES

A
Comedy, Presented at the Black
Fryers, And lately before
his Maiestie.

Written by *George Chapman*.

AT LONDON,
Printed for Thomas Thorpe.
1 6 0 5.

Actors

GOSTANZO. } Knights.
MARC ANTONIO.
VALERIO, *son to Gostanzo*, [*secretly married to Gratiana*].
FORTUNIO, *elder son to Marc Antonio*, [*in love with Bellanora*].   5
RINALDO, *the younger* [*son to Marc Antonio*].
DARIOTTO. } *Courtiers.*
CLAUDIO.
CORNELIO, *a start-up gentleman*, [*married to Gazetta*].
CURIO, *a Page.*   10
[NOTARY.]
FRANCIS POCK, *a Surgeon.*
GAZETTA, *wife to Cornelio.*
BELLANORA, *daughter to Gostanzo.*
GRATIANA, *stolen wife to Valerio.*   15
[A Drawer or two, a Page.]

---

2. MARC] *Shepherd*; Mar. *Q*.   3. *secretly married to Gratiana*] *This ed.; not in Q.*
4. *in love with Bellanora*] *This ed.; not in Q.*
5. *son to Marc Antonio*] *This ed.; not in Q.*
8. *married to Gazetta*] *This ed.; not in Q.*
10. NOTARY] *This ed.;* Kyte, a Scrivener *Q*.   15.] *This ed.; not in Q.*

---

2. MARC ANTONIO] Chapman's combination of the French 'Marc' with the Italian 'Antonio' caused no end of confusion for the printer. *Q* sometimes has Marc. Antonio, as if Marc were short for Marco, creating an obtrusive full stop in the middle of a sentence. Shepherd (1874) was the first editor to regularise everything to Marc, but, for some reason, the next modern-spelling edition reverted to Marc., even though the editor's name was Thomas Marc Parrott.

5. RINALDO] Rinaldo being a trickster, his name may allude to Reynard, the cunning fox of medieval folklore.

8. CORNELIO, a start-up gentleman] His name taken from the Latin *cornu* (horn), Cornelio has an obsessive fear of being cuckolded. 'Start-up' is synonymous with 'upstart', a newcomer to his social class. Both forms were common at this time.

10. NOTARY] *Q* has 'Kyte, a Scrivener'. He is known only as 'Notary' in the play, however—neither 'Kyte' nor 'scrivener' appears in speech prefixes, stage directions, or the spoken text.

14. *stolen*] secret (*OED* adj. 2a).

Prologue

The fortune of a stage, like Fortune's self,
Amazeth greatest judgements, and none knows
The hidden causes of those strange effects
That rise from this hell, or fall from this heaven.
Who can show cause why your wits, that in aim　　　5
At higher objects, scorn to compose plays—

---

0. Prologue] *This ed.;* PROLOGUS *Q.*

---

0. Prologue] Chapman wrote *All Fools* in 1599 for the Admiral's Men, then performing at the Rose. A year or two later, he began his association with the Chapel Children at the Blackfriars, and the play was presented there. References to the 'Stage War', at its height during 1600 and 1601, and to the fashion of sitting on the stage (ll. 14–15, 30–3), show that the Prologue was written for the Blackfriars. However, the text of the play itself represents, as far as can be known, what spectators saw at the Rose in 1599. It shows no clear sign of revision, nor any reference to external events post 1599.

1–4.] The first four lines introduce a series of questions wherein Chapman, as Leo Salingar notes, ponders 'the inscrutable 'fortune' of the stage and the lordly presumption of spectators at Blackfriars' (p. 17). Chapman walks a fine line between flattering the audience and scorning its pretensions—Michael Shapiro observes that Chapman's 'manner of addressing his private theatre audiences was neither as brusque as Jonson's nor as obsequious as Lyly's or Marston's' (Shapiro, p. 74; cf. Smith, *Blackfriars*, pp. 414–21).

1. *like Fortune's self*] like Dame Fortune herself.
2. *Amazeth*] bewilders, perplexes (*OED* v. 2).

judgements] those possessing good judgement and critical taste (*OED* n. 8c).

3–4. *effects ... heaven*] One might assume that 'effects' are stage effects coming from hell (trap door) and heaven (stage canopy), included in the design of the Blackfriars, but then Chapman would be anticipating *OED*'s first recorded use of the word in this sense by more than two centuries. Furthermore, *All Fools* is without any such effects, so the speaker probably means 'results', particularly the reception, of the poet's and players' efforts. 'Effects' is used in the same sense at 1.1.2 (cf. *OED* effect n. 2b, 4c; Gurr, *Shakespearean Stage*, pp. 198–9).

5. *wits*] Chapman plays cleverly with this word in the prologue. Here, he employs the metonymic sense of wits as people with a fine intellect (*OED* n. 9), particularly those who have, or think they have, good aesthetic judgement. Shakespeare, in Sonnet 59, ponders the difficulty a poet has in trying to be original, but concludes 'O sure I am the wits of former days / To subjects worse have given admiring praise' (13–14).

6. *objects*] goals, objectives (*OED* n. 2).

6–9. *scorn to compose ... those that make*] Nothing is quite as galling to a writer as the condescending attitude of those who have not written anything, yet are always

58

PRO.]   ALL FOOLS   59

Though we are sure they could, would they vouchsafe it!—
Should, without means to make, judge better far
Than those that make? And yet ye see they can.
For without your applause, wretched is he   10
That undertakes the stage, and he's more blest
That with your glorious favours can contest.
Who can show cause why th'ancient comic vein
Of Eupolis and Cratinus—now revived,
Subject to personal application—   15

---

ready to criticise the work of others. In *The Scourge of Villainy*, Marston rails at the critic who, 'with his late-kissed hand my book doth grace / Straight reads, then smiles and lisps, 'tis pretty good' / And praiseth that he never understood' (*Satire* 6.78–80).

7. *vouchsafe it*] condescend to try (*OED* v. 3a).

8. *make*] write plays.

9. *ye see they can*] The speaker is careful to separate 'ye', the present audience, from 'they', those other critics with poor judgement.

11. *undertakes the stage*] ventures to write plays.

12.] 'With' seems to mean 'with the help of'. The poet is more likely to 'contest' (compete) successfully, if he has the support of the spectators' 'favours', i.e., indulgences, good wishes (*OED* n. 3).

13. *th'ancient comic vein*] the Old Comedy of ancient Athens, which flourished from about 440 to 380 BC.

14. *Eupolis and Cratinus*] The barest fragments of their work survive, but in their day Eupolis and Cratinus were esteemed as major comic poets, and important rivals of Aristophanes. Chapman draws on the Roman satirists Persius and Horace: Persius hopes that his readers will be like those who appreciated the Athenian masters: 'If you've caught the spirit of brave Cratinus, / or are pale from devotion to angry Eupolis and the Grand Old Man [Aristophanes], / if you've an ear for a concentrated brew, then have a look at this' (1.124–6). Horace is more explicit about what Old Comedy poets did: 'Take the poets Eupolis, Cratinus, and Aristophanes, and also / the other men who go to make up the Old Comedy. / If any person deserved to be publicly exposed for being / a crook and a thief, an adulterer or a cut-throat, for being notorious / in some other way, they used to speak right out and brand him' (*Satires* Bk. I, 4.1–5).

14–15. *now revived ... personal application*] The Prologue sees a revival of Old Comedy in the current fad for satire and personal attacks of the Stage War, fought mostly between Ben Jonson and John Marston. From Horace's description (prev. n.), we see that a distinguishing feature of the Old Comedy was the vituperation the poets levelled at public figures. What Horace does not mention, and what is more relevant to the situation at the Blackfriars, is that they also directed it at each other. Cratinus was much older than Aristophanes, but he was still active when Aristophanes wrote his earliest extant comedy, *The Acharnians*. The younger dramatist offers this tribute to his elderly rival, assuring the audience: 'Your tortured nose can take a rest: It won't meet in this mart that poet who offends in both his armpits and his art, that overfacile scratcher, that drooling fossil lecher, his head no balder than his name is void of any virtue, that staggering aesthetic zero, mighty moral minus, and ninety-year-old nullity— we mean, of course, Kratinos!' (p. 74).

Should be exploded by some bitter spleens,
Yet merely comical and harmless jests—
Though ne'er so witty—be esteemed but toys,
If void of th'other satirism's sauce?
Who can show cause why quick venerian jests   20
Should sometimes ravish, sometimes fall far short
Of the just length and pleasure of your ears,
When our pure dames think them much less obscene
Than those that win your panegyric spleen?
But our poor dooms, alas, you know are nothing.   25

---

16. *exploded*] hissed or clapped off the stage, from the Latin *explōdere* (*OED* explode, v.). Horace uses the word in describing how the actress Arbuscula was so treated by a Roman audience (*Satires* Bk. 1, 10.77.) The association of 'explode' with the ignition of gunpowder dates from the eighteenth century.

bitter spleens] Writers of treatises on the humours differed widely on the properties and functions of various parts of the body. This was particularly true of the spleen. Depending upon which humours it stored and emitted, the spleen might bring about laughter and merriment, melancholy and morose feelings, rashness, capriciousness, hot and violent anger, or, as it does here in Chapman's putative critical audience, irritability and peevishness (*OED* spleen n.; Hoeniger, pp. 103–6).

18. *toys*] worthless trifles, often used in regard to literary works (*OED* n. 3a, 5).

19.] The speaker cannot understand why those who reject satire also discount the 'harmless jests' (l. 17) of other writers. 'Satirism', a rare word denoting the 'satirical temper' (*OED* n.), is found in Dekker's contribution to the Stage War, *Satiro-mastix*, as Crispinus threatens Horace (Ben Jonson) with an emetic to cure him 'Of bitter satirism, of arrogance / Of self-love, of detraction, of a black / And stinging insolence' (5.2.220–2).

20. *quick venerian jests*] lively, risqué jokes (*OED* quick adj. 12, venerian adj.).

21. *ravish*] captivate, delight (*OED* v. 3b).

22. *just ... ears*] One's jests, like poorly executed artillery fire, may 'fall far short' of the just, i.e., exact, length required to hit the target. 'Just length' may also be the right and proper size of the audience's ears, anticipating the reference to the long ass's ears that King Midas earned for being a bad critic (Prol. 35 n.).

23. *pure dames*] Puritan ladies. Presumably, if pure dames do not find 'venerian jests' obscene, then no one else should, but one never knows how pure the dames really are. Simion Grahame, in *The Anatomy of Humours* (1609), ironically advises a gallant that his best choice of mistress is a 'quick-witted lady ... who in a venerian discourse, with the want of shame, will make her fan serve to cover the bloodless blush of her never blushing face' (sig. C3v).

24. *panegyric spleen*] The 'bitter' spleen (l. 16) is now benign, and capable of encouraging an elaborate speech of praise in honour of the poet, or at least his jokes.

25. *dooms*] judgements, opinions (*OED* n. 3).

To your inspired censure ever we
Must needs submit, and there's the mystery.
Great are the gifts given to united heads.
To gifts, attire, to fair attire the stage
Helps much. For if our other audience see 30
You on the stage depart before we end,
Our wits go with you all, and we are fools.
So Fortune governs in these stage events,
That merit bears least sway in most contents.

---

27. mystery] *Reed;* mistery *Q(u);* misery *Q(c).*

26. *censure*] critical opinion, not necessarily negative, and often used in a theatrical situation. In *The Gull's Horn-Book*, Dekker tells gallants to be sure to pay extra and sit on the stage, for then 'you have a signed patent to engross the whole commodity of censure' (2: 248).

27. *mystery*] something inexplicable, as in the usual modern meaning (*OED* n.¹ 5a). During the printing of the quarto, 'mystery' was changed to 'misery', a 'correction' adopted only by Collier. As Evans notes (p. 308), the uncorrected reading makes more sense in context.

28. *gifts*] faculties, powers (*OED* n.¹ 6b).

united heads] people with a specific mental ability (*OED* n.¹ 11), in this context artistic taste. If the audience is united in a single critical attitude, it has the power to determine a play's success. Subsequent lines show that Chapman's special concern is the privileged spectators sitting on the stage. 'Heads' leads nicely to the next line, since these spectators would all be attired in fashionable hats.

29-30. *To gifts ... Helps much*] No previous editor has even tried to parse these seemingly incomprehensible lines. Chapman is so frequently obscure that one hesitates to assume textual corruption, and since no obvious emendation presents itself, we are forced to deal with what we have. The initial 'to gifts' might be read as 'to those gifts' of the 'united' patrons, introduced in the previous lines. Play on 'attire' follows—first as a subject noun in the sense of the fashionable clothing worn by the stage-sitters. Such attire, along with the aforementioned gifts, 'helps much' to 'fair attire', i.e., handsomely adorn, the stage (*OED* attire n., v.¹, fair adv.). In *Every Man Out of His Humour*, Buffone tells the would-be gallant Sogliardo, when at the theatre, 'sit o' the stage and flout, provided you have a good suit' (1.2.52).

30-1. *other audience ... before we end*] The 'other' audience is everyone except those on the stage, who liked to make a show of leaving early. *The Gull's Horn-Book* has this advice for the gallant who has something against the dramatist: 'in the middle of the play, be it pastoral, moral, comedy or tragedy ... rise with a screwed and discontented face from your stool and be gone' (2: 253).

32. *Our wits ... all*] If the 'wits' (l. 5) leave, we are at our wits' end.

34. *contents*] the plural of the abstract noun 'content', in the sense of 'satisfaction, pleasure' (Parrott).

Auriculas asini quis non habet? 35
How we shall then appear, we must refer
To magic of your dooms, that never err.

35.] 'Who is without an ass's ears?' This is a direct quotation from Persius's first *Satire* (1.121), offering the artist's traditional complaint that most critics are completely unable to recognise quality. The ears belong to King Midas, who attained them in an incident separate from the unfortunate business of the golden touch. As Ovid tells the story, Pan once boasted that he played better music on his pipes than Apollo did on his lyre. So a talent contest was arranged, with the mountain-god Tmolus as judge. When Tmolus awarded the prize to Apollo, Midas, who 'chanced / to be there when he played', called the decision 'unfair'. The irate Apollo 'couldn't allow such insensitive ears to preserve / their human appearance. He lengthened them out; he filled them with shaggy / grey hairs; he made them floppy and able to waggle their tips' (*Metam.* 11.161-2, 173, 174-6).

36. *How we shall then appear*] how successful we shall be.

Act 1

ACT 1, SCENE 1

Enter RINALDO, FORTUNIO, VALERIO.

Rinaldo. Can one self cause, in subjects so alike
As you two are, produce effects so unlike?
One like the turtle, all in mournful strains
Wailing his fortunes, th'other like the lark,
Mounting the sky, in shrill and cheerful notes 5
Chanting his joys aspired, and both for love.
In one, love raiseth by his violent heat
Moist vapours from the heart into the eyes,

---

0. Act 1, Scene 1] *Hudston (subst.);* Actus primi. Scaena prima *Q.*
1. SP.] *Collier; Ryn. Ry. Rin. Q.*   2. effects] *Q(c);* effect *Q(u).*
3. strains] *Reed;* straines *Q(c);* steaines *Q(u).*

---

0. *Act 1, Scene 1*] As in so many Elizabethan plays, the audience only becomes aware of the fictional locale gradually. The title gives nothing away. Once a few characters' names are spoken, we get the impression that we are in Italy, but the city, Florence, is not named until 4.1.297. In this initial scene, the comings and goings of the characters and their chance meetings tell us that we are outdoors.

1. *one self*] one and the same (*OED* self adj. B1d).
   subjects] persons under the influence of an external cause (*OED* n. 12), as in Juliet's 'Alack, alack, that heaven should practise stratagems / Upon so soft a subject as myself' (3.5.209-10).

3. *turtle*] a type of dove, usually a stand-alone word in this period. 'Turtle-dove' is seen, but less frequently. There was no confusion with the reptile, as that usage, apparently a corruption of the French *tortue*, does not occur until the mid-1600s (*OED* n.^{1}, n.^{2}).
   strains] songs (*OED* n.^{2} 13). The 'mourning' of the dove for its lost mate is a common image, e.g., Vandome to Marcellina in Chapman's *Monsieur D'Olive*, 'While you, poor turtle, sit and mourn at home / Mew'd in your cage, your mate he flies abroad' (5.1.86-7).

6. *aspired*] lofty, elevated (*OED* adj.).

7. *In one*] Rinaldo would indicate Fortunio here, and Valerio at l. 10.

8. *vapours*] The 'vapours' Fortunio feels are synonymous with 'psychic pneuma' or 'spirits', an idea initiated by the stoics, taken up by Galen in a medical sense, and then by the neo-Platonists in a philosophical one. This invisible substance serves as the medium by which emotions and feelings, created by the humours, are transmitted from one part of the body to another, and from the body to the soul. Marsilio Ficino, in his *Commentary on Plato's Symposium*, one of the central texts of neo-Platonic thought,

From whence they drown his breast in daily showers.
In th'other, his divided power infuseth   10
Only a temperate and most kindly warmth,
That gives life to those fruits of wit and virtue,
Which the unkind hand of an uncivil father
Had almost nipped in the delightsome blossom.
Fortunio. Oh, brother, love rewards our services   15
With a most partial and injurious hand,
If you consider well our different fortunes.
Valerio loves, and joys the dame he loves.
I love, and never can enjoy the sight
Of her I love, so far from conquering   20
In my desire's assault, that I can come

---

15. SP.] Reed; *Fort. For.* Q.

writes that 'soul and body, naturally very different from each other, are joined by the median, spirit, which is a certain very thin clear vapour, created through the heat of the heart from the purest part of the blood; and thence diffused through all the parts. This spirit receives the powers of the soul and transfers them into the body' (p. 189).

10. *divided power*] Love's power is 'divided' in the sense of its ability to spread in all directions. In the sixth of his *Amoretti* sonnets, Spenser likens this action to the burning of an oak: 'The durefull oak, whose sap is not yet dried / Is long ere it conceive the kindling fire / But when it once doth burn, it doth divide / Great heat, and makes his flames to heaven aspire' (5–8).

11. *kindly*] natural, inherent, along with the more general sense of pleasant, agreeable (*OED* adj. 1b, 6).

12.] Love's ability to inspire 'wit and virtue' in men is a major theme of Castiglione's *Book of the Courtier*, which gained wide currency in England with Sir Thomas Hoby's translation of 1561. Castiglione has Lord Cesar Gonzaga speak of the inspiration the love of a woman gives to the true courtier: 'for like as no court, how great ever it be, can have any sightliness, or brightness in it, or mirth without women, nor any courtier can be gracious, pleasant or hardy, nor at any time undertake any gallant enterprise of chivalry unless he be stirred with the conversation and with the love and contentation [contentment] of women, even so in like case the courtier's talk is most unperfect ever more, if the intercourse of women give them not a part of the grace wherewithal they make perfect and deck out their playing the courtier' (Hoby, pp. 214–15).

13. *unkind*] Playing on 'kindly' in line 11, Rinaldo says that Valerio's father is both lacking in warmth, and acting in a way that is contrary to the natural feelings of kindred that should exist between father and son (*OED* adj. 2b, 6a).

14. *nipped ... blossom*] synonymous with the proverbial 'nipped in the bud' (Dent B702). Delightsome, as a form of delightful, was common in the seventeenth century.

16. *partial*] unfair, biased (*OED* adj. 4a). 'Partial' and 'injurious' are often seen together. William Camden assures the readers of his *Britain* (1610) that he will offer praise to those who deserve it, for 'God forbid that we should be so partially injurious as to think our times under most worthy princes to be barren of praiseworthy persons' (sig. ¶5r).

18. *joys*] enjoys, delights in (*OED* v. 2).

> To lay no batt'ry to the fort I seek,
> All passages to it so strongly kept
> By strait guard of her father.
> *Rinaldo.*   I dare swear,
> If just desert in love measured reward,   25
> Your fortune should exceed Valerio's far.
> For I am witness, being your bedfellow,
> Both to the daily and the nightly service
> You do unto the deity of love
> In vows, sighs, tears, and solitary watches.   30
> He never serves him with such sacrifice,
> Yet hath his bow and shafts at his command.
> Love's service is much like our humorous lords',
> Where minions carry more than servitors:
> The bold and careless servant still obtains,   35
> The modest and respective nothing gains.
> You never see your love unless in dreams;

---

22. *batt'ry*] an artillery assault or bombardment, and a common trope for a lover's romantic advances. In *Venus and Adonis*, the goddess is told, 'Dismiss your vows, your feigned tears, your flatt'ry / For where a heart is hard they make no batt'ry' (425–6).

23. *kept*] guarded, defended (*OED* keep v. 14).

24. *strait*] strict, rigorous (*OED* adj. 8b).

25. *desert*] deserving, worthiness (*OED* n.¹).

measured] were commensurate with (*OED* measure v. 2).

27. *your bedfellow*] not only your brother but your close friend. In *The Battle of Alcazar*, King Sebastian welcomes Christophero de Tavora as 'next unto myself, / My good Hephaestion and my bedfellow' (2.4.75–6), Hephaestion being the companion of Alexander the Great.

29. *deity of love*] Cupid, as we learn from the 'bow and shafts' at l. 32.

30. *watches*] vigils, nights without sleep (*OED* n. 1).

31–2.] Valerio never serves Cupid with any ceremony, and yet Cupid is always ready to do his bidding.

33. *humorous*] a word with a variety of meanings, all of them explored in Chapman's *An Humorous Day's Mirth*. Here, where love's service and the service to a lord are equated, 'capricious' or 'whimsical' is most appropriate.

34. *minions*] favourites, close companions. In early use, there was often connotation of a homosexual relationship. As so often happens with Chapman, the syntax is less than helpful, although the sense is clear enough. Minions 'carry' (succeed) more often than do honest 'servitors'—a convenient three-syllable synonym for servants (*OED* minion n.¹ 1, carry v. 15, servitor n.).

35. *bold*] used here in the negative sense of presumptuous (*OED* adj. 4).

obtains] wins, succeeds (*OED* v. 4b). In *The Conspiracy of Charles, Duke of Byron*, the Duke of Savoy says 'La Fin is in the right, and will obtain' (3.2.1).

36. *respective*] respectful (*OED* adj.) Both words were common at this time.

37–8.] The 'you' of these two lines is Fortunio, the 'He' is Valerio.

He, Hymen puts in whole possession.
What different stars reigned when your loves were born,
He, forced to wear the willow, you the horn.   40
But, brother, are you not ashamed to make
Yourself a slave to the base lord of love,
Begot of fancy and of beauty born?
And what is beauty? A mere quintessence,
Whose life is not in being, but in seeming,   45

---

38. *Hymen*] the god of marriage, usually represented as a young man carrying a torch and veil (*OED* n.). This is the first indication that Valerio and Gratiana are secretly married.

39.] The influence of the stars and planets on the success or failure of love is found everywhere in medieval and Renaissance literature. Their most positive achievement would be Chaucer's Wife of Bath, who was born when Taurus was in the ascendant, 'and Mars therinne'. As she explains in her Prologue, 'I folwed ay myn inclinacioun / By vertu of my constellacioun; / That made me I koude noght withdrawe / My chambre of Venus from a good felawe' (613, 615–16). Her reasoning seems sound, since 'Housbondes at chirche dore she hadde fyve / Withouten oother compaignye in youthe' (Gen. Prol. 460–1).

40.] 'He' is now Fortunio, who wears the willow, the proverbial trope for unrequited or unattainable love (Dent W403). The pronouns are confusing on the page, but present no problem in the theatre, provided that the actor playing Rinaldo knows where to look. Rinaldo displays his cynicism in telling the newly married Valerio that he already wears the horn, the symbol of cuckoldry in so many European cultures (Dent H625, C889.)

43.] That love is a child 'of fancy and of beauty' is part of the neo-Platonic philosophy of Marsilio Ficino, which holds a central place in Chapman's work, especially the early poems such as *The Shadow of Night* (1594) and *Ovid's Banquet of Sense* (1595). As we read in Plato's *Symposium* and Ficino's *Commentary* on it, the sight of a beautiful person is the first step to love (Plato, p. 493; Ficino, p. 183). This process, however, may be complicated by the influence of fancy, a contraction of the word 'fantasy', and synonymous with it (*OED* n. 1). In Pierre de la Primaudaye's *The French Academy*, first printed in English in 1586 and reprinted with additions no less than nine times, four French noblemen withdraw from society to discuss the nature of ethics, love, good conduct, and true knowledge. La Primaudaye regards fantasy as a powerful faculty, antagonistic to reason, that takes information from the external senses and alters it beyond recognition as it proceeds via the spirit (cf. 1.1.8 n.) to the soul: 'even in the time of sleep it hardly taketh any rest, but is always occupied in dreaming and doting, yea even about those things which never have been, shall be, or can be ... there is nothing but the fantasy will imagine and counterfeit, if it have any matter and foundation to work upon' (p. 414).

44. *quintessence*] a non-material and invisible element, existing in addition to the four elements of earth, air, fire, and water. It was often represented as the purest form of any substance, as in Hamlet's depiction of man as a 'quintessence of dust' (2.2.308).

45.] Spenser would consider Rinaldo to be one of those 'fond men' who believe beauty to be 'an outward show of things, that only seem'. Although the beauty of the body will assuredly 'fade and fall away', true beauty of the spirit, 'shall never be extinguished, nor decay' (*Hymn in Honour of Beauty*, 90–1, 95, 101).

SC. I]   ALL FOOLS   67

>   And therefore is not to all eyes the same,
>   But like a cozening picture, which one way
>   Shows like a crow, another like a swan.
>   And upon what ground is this beauty drawn?
>   Upon a woman, a most brittle creature,   50
>   And would to God, for my part, that were all.
> *Fortunio.* But tell me, brother, did you never love?
> *Rinaldo.* You know I did, and was beloved again,
>   And that of such a dame as all men deemed
>   Honoured, and made me happy in her favours.   55
>   Exceeding fair she was not, and yet fair
>   In that she never studied to be fairer
>   Than nature made her. Beauty cost her nothing.
>   Her virtues were so rare, they would have made
>   An Ethiope beautiful, at least so thought   60
>   By such as stood aloof, and did observe her
>   With credulous eyes. But what they were indeed

---

47. *cozening*] cheating, deceitful (*OED adj.*). Rinaldo likens love to an 'optic' or 'perspective' picture, one that changes according to the angle from which it is viewed. A familiar example, cited by Hudston, is Holbein's *The Ambassadors*, wherein a skull, placed at the bottom centre, can be seen only from the side of the painting. In *Ovid's Banquet of Sense*, Chapman has Corinna bathing in a fountain fed by a statue of the weeping Niobe, 'So cunningly to optic reason wrought, / That afar off, it showed a woman's face, / Heavy, and weeping; but more nearly viewed, / Nor weeping, heavy, nor a woman showed' (3.6–9).

49. *ground*] material, in the sense of a painter's canvas, or the cloth used as a basis for embroidery or decoration (*OED* n. 1, 6).

50. *brittle*] inconstant, fickle (*OED* adj. 2).

53. *again*] in return (*OED adv.* 2).

54. *of*] by.

57–8.] She had no need of cosmetics. From the day the prophet Jeremiah told women, 'though thou paintest thy face with colours, yet shalt thou trim thy self in vain, for thy lovers will abhor thee and seek thy life' (4.30), the use of makeup has often been the subject of disapproval. This point of view was not always held, however. In the delightful *On Facial Treatment for Ladies*, Ovid advises, 'Girls, learn from me what treatment will embellish / Your complexions, how beauty is best preserved', and offers an elaborate recipe for face cream, including barley imported from Libya and powdered antler horn: 'Any girl / Who uses a face-pack according to this prescription / Will shine brighter than her own / Mirror' (1–2, 66–9).

59. *rare*] splendid, excellent (*OED a.*[1] 6b).

60. *Ethiope*] a common term for an unattractive woman. At this time, a fair skin was considered essential to beauty.

61. *aloof*] at a distance (*OED* adj. 2a).

62. *credulous*] easily fooled (*OED* adj. 2).

they] her virtues (l. 59).

indeed] 'in fact' or 'in reality' (*OED* advb. phr. 1), not merely an insertion to add emphasis.

ALL FOOLS [ACT I

I'll spare to blaze, because I loved her once.
Only I found her such, as for her sake
I vow eternal wars against their whole sex, 65
Inconstant shuttlecocks, loving fools and jesters,
Men rich in dirt and titles, sooner won
With the most vile than the most virtuous,
Found true to none. If one amongst whole hundreds
Chance to be chaste, she is so proud withal, 70
Wayward and rude, that one of unchaste life
Is oftentimes approved a worthier wife.
Undressed, sluttish, nasty to their husbands,
Sponged up, adorned, and painted to their lovers,

---

63. *blaze*] describe, set forth (*OED* v.² 4a), as in Spenser's *Shepherd's Calendar*: 'Help me to blaze / Her worthy praise, / Which in her sex doth all excel' (April, 43–5).

64. *as for her sake*] that because of her (Abbott 109; *OED* sake n.¹ 7b).

65.] Chapman abruptly shifts from a neo-Platonic discourse on love to a diatribe against womanhood, based on Juvenal's notoriously misogynistic sixth *Satire*.

66. *Inconstant*] fickle, changeable (*OED* adj. 10).

shuttlecocks] Often spelled 'shittlecock', a shuttlecock is a small piece of cork, fitted with a crown or circle of feathers. It was batted back and forth in the game of 'battledore and shuttlecock', similar to modern badminton, whose players appropriated the word. As something that flies about so freely, it is a useful metaphor for 'harlot' or 'slut', both here and in Middleton's *The Ant and the Nightingale* (1604), where 'such shuttlecocks' are women who 'will rather venture a maidenhead than want a headtire' (ll. 587–8).

67. *Men rich in dirt*] wealthy landowners, as in Hamlet's decription of Osric, who is 'spacious in the possession of dirt' (5.2.87–8).

titles] social status, possession of lands (*OED* n. 5).

68. *With the most vile*] The sense seems to be that women seek out rich men, no matter how vile; this use of 'with' is often seen in Elizabethan texts (Abbott 193).

69. *Found true to none*] The antecedent of 'found' must be the 'shuttlecocks' of line 66—they love all sorts of awful men, and are true to none of them. An actor would have a tough time making Chapman's syntax clear in lines such as these.

69–72. *If one ... worthier wife*] That a noble and chaste wife is bound to be insufferably proud of her own virtue comes directly from Juvenal. He responds to the suggestion that there must be at least one woman somewhere who would make an excellent wife—'beauty and charm, fertile, wealthy'—by describing what it would be like to marry Cornelia, the daughter of Scipio Africanus and the mother of the noble Tiberius and Gaius Gracchus: 'Who could stomach such wifely perfection? I'd far far sooner / Marry a penniless tart than take on that virtuous / Paragon Cornelia, Mother of Statesmen, so haughty, / So condescending a prig' (*Satires* 6.162, 165–8).

73–4.] Juvenal has much to say about a woman who 'takes no trouble about / The way she looks at home', but applies huge amounts of makeup for her lover: 'First one layer, then the next: at last the contours emerge / Till she's almost recognisable ... you wonder what's underneath, a face or a boil' (*Satires* 6.464–5, 466–7, 474).

73. *Undressed*] not properly or fully dressed (1st cit. *OED* adj. 8a).

74. *Sponged*] spruced, smartened (*OED* sponge v. 2).

SC. I]   ALL FOOLS   69

    All day in ceaseless uproar with their households,   75
    If all the night their husbands have not pleased them.
    Like hounds, most kind, being beaten and abused;
    Like wolves, most cruel, being kindliest used.
Fortunio. Fie, thou profan'st the deity of their sex.
Rinaldo. Brother, I read that Egypt heretofore   80
    Had temples of the richest frame on earth,
    Much like this goodly edifice of women.
    With alabaster pillars were those temples
    Upheld and beautified, and so are women;
    Most curiously glazed, and so are women;   85
    Cunningly painted too, and so are women;
    In outside wondrous heavenly, so are women.
    But when a stranger viewed those fanes within,
    Instead of gods and goddesses, he should find

---

81. richest] *Reed;* riches *Q.*

75–6.] This also comes directly from Juvenal: 'If her husband, the night before, has slept with this back to her, then / The wool-maid's had it, the dressers are stripped and flogged, / The litter-bearer's accused of coming late. One victim / Has rods broken over her back, another bears bloody stripes / From the whip, a third is lashed with cat-o'-nine tails: / Some women pay their floggers an annual salary' (*Satires* 6.475–80).

77.] Chapman substitutes a hound for the traditional spaniel in the proverb, 'The spaniel that fawns when he is beaten, will never forsake his master' (Dent S705). Lyly's version in *Euphues: The Anatomy of Wit* is 'the kind spaniel, which the more he is beaten the fonder he is' (p. 90).

78.] We find a similar sentiment in Erasmus's *Adages*: 'A wolf may change his hair, but not his heart' (34: 288).

79. *deity*] divine quality or character (*OED* n. 1b); cf. 1.1.29 n.

80–91.] Rinaldo now moves from Juvenal to Lucian's *Essays in Portraiture*, the source for his likening of women to an Egyptian temple: 'Perfect beauty, to my mind, is when there is a union of spiritual excellence and physical loveliness. In truth, I could point you out a great many who are well endowed with good looks, but in every way discredit their beauty. Such women seem to me like the temples of Egypt, where the temple itself is fair and great, built of costly stones and adorned with gold and with paintings, but if you seek out the god within, it is either a monkey or an ibis or a goat or a cat. Women of that sort are to be seen in plenty' (4: 277). Nashe appropriates the same passage in *The Anatomy of Absurdity* (1: 34).

81. *frame*] structure (*OED* n. 17), as in *The Faerie Queene*: 'Long were it to describe the goodly frame / And stately port of Castle Joyous' (3.1.31.1–2).

83. *alabaster*] Sometimes spelled 'alablaster', this white or translucent Egyptian stone is of great beauty. Othello promises, 'Yet I'll not shed her blood / Nor scar that whiter skin of hers than snow, / And smooth as monumental alabaster' (5.2.3–5).

85. *glazed*] given a lustrous coating (*OED* glaze v.^{1} 3a).

88. *fanes*] temples (*OED* n.^{2}). The 'Argument of the First Sestiad' of Marlowe's *Hero and Leander* begins, 'Hero's description, and her love's, / The fane of Venus, where he moves / His worthy love suit' (1–2).

A painted fowl, a fury, or a serpent, 90
And such celestial inner parts have women.
Valerio. Rinaldo, the poor fox that lost his tail
Persuaded others also to lose theirs.
Thyself, for one perhaps that for desert
Or some defect in thy attempts refused thee, 95
Revil'st the whole sex—beauty, love, and all.
I tell thee love is nature's second sun,
Causing a spring of virtues where he shines.
And as without the sun, the world's great eye,
All colours, beauties, both of art and nature, 100
Are given in vain to men, so without love
All beauties bred in women are in vain,
All virtues born in men lie burièd.
For love informs them as the sun doth colours;
And as the sun, reflecting his warm beams 105

92. SP.] *Reed; Val. Vale. Q.*   97. sun] *Shepherd (subst.); sonne Q.*

---

90. *fury*] Furies (Latin), or Erinyes (Greek), are the mythological creatures sent by the gods to avenge blood-crimes. Ovid describes them as 'daughters of Night, who were sitting in front of the prison of hell, / with its great iron gates, and combing the black snakes out of their hair' (*Metam.* 4.453–4).

91. *celestial*] Furies and other monsters come from the same place as do the gods.

92–3.] In Aesop's fable, the only way a fox could escape a trap was to cut off its own tail. Embarrassed about its appearance, it tried to convince the other foxes that life was much better without one, and they should all remove theirs. An elder fox replied, 'I rather think, my friend, that you would not have advised us to part with our tails if there were any chance of recovering your own' (Aesop, p. 35).

93. *Persuaded*] urged, advised (*OED* persuade v. 3).

94. *for one*] because of one woman Rinaldo once loved.

for desert] for good reason, as in 'just desert' (1.1.25).

95. *defect in thy attempts*] deficiency or lack of quality in your wooing.

98. *spring*] often used figuratively as any sort of source.

99. *the world's great eye*] The eye was believed to be similar to the sun in that it projected beams of light. Plato, in the *Timaeus*, describes how sight is created by a type of fire in the body, 'not for burning but for providing a gentle light', which would be 'made to flow through the eyes', strike an external object, and then return to the eye, and transport an image via these spirits to the soul. Galen took up the idea, calling the beams 'shining pneumata'; it became one of the most common tropes to be found in Renaissance poetry. In his translation of Grammaticus Musaeus's *Divine Poem*, Chapman writes, 'But now the love-brand / In his eye-beam burned / And with th'unconquer'd fire / His heart was turn'd / Into a coal' (sig. D4v; cf. Plato, p. 1248; Hoeniger, pp. 95–9).

104. *informs*] fashions, gives shape to (*OED* v. 6).

105. *reflecting*] shining, projecting (*OED* v. 4). The modern sense of light turning back after striking a surface was also in use at this time, and context was the only means of a precise definition.

SC. I]   ALL FOOLS   71

    Against the earth, begets all fruits and flowers,
    So love, fair shining in the inward man,
    Brings forth in him the honourable fruits
    Of valour, wit, virtue, and haughty thoughts,
    Brave resolution, and divine discourse.   110
    Oh, 'tis the paradise, the heaven of earth.
    And didst thou know the comfort of two hearts
    In one delicious harmony united,
    As to joy one joy, and think both one thought,
    Live both one life, and therein double life.   115
    To see their souls met at an interview

107–10.] Chapman returns to the subject of love's power to inspire virtuous deeds, briefly introduced at 1.1.12. Castiglione has Cesar Gonzaga expand upon the topic in *The Courtier*: 'certes it is not possible, that in the heart of man, where once is entered the flame of love, there should at any time reign cowardliness. For he that loveth ... passeth not to go a thousand times in a day to his death, to declare himself worthy of that love.' Romantic love is also the source of artistic and literary achievement: 'Do you not see that of all comely exercises and which delight the world, the cause is to be referred to no earthly thing, but to women? Who learneth to dance featly [fitly] for other, but to please women? Who applieth the sweetness of music for other cause, but for this? Who to write in metre, at the least in the mother tongue, but to express the affections caused by women?' (Hoby, p. 264).

109. *haughty*] elevated, lofty (*OED* adj. 2). The word often carried connotations of arrogance, but not always so.

111.] proverbial (Dent H349.1), as the Nurse tells Ascanius in Marlowe's *Dido Queen of Carthage*, 'If there be any heaven on earth, tis love' (4.5.27).

112–15.] In Plato's *Symposium*, Aristophanes's discourse on the nature of love begins with a strange creation story. The first humans had two or more of everything, but the gods divided them, so now love is the joining together to make things complete again: 'Love is born into every human being: it calls back the halves of our original nature together; it tries to make one out of two and heal the wound of human nature'. He goes on to describe what happens when lovers meet: 'the two are struck from their senses by love, by a sense of belonging to one another, and by desire, and they don't want to be separated from one another, not even for a moment' (Plato, p. 475). Ficino addresses this idea in his *Commentary*: 'This desire of restoring the whole—this force—has received the name of love. This love is the greatest blessing to us, for the present when it unites with its own each of the once most intimate halves, and for the future when it proposes to those of us who piously worship God, to make us most blessed by restoring us to our former shapes and healing us' (p. 155).

113. *delicious*] delightful (*OED* adj. 1), relating to all the senses, not only taste.

115. *double*] used here as a verb. Love makes life twice as valuable.

116. *To see*] 'If you (Rinaldo) did see', leading to 'Thou wouldst abhor' at l. 121.

interview] mutual view (*OED* n. 2). The meeting of souls through sight is a physical process, brought about by the collision and intertwining of lovers' eye-beams as they are projected toward and received by each other. Donne's poem *The Ecstasy* tells how he and his love sat together: 'Our eye-beams twisted, and did thread / Our eyes, upon one double string' (ll. 7–8; cf. 1.1.99 n.).

In their bright eyes, at parley in their lips,
Their language kisses, and t'observe the rest,
Touches, embraces, and each circumstance
Of all love's most unmatchèd ceremonies, 120
Thou wouldst abhor thy tongue for blasphemy.
Oh, who can comprehend how sweet love tastes
But he that hath been present at his feasts?
Rinaldo. Are you in that vein too, Valerio?
'Twere fitter you should be about your charge, 125
How plough and cart goes forward. I have known
Your joys were all employed in husbandry,
Your study was how many loads of hay
A meadow of so many acres yielded,
How many oxen such a close would fat. 130
And is your rural service now converted

---

117. parley] *Reed;* parle *Q.*

117–18. *parley ... kisses*] Although the most common use of 'parley' was (and is) a meeting of two sides in a war or other dispute, it could also be any conversation (*OED* n.¹). In making kisses the language of such a parley, Chapman draws on concepts spoken by the poet and scholar Pietro Bembo in the fourth book of *The Courtier.* He regards a kiss as a powerful expression of rational, as well as sensual love. Just as lovers' eye-beams are the media to bring together two souls, in kissing their souls' spirits pass between them by the meeting of their lips, and 'be so mingled together, that each of them hath two souls, and one alone so framed of them both ruleth (in a manner) two bodies' (Hoby, pp. 355-6).

123–32.] The philosophical discourse on love is concluded with Rinaldo's reminder to Valerio that he would be better off looking after the farm as he is supposed to be doing. After 122 lines about love, the subject is never raised again; romance or love takes no part in the proceedings, unless it is being lampooned. This is unusual for an Elizabethan comedy, but not for Chapman—*An Humorous Day's Mirth* is exactly the same in this regard.

125. *charge*] task, duty (*OED* n.¹).

126. *goes*] The plural subject taking a singular verb is common in early modern usage (Abbott 333).

127. *husbandry*] farming, including both tillage of the soil and raising poultry or livestock (*OED* n. 2a).

128–9.] Early modern experts recognise the importance of maximising the yield of hay from a pasture. In his *Four Books of Husbandry* (1577), the German authority Conrad Heresbach writes of 'two kinds of pasture ground, whereof one is always dry, the other overflown. The good and the rich ground hath no need of overflowing, the hay being much better that groweth of the self goodness of the ground, than that which is forced by water' (sig. F4r).

130. *close*] an enclosed pasture (*OED* n.¹ 1).
fat] fatten.

SC. I] ALL FOOLS 73

    From Pan to Cupid, and from beasts to women?
    Oh, if your father knew this, what a lecture
    Of bitter castigation he would read you!
Valerio. My father? Why my father? Does he think   135
    To rob me of myself? I hope I know
    I am a gentleman, though his covetous humour
    And education hath transformed me bailie
    And made me overseer of his pastures,
    I'll be myself, in spite of husbandry.   140

        Enter GRATIANA.

    And see, bright heaven, here comes my husbandry.
                                 [*He embraces her.*]

---

141. SD. *He embraces her*] Reed; *Amplecti-tur eam* Q.

---

    132. *Pan*] the shepherd-god (cf. Prol.35 n.).
    to women] A few moments ago, Valerio was a man who 'loves, and joys the dame he loves' (1.1.18), but must keep his marriage a secret. Now, according to Rinaldo, he is a secret rake who spends his time chasing women. These two seemingly irreconcilable attitudes are apparent throughout the play. Chapman never fully discloses which Valerio is the 'real' one, although we hear more about 'cards, tennis, wenching, dancing, and what not' (1.1.154) as the play proceeds.
    133–4. *lecture … read you*] a common expression in which 'read' is not meant literally, but in the more general sense of 'deliver' (*OED* read v. phr.2). Corvino, in *Volpone*, warns Celia 'I will make thee an anatomy, / Dissect thee mine own self, and read a lecture / Upon thee to the city, and in public' (2.5.70-2).
    135–40.] Valerio's description of his rural upbringing, denied an education by his parsimonious father Gostanzo, is similar to what Orlando says about the treatment he receives from his brother-guardian Oliver in *As You Like It* (1.1.1–25).
    136. *myself*] my true self (*OED* pron. 4).
    137. *humour*] Here, humour denotes Gostanzo's nature, disposition, or in a slightly stronger sense, obsessive behaviour.
    138. *education*] Valerio would be referring to the poor education he has been given, due to his father's stinginess.
    bailie] a form of 'bailiff', a farm superintendent (*OED* bailiff n. 3).
    140–1. *I'll be myself … my husbandry*] Valerio is determined to live the high life in spite of being kept on the farm. These lines are the first indication that Chapman has based *All Fools* on the comedies of Terence. Those in the original audience who went to grammar school, where they studied, memorised, translated, and acted Terence from the time they were nine years old, would have recognised the similarity of Valerio's situation to that of young Ctesipho in Terence's *The Brothers*.
    141.1 SD. *He embraces her*] Q's stage direction, *amplecti-tur eam*, shows that Valerio is glad to see the woman to whom he is secretly married, but, in the ensuing dialogue, his lines are addressed to Fortunio or Rinaldo. He says nothing directly to her, and she remains mute the entire scene. Chapman draws from Terence here—in all his plays, words of endearment between lovers are never spoken (Barsby, 1: 119).

  Here shall my cattle graze, here nectar drink.
  Here will I hedge and ditch, here hide my treasure.
  O poor Fortunio, how wouldst thou triumph,
  If thou enjoy'dst this happiness with my sister!   145
Fortunio. I were in heaven if once 'twere come to that.
Rinaldo. And methinks 'tis my heaven that I am past it.
  And should the wretched Machiavellian,
  The covetous knight, your father, see this sight,
  Lusty Valerio?
Valerio.   'Sfoot, sir, if he should,   150
  He shall perceive ere long my skill extends
  To something more than sweaty husbandry.
Rinaldo. I'll bear thee witness, thou canst skill of dice,
  Cards, tennis, wenching, dancing, and what not,
  And this is something more than husbandry.   155
  Thou'rt known in ordinaries and tobacco shops,
  Trusted in taverns and in vaulting houses,

---

  143. *hedge and ditch*] John Fitzherbert's *Book of Husbandry* (1540) advises, 'if a husband shall keep cattle well to his profit, he must have several closes and pastures to put his cattle in, the which would be well quicksetted, ditched, and hedged' (p. 52). Along with the literal meaning, Valerio is making a bawdy pun on these words to mean 'fornicate' (Williams, pp. 394, 656).
  hide my treasure] Like 'head and ditch', this offers another sexual innuendo.
  145. *my sister*] Bellanora.
  146. *were*] 'would be', typical in Elizabethan grammar (Abbott 301).
  148. *Machiavellian*] The ideas of Machiavelli (1469–1527), either directly from his books or second-hand, were well known in Elizabethan England. His name, perhaps unfairly, became synonymous with self-interested scheming, godlessness, and duplicity.
  150. *Lusty*] Applied to Valerio, the term means both lively and having a healthy libido (*OED* adj. 1a, 4).
  'Sfoot] By God's, or Christ's foot, a common oath.
  153. *thou canst*] you know (*OED* can v.[1]).
  156. *ordinaries and tobacco shops*] Ordinaries were popular inns or taverns where meals were served, usually at a fixed price, and where gambling also occurred. To supply the national mania for smoking, tobacco was sold nearly everywhere, including specialist shops that offered nothing else. As Barnabe Rich writes in *The Honesty of this Age* (1614), tobacco is 'a commodity that is now as vendible in every tavern, inn, and alehouse, as either wine, ale, or beer, and for apothecary's shops, grocer's shops, chandler's shops, they are (almost) never without company, that from morning till night are still taking of tobacco, what a number are there besides, that do keep houses, set open shops, that have no other trade to live by, but by the selling of tobacco' (pp. 25–6).
  157. *vaulting houses*] brothels (*OED* vaulting n.[2] 3). In Dekker's *The Seven Deadly Sins of London*, 'Lechery is patron of all your suburb colleges, and sets up vaulting houses, and dancing schools' (2: 52).

sc. 1]   ALL FOOLS   75

  And this is something more than husbandry.
  Yet all this while, thy father apprehends thee
  For the most tame and thrifty groom in Europe. 160
Fortunio. Well, he hath ventured on a marriage
  Would quite undo him, did his father know it.
Rinaldo. Know it? Alas, sir, where can he bestow
  This poor gentlewoman he hath made his wife
  But his inquisitive father will hear of it, 165
  Who, like the dragon to th'Hesperian fruit,
  Is to his haunts? 'Slight, hence! The old knight comes!

    [*Enter*] GOSTANZO.

    [*Exeunt* VALERIO, GRATIANA, *and* FORTUNIO, *running.*]
Gostanzo. Rinaldo!
Rinaldo.   Who's that calls? What, Sir Gostanzo?
  How fares your knighthood, sir?
Gostanzo.   Say, who was that
  Shrunk at my entry here? Was't not your brother? 170
Rinaldo. He shrunk not, sir. His business called him hence.
Gostanzo. And was it not my son that went out with him?
Rinaldo. I saw not him. I was in serious speech
  About a secret business with my brother.

167.1. SD. *Enter*] Reed; *Intrat* Q.
167.2. SD.] *This ed.; Omnes aufugiunt* Q; *All go out except Rinaldo* Reed.
168. SP.] *Reed; Gost.* Q.

---

 160. *groom*] boy or young man, often applied to shepherds (*OED* n.[1] 1, 2). The term was rarely seen at this time as a shortened form of bridegroom, except in the phrase 'bride and groom'.
 161. *he*] Valerio.
 162. *Would*] that would.
 166–7. *dragon ... haunts*] According to Rinaldo, Gostanzo guards his house and farm as zealously as Ladon, the hundred-headed serpent who never sleeps. Along with nymphs known as the Hesperides, it guarded the golden apples, but was no match for Hercules, whose eleventh labour was to fetch them.
 167. *'Slight*] By God's light, another common oath.
 168. *Who's that calls?*] Who is it that calls? Early modern writers frequently omit the relative pronoun (Abbott 244).
 168.2 SD.] Q has *Omnes aufugiunt* (all flee), but of course Rinaldo remains.
 168–9. *Sir Gostanzo ... your knighthood*] The rather absurd 'your knighthood' implies mock servility on Rinaldo's part. In Beaumont's *The Woman Hater*, the Duke seems to employ the same irony when he asks Arrigo, 'and what thinks your knighthood of it?' (1.1.12).
 170. *Shrunk*] who withdrew furtively (cit. *OED* shrink v. 6a). As in the previous line, the relative pronoun is omitted.

Gostanzo. Sure 'twas my son. What made he here? I sent him 175
  About affairs to be dispatched in haste.
Rinaldo. Well, sir, lest silence breed unjust suspect,
  I'll tell a secret I am sworn to keep,
  And crave your honoured assistance in it.
Gostanzo. What is't, Rinaldo?
Rinaldo.   This, sir: 'twas your son. 180
Gostanzo. And what young gentlewoman graced their company?
Rinaldo. Thereon depends the secret I must utter.
  That gentlewoman hath my brother married.
Gostanzo. Married? What is she?
Rinaldo.   'Faith, sir, a gentlewoman,
  But her unnourishing dowry must be told 185
  Out of her beauty.
Gostanzo.   Is it true, Rinaldo?
  And does your father understand so much?
Rinaldo. That was the motion, sir, I was entreating
  Your son to make to him, because I know
  He is well spoken, and may much prevail 190
  In satisfying my father, who much loves him,
  Both for his wisdom and his husbandry.

185. unnourishing] *Q(c) (subst.);* unusuring *Q(u).*

175–6.] Gostanzo's first asks what Valerio was doing here, when he had sent his son off on an important errand. His question about the identity of the woman comes as an afterthought, showing he has no suspicion at this point of Valerio's true nature.

177. *suspect*] suspicion (*OED* n.[1] 1).

178–83.] These lines set the main action of the play, taken from Terence's *The Self-Tormenter,* in motion. Rinaldo could easily have satisfied Gostanzo with a simple lie about the identity of the 'gentlewoman'; instead he makes up a secret that he 'reluctantly' shares with the old man: that she is Fortunio's secret bride. In Terence, the role of the cunning slave Syrus is to solve a crisis. In *All Fools*, Rinaldo's role is to *create* a crisis, purely for the fun of employing some ingenious scheme to solve it (cf. Introduction, pp. 17–18).

185. *unnourishing*] a word possibly coined by Chapman (1st cit. *OED adj.*). *Q*'s original 'unusering' was corrected while the play was being printed. Evans's preference for the uncorrected 'unusering dowry', i.e., one that offers no increase in value, does have some sense to it, but 'unnourishing' fits the context perfectly. Rinaldo is exploiting what he knows to be Gostanzo's idea of money as one of the basic food groups (cf. Evans, p. 308).

told] counted, reckoned (*OED* tell v.20).

188–91] So far Rinaldo's tall tale has nothing to do with Valerio. Now, by saying he has asked Valerio to put things right with Marc Antonio on Fortunio's behalf, Rinaldo brings everyone into the game, and is making things more dangerous for Valerio in the process.

192.] With praise of Valerio's supposed virtues, Rinaldo begins his flattery of Gostanzo, for he knows that the old man will take credit for instilling them in his son. The slave Syrus uses exactly the same technique when duping the old man Demea in *The Self-Tormentor.*

SC. I]   ALL FOOLS   77

Gostanzo. Indeed he's one can tell his tale, I tell you.
   And for his husbandry—
Rinaldo.   Oh, sir, had you heard
   What thrifty discipline he gave my brother   195
   For making choice without my father's knowledge
   And without riches, you would have admired him.
Gostanzo. Nay, nay, I know him well. But what was it?
Rinaldo. That in the choice of wives men must respect
   The chief wife, riches, that in every course   200
   A man's chief lodestar should shine out of riches,
   Love nothing heartily in this world but riches,
   Cast off all friends, all studies, all delights,
   All honesty, and religion for riches,
   And many such, which wisdom sure he learned   205
   Of his experient father. Yet my brother
   So soothes his rash affection, and presumes

---

193. *tell his tale*] speak eloquently.
194. *for*] as for.
194-206.] By inventing the story that Valerio scolded Fortunio vehemently for abandoning all notions of filial behaviour and eloping, i.e., doing what he actually did himself, Rinaldo appeals to Gostanzo's belief that he has raised a wise son, whose qualities were acquired by following his father's example.
195. *thrifty discipline*] proper chastisement (*OED* thrifty adj. 2b; discipline n. 7a).
199-200. *choice of wives … riches*] While Gostanzo may believe that money is the only concern in choosing a wife, those who follow this practice in Roman comedy always regret it. In Plautus's *The Comedy of Asses*, Artemona, the wealthy wife of Demaenaetus, is not shy about exerting her authority over the family finances, leading Demaenaetus to admit that even his wife's slave is probably better off than he is: 'I took the money, and sold my authority for the dowry' (88-9). Similarly, when Apoecedes, an elderly gentleman in *Epidicus*, remarks 'a dowry is beautiful money', his friend Periphanes reminds him, 'Yes, if it comes without a wife' (180-1).
201. *lodestar*] guiding star (*OED* n. 2).
206. *experient*] an older form of 'experienced' (*OED* adj.)
206-9. *Yet my brother … home to him*] Fortunio is so assured of his father Marc Antonio's forgiving nature that he is about to bring his new bride home. Here Chapman introduces a new theme, taken from Terence's *The Brothers*, where Gostanzo's counterpart, old Demea, is supremely confident that his strict, disciplinary approach to raising a son is superior to the kind and lenient approach of his brother Micio.
207. *soothes*] glosses over (*OED* soothe v. 6a). To 'soothe', in the sense of render calm, is a later usage.
   affection] passion, desire. The French lords of *Love's Labour's Lost* promise to 'make war against [their] own affections / And the huge army of the world's desires' (1.1.9-10). These feelings, the enemy of our rational side, are the work of the psychic 'spirits' that excite our imaginations or fantasies (cf. 1.1.43 n.). In *Nosce Tiepsum*, Chapman's friend Sir John Davies writes, 'these spirits of sense, in fantasy's high court / Judge of the forms of objects, ill or well; / And so they send a good or ill report / Down to the heart, where all affections dwell' (ll. 1125-8).

	So highly on my father's gentle nature,	
	That he's resolved to bring her home to him.	
	And like enough he will.	

Gostanzo.   And like enough   210
Your silly father, too, will put it up.
An honest knight, but much too much indulgent
To his presuming children.
Rinaldo.   What a difference
Doth interpose itself 'twixt him and you
Had your son used you thus!
Gostanzo.   My son? Alas,   215
I hope to bring him up in other fashion;
Follows my husbandry, sets early foot
Into the world. He comes not at the city
Nor knows the city arts—
Rinaldo. [*Aside*]   But dice and wenching—
Gostanzo. Acquaints himself with no delight but getting,   220
A perfect pattern of sobriety,
Temperance, and husbandry to all my household.
And what's his company, I pray? Not wenches.
Rinaldo. Wenches? I durst be sworn he never smelt
A wench's breath yet, but methinks 'twere fit   225
You sought him out a wife.
Gostanzo.   A wife, Rinaldo?
He dares not look a woman in the face.
Rinaldo. 'Sfoot, hold him to one. Your son such a sheep?
Gostanzo. 'Tis strange, in earnest.
Rinaldo. Well, sir, though for my thriftless brother's sake,   230

---

219. SD. *Aside*] Reed; *Aversus Q.*

---

210. *like*] likely.
211. *put it up*] submit to it.
213. *presuming*] presumptuous, arrogant (*OED* adj.).
217. *Follows*] in such a way that he follows. The ellipsis of the subject is not unusual (Abbott 399–402).
217–18. *sets early foot / Into the world*] Explicit advice to rise early is curiously absent from the classic works on husbandry, such as Hesiod's *Works and Days*, Cato's *On Agriculture*, or Virgil's *Georgics*, perhaps because it was too glaringly obvious to be worth mentioning.
218. *at*] to. Prepositions were very freely used in this period, particularly by Chapman.
220. *getting*] gaining, earning (*OED* n. 2), perhaps with the unintended bawdy meaning of 'begetting, procreating'.
224–6. *Wenches ... wife*] Q crowds these two and a half lines into two long ones, probably to save space near the end of the page (sig. B3r).

I little care how my wronged father takes it.
Yet for my father's quiet, if yourself
Would join hands with your wise and toward son,
I should deserve it some way.
Gostanzo.   Good Rinaldo,
I love you and your father, but this matter   235
Is not for me to deal in, and 'tis needless.
You say your brother is resolved, presuming
Your father will allow it.

Enter MARC ANTONIO.

Rinaldo.   See, my father!
Since you are resolute not to move him, sir,
In any case conceal the secret by way   240
Of an atonement. Let me pray you will.
Gostanzo. Upon mine honour.
Rinaldo.   Thanks, sir.   [*He hides.*]
Marc Antonio. God save thee, honourable knight Gostanzo.
Gostanzo. Friend Marc Antonio, welcome! And I think
I have good news to welcome you withal.   245
Rinaldo. [*Aside*] He cannot hold.
Marc Antonio.   What news, I pray you, sir?
Gostanzo. You have a forward, valiant, eldest son,
But wherein is his forwardness and valour?
Marc Antonio. I know not wherein you intend him so.

---

233. wise] *Shepherd; wife Q.*   242. SD. *He hides*] *Reed; Abscondit se Q.*
243. SP.] *Manley; Mar. Marc. Marc-Ant. Q.*   246. SD.] *Collier; not in Q.*

232–3. *if yourself ... toward son*] By asking Gostanzo to join with 'wise' Valerio in an effort to appease Marc Antonio, Rinaldo is making things more and more complicated. Nothing Rinaldo has said will help Valerio keep his marriage a secret; if anything, it makes it more difficult. Rinaldo cares only about adding to the day's amusement.

233. *toward*] obliging, docile (*OED* adj. 4a). Rinaldo senses he has Gostanzo hooked, and is pouring on the flattery.

234. *deserve*] repay, requite (*OED* v. 6).

240–2.] Rinaldo knows Gostanzo's assurance that he will keep his knowledge of the affair secret will last approximately ten seconds. The idea is taken from *The Self-Tormentor*, where old Chremes is well-meaning but an incorrigible busybody.

241. *atonement*] act of friendship or reconciliation (*OED* n.¹). The word was not exclusive to a theological context.

242. SD] Q has *Abscondit se* at l. 240, but it makes little sense for Rinaldo to hide before speaking.

247. *forward*] spirited (*OED* adj. 6c).

249. *intend*] judge, estimate (*OED* v. 15).

Gostanzo. Forward before, valiant behind his duty, 250
That he hath dared before your due consent
To take a wife.
Marc Antonio. A wife, sir? What is she?
Gostanzo. One that is rich enough: her hair pure amber,
Her forehead mother of pearl, her fair eyes
Two wealthy diamonds, her lips mines of rubies. 255
Her teeth are orient pearl, her neck pure ivory.
Marc Antonio. Jest not, good sir, in an affair so serious.
I love my son, and if his youth reward me
With his contempt of my consent in marriage,
'Tis to be feared that his presumption builds not 260
Of his good choice that will bear out itself,
And being bad, the news is worse than bad.
Gostanzo. What call you bad? Is it bad to be poor?
Marc Antonio. The world accounts it so. But if my son
Have in her birth and virtues held his choice 265
Without disparagement, the fault is less.
Gostanzo. Sits the wind there? Blows there so calm a gale
From a contemnèd and deservèd anger?
Are you so easy to be disobeyed?
Marc Antonio. What should I do? If my enamoured son 270
Have been so forward, I assure myself
He did it more to satisfy his love
Than to incense my hate, or to neglect me.

---

264. son] *Reed; soone Q.*

253–7.] Spenser offers a similar catalogue of his mistress's virtues in the *Amoretti*: 'If sapphires, lo, her eyes be sapphires plain, / If rubies, lo, her lips be rubies sound: / If pearls, her teeth be pearls both pure and round; / If ivory, her forehead ivory ween; / If gold, her locks are finest gold on ground; / If silver, her fair hands are silver sheen …' (15.7–12). Gostanzo thinks he is rubbing it in by saying that Fortunio's wife is rich, then adding she is rich only in beauty.

260–2.] We have some of Chapman's legendary obscurity here. Marc Antonio is worried about Fortunio's 'presumption'—not only for having married without permission but also for possibly making a poor choice of a wife. If that choice turns out to be a good one, however, it would in some way 'bear out', i.e., justify, his actions.

264–5. *if my son / Have*] This now archaic use of the subjunctive is often found in Elizabethan texts (Abbott 366).

265. *held*] made.

266. *disparagement*] the dishonour involved in marrying someone of lower rank (*OED* n. 1).

267. *Sits the wind there*] proverbial (Dent W.429.11), similar to Benedick's 'Sits the wind in that corner?' in *Much Ado* (2.3.98).

268. *contemnèd*] treated with contempt (*OED* adj.).

SC. I]   ALL FOOLS   81

Gostanzo. A passing kind construction. Suffer this,
    You ope him doors to any villainy.   275
    He'll dare to sell, to pawn, run ever riot,
    Despise your love in all, and laugh at you.
    And that knight's competency you have gotten
    With care and labour, he with lust and idleness
    Will bring into the stipend of a beggar,   280
    All to maintain a wanton whirligig,
    Worth nothing more than she brings on her back,
    Yet all your wealth too little for that back.
    By heaven, I pity your declining state,
    For, be assured, your son hath set his foot   285
    In the right pathway to consumption:
    Up to the heart in love, and for that love
    Nothing can be too dear his love desires.
    And how insatiate and unlimited
    Is the ambition and the beggarly pride   290
    Of a dame hoisèd from a beggar's state

274–6] These lines are taken directly from the *Self-Tormenter*: 'If once he realises how you feel, how you'll abandon your life and all your money rather than losing your son—well! What a window on wickedness you'll be opening' (478–80).

274. *passing*] pre-eminently, exceedingly (*OED* adv. a).

Suffer] allow, tolerate (*OED* v. 12).

275. *ope him*] open for him. This shortened form of 'open' is common, almost always used for metrical purposes.

276. *ever*] always (Abbott 39).

278. *competency*] sufficient income (*OED* n. 3).

281. *whirligig*] a top or other spinning toy (*OED* n.). The most famous figurative use is Feste's 'whirligig of time' in *Twelfth Night* (5.1.88); here it is a fitting metaphor for a fickle or inconstant person.

283.] All your wealth could not pay for her wardrobe.

284–6.] Chremes, Gostanzo's counterpart in *The Self-Tormenter*, makes the identical prediction to Menedemus, the model for Marc Antonio: 'What do you think will become of you when they are eating you up all the time? I can assure you, I did feel sorry for your fate, Menedemus' (461–4). Overall, the long-suffering husband who bemoans his wife's extravagance is more a feature of Plautus than Terence. Megadorus, in *The Pot of Gold*, worries over the dangers that await should he marry a rich woman who expects to maintain her lifestyle. In a long and hilarious rant, he lists all the people to whom he will owe money, starting with 'the launderer, the embroider, the goldsmith, the woollen worker', and naming many others before concluding with 'the sellers of girdles' (508–20).

286. *consumption*] destruction, wasting away (*OED* n.1,2). In *2 Henry IV*, Falstaff complains, 'I can get no remedy for this consumption of the purse' (1.2.236–7).

287. *up to the heart in love*] proverbial, although, even for love, 'up to the ears' is more common (Dent H268).

291. *hoisèd*] raised aloft, originally a nautical term (*OED* v.).

	To a state competent and plentiful?	
	You cannot be so simple not to know.	
Marc Antonio.	I must confess the mischief, but, alas,	
	Where is in me the power of remedy?	295
Gostanzo.	Where? In your just displeasure. Cast him off,	
	Receive him not. Let him endure the use	
	Of their enforcèd kindness that must trust him	
	For meat and money, for apparel, house,	
	And everything belongs to that estate,	300
	Which he must learn with want of misery,	
	Since pleasure and a full estate hath blinded	
	His dissolute desires.	
Marc Antonio.	What should I do?	
	If I should banish him my house and sight,	
	What desperate resolution might it breed	305
	To run into the wars, and there to live	
	In want of competency and perhaps	
	Taste th'unrecoverable loss of his chief limbs,	
	Which, while he hath in peace at home with me,	
	May, with his spirit, ransom his estate	310
	From any loss his marriage can procure.	
Gostanzo.	Is't true? Nay, let him run into the war	
	And lose what limbs he can. Better one branch	
	Be lopped away, than all the whole tree should perish;	
	And for his wants, better young want than old.	315

---

292. *competent*] with income appropriate to her rank (*OED* adj. 2; cf. 1.1.278n.).

294. *confess*] acknowledge (*OED* v. 2). Confessing is not limited to admitting one's own wrongdoings; the 'mischief', Marc Antonio believes, is Fortunio's.

297–301.] Chapman's love for correct but unusual definitions renders these lines difficult. Gostanzo thinks that Fortunio should suffer the indignity of being broke—the 'use' to be endured is the use of money borrowed at interest. The 'enforced kindness' is that of the usurers, who will 'trust', i.e., extend credit, for Fortunio's purchases (*OED* use n. 5a; trust v. 7a).

301. *want of misery*] miserable poverty (Parrott).

302–3. *blinded ... desires*] blinded him to the consequences of his behaviour.

306. *run into the wars*] What Marc Antonio fears has already happened in *The Self-Tormentor*, where young Clinia 'went off to Asia to fight for the king' (116). He has just returned as the play begins.

309–11.] If Fortunio stays home, the limbs he might have lost at war could be put to hard work, and with his 'spirit', i.e., his mettle or ardour, pay his debts (*OED* spirit n. 13a).

313–14. *Better ... perish*] similar to the proverbial 'better one die than all' (Dent O42).

SC. I]   ALL FOOLS   83

>   You have a younger son at Padua.
>   I like his learning well. Make him your heir,
>   And let your other walk. Let him buy wit
>   At's own charge, not at's father's; if you lose him.
>   You lose no more than that was lost before;   320
>   If you recover him, you find a son.
> *Marc Antonio.* I cannot part with him.
> *Gostanzo.*   If it be so,
>   And that your love to him be so extreme,
>   In needful dangers ever choose the least.
>   If he should be in mind to pass the seas,   325
>   Your son Rinaldo, who told me all this,
>   Will tell me that, and so we shall prevent it.
>   If by no stern course you will venture that,
>   Let him come home to me with his fair wife,
>   And if you chance to see him, shake him up,   330
>   As if your wrath were hard to be reflected,
>   That he may fear hereafter to offend
>   In other dissolute courses. At my house,
>   With my advice and my son's good example,

316.] Rinaldo is a student at the famous University of Padua, 'nursery of arts', where Shakespeare's Lucentio plans to follow 'a course of learning and ingenious studies' (*Shrew* 1.1.2, 9).

318–19. *Let … charge*] Fortunio needs to learn from his own experience. The proverbs 'bought wit is best' and 'wit is never good till it be bought' were popular with early modern writers (Dent W545, W567).

318. *your other*] your other son Fortunio.

324.] 'Always choose the lesser of two evils' must have been already old when Cicero quoted it in *De Officiis*, as he precedes the expression with 'they say' (3.29.105).

325. *pass*] cross, traverse (*OED* v. 17a).

327. *tell me that*] tell me if Fortunio decides to run away to the wars. The sense is clear if the actor stresses 'this' in the previous line and 'that' in this one.

328. *venture that*] try to reform your son.

329.] In Terence's *The Self-Tormenter*, the slave Syrus comes up with the idea that the young 'tart' (l. 598) should stay at old Chremes's house. Here, with no prompting from Rinaldo, Gostanzo himself decides to offer Gratiana hospitality. To Rinaldo, this is pure luck, which he happily acknowledges at 1.2.123–4.

330. *shake him up*] chastise him soundly (*OED* shake v. phr. 6).

331. *reflected*] turned away, diverted (*OED* reflect 2a; cf. 1.1.105n.).

332–3. *That he may fear … courses*] In following Terence closely, Chapman makes a key departure from what we expect to see in comedies of this type, where the father usually wants to prevent his child's marriage. There is no question of that happening here, since the wedding has already occurred. The only benefit to be derived from Fortunio and his supposed bride residing with Gostanzo is that the young man will be less likely to commit some other offence in the future.

84   ALL FOOLS   [ACT I

    Who shall serve as a glass for him to see 335
    His faults, and mend them to his precedent,
    I make no doubt but of a dissolute son
    And disobedient, to send him home
    Both dutiful and thrifty.
Marc Antonio.   O Gostanzo!
    Could you do this, you should preserve yourself 340
    A perfect friend of me, and me a son.
Gostanzo. Remember you your part, and fear not mine.
    Rate him, revile him, and renounce him too.
    Speak, can you do't, man?
Marc Antonio.   I'll do all I can.   *Exit.*
Gostanzo. Alas, good man, how nature overweighs him! 345
                                RINALDO *comes forth.*
Rinaldo. God save you, sir.
Gostanzo.   Rinaldo, all the news
    You told me as a secret, I perceive
    Is passing common, for your father knows it.
    The first thing he related was the marriage.
Rinaldo. And was extremely moved?
Gostanzo.   Beyond all measure. 350
    But I did all I could to quench his fury,
    Told him how easy 'twas for a young man
    To run that amorous course, and though his choice
    Were nothing rich, yet she was gently born,
    Well qualified, and beautiful. But he still 355
    Was quite relentless, and would needs renounce him.
Rinaldo. My brother knows it well, and is resolved

---

  335. *glass*] mirror.
  336. *precedent*] example (*OED* n. 4a). As we shall see, Valerio does indeed serve as a role model for Fortunio, but not in the way Gostanzo thinks.
  337. *I make no doubt*] I am certain (*OED* doubt n.¹ 4a).
  339. *thrifty*] respectable (*OED* adj. 2a), although 'prudent with money' is also implied, given the speaker.
  340–1.] If you are successful, both your friendship with me and my son's character would be strengthened.
  343. *Rate*] scold (*OED* v.¹).
  345. *nature*] in early usage, natural feeling or affection, especially that between parent and child (*OED* n. 6).
  overweighs] oppresses, overburdens (*OED* v.).
  348. *passing*] extremely.
  350. *moved*] perturbed, angry (*OED* move v. 25a).
  353. *his choice*] his choice of a bride.
  354. *nothing*] not at all.
  gently] of the gentility (*OED* adv.1b).
  355. *qualified*] of good quality, from the upper class (*OED* adj. 4).
  he] Marc Antonio.

            To trail a pike in field, rather than bide
            The more feared push of my vexed father's fury.
Gostanzo. Indeed, that's one way. But are no more means   360
            Left to his fine wits, than t'incense his father
            With a more violent rage and to redeem
            A great offence with greater?
Rinaldo.   So I told him,
            But to a desperate mind all breath is lost.
Gostanzo. Go to, let him be wise, and use his friends,   365
            Amongst whom I'll be foremost, to his father.
            Without this desperate error he intends
            Joined to the other, I'll not doubt to make him
            Easy return into his father's favour,
            So he submit himself, as duty binds him.   370
            For fathers will be known to be themselves,
            And often when their angers are not deep
            Will paint an outward rage upon their looks.
Rinaldo. All this I told him, sir. But what says he?
            'I know my father will not be reclaimed.   375
            He'll think that if he wink at this offence,
            'Twill open doors to any villainy.
            I'll dare to sell, to pawn, and run all riot,
            To laugh at all his patience, and consume
            All he hath purchased to an honoured purpose   380
            In maintenance of a wanton whirligig
            Worth nothing more than she wears on her back.'
Gostanzo. [*Aside*] The very words I used t'incense his father.—
            But, good Rinaldo, let him be advised.

---

383. SD.] *Collier; not in Q.*

    358. *trail a pike*] What Ancient Pistol of *Henry V* calls 'the puissant pike' (4.1.40) was a wooden shaft, perhaps eighteen feet long, with a pointed head of iron or steel. A pikeman would either 'port' his weapon on his shoulder, or hold the staff near the head and 'trail' the butt on the ground (cf. Edelman, *Military*, pp. 252–5).

    bide] encounter, withstand (*OED* v. 7).

    359. *push*] Marc Antonio's fury would be worse than the 'push', or thrust, of the aforementioned pike.

    362. *redeem*] repay.

    365. *Go to*] a common locution expressing impatience or dismissiveness.

    367–8. *Without ... other*] Fortunio 'intends' to add the 'desperate error' of joining the army to the error of getting married.

    368. *I'll not doubt to*] I have no doubt that I can. A similar construction occurs in *Epicene*, with Truewit's 'a man should not doubt to overcome any woman' (4.1.53).

    368–9. *make him / Easy return*] presumably 'make for him an easy return'. This sort of elision is typical of Chapman.

    375. *reclaimed*] won over (*OED* reclaim v. 9b).

    379. *patience*] forbearance, tolerance (*OED* n.¹b).

How would his father grieve, should he be maimed,	385
Or quite miscarry in the ruthless war?	
Rinaldo. I told him so. But 'Better far', said he,	
'One branch should utterly be lopped away,	
Than the whole tree of all his race should perish;	
And for his wants, better young want than old'.	390
Gostanzo. [*Aside*] By heaven, the same words still I used t'his father.	
Why comes this about?—Well, good Rinaldo,	
If he dare not endure his father's looks,	
Let him and his fair wife come home to me,	
Till I have qualified his father's passion.	395
He shall be kindly welcome, and be sure	
Of all the intercession I can use.	
Rinaldo. I thank you, sir. I'll try what I can do,	
Although I fear me I shall strive in vain.	
Gostanzo. Well, try him, try him.	
Rinaldo. Thanks, sir, so I will.	400

Exit [GOSTANZO].

See this old, politic, dissembling knight.	
Now he perceives my father so affectionate,	
And that my brother may hereafter live	
By him and his with equal use of either,	
He will put on a face of hollow friendship.	405
But this will prove an excellent ground to sow	
The seed of mirth amongst us. I'll go seek	
Valerio and my brother, and tell them	
Such news of their affairs as they'll admire. *Exit.*	

---

390. old] *Reed;* eld *Q.*   391. SD.] *Collier; not in Q.*

---

386. *miscarry*] come to harm (*OED* v. 1).

390. *old*] *Q* has the archaic 'eld', which is perfectly acceptable, but Rinaldo is repeating Gostanzo's words, and Gostanzo said 'better young than old'.

395. *qualified*] appeased (*OED* qualify v. 10).

399. *I fear me*] I fear. Such reflexive forms are often seen in Elizabethan texts (Abbott 296).

401. *politic*] scheming *(OED* adj. 2.c).

403-4.] Fortunio will live at Gostanzo's house, enjoying both the old man's hospitality and the favours of his daughter Bellanora.

406-7. *But this ... amongst us.*] Rinaldo reviews the day so far by promising that the game is only starting. Soliloquies by schemers, be they malicious like Richard III or purely fun-loving like Rinaldo, are often addressed directly to the spectators; the 'us' in 'amongst us' would include everyone in the audience.

409. *admire*] be astonished (*OED* v. 1), as in Sir Andrew Aguecheek's challenge to 'Cesario': 'thou art but a scurvy fellow ... Wonder not, nor admire not in thy mind why I do call thee so' (3.4.148–51).

ACT 1, SCENE 2

Enter GAZETTA, BELLANORA, GRATIANA.

Gazetta. How happy are your fortunes above mine,
    Both still being wooed and courted, still so feeding
    On the delights of love that still you find
    An appetite to more, where I am cloyed,
    And, being bound to love-sports, care not for them.   5
Bellanora. That is your fault, Gazetta. We have loves
    And wish continual company with them
    In honoured marriage rites, which you enjoy,
    But seld or never can we get a look
    Of those we love. Fortunio, my dear choice,   10
    Dare not be known to love me, nor come near
    My father's house, where I as in a prison
    Consume my lost days and the tedious nights,
    My father guarding me for one I hate.
    And Gratiana here, my brother's love,   15
    Joys him by so much stealth that vehement fear
    Drinks up the sweetness of their stol'n delights,

---

0. Act 1, Scene 2] *Parrott¹ (subst.); not in Q.*   1. SP.] *Reed; Gaze. Gaz. Q.*
6. SP.] *Reed; Bell. Q,*

---

    0. *Act 1, Scene 2*] Q has no scene break here, but Rinaldo would probably make a complete exit before the women enter. This scene introduces us to the main subject of the subplot, Cornelio's obsessive fear that his wife Gazetta is cuckolding him.
    1. *happy*] lucky, propitious (*OED* adj. 1).
    your fortunes] Gazetta is addressing both Bellanora and Gratiana.
    4. *cloyed*] surfeited, sated (*OED* adj.).
    5. *bound to love-sports*] required, as a wife, to take part in love-making. In Philemon Holland's 1603 translation of Plutarch's *Moralia*, one of the 'Precepts of Wedlock' is that 'it would become an honest matron and huswife to behave herself toward her husband, that she neither reject and disdain dalliance and love-sports with him' (p. 319).
    9. *seld*] seldom (*OED* adv. 1), a now-obsolete synonym, rather than an abbreviation. Having only one syllable, it is useful in blank verse.
    14. *one I hate*] This rather mysterious reference to a rival suitor must be accounted a false start, as he never appears, nor does Gostanzo, Bellanora's father, ever mention him. Indeed, Gostanzo never speaks of his plans for Bellanora at all. What might be called a standard situation of Elizabethan drama, a father's determination to select a husband for his daughter, who loves someone else, has no place in *All Fools* (cf. Introduction, pp. 19–20).
    15. *my brother's*] Valerio's.
    17.] possibly a play on Proverbs, 9.17: 'stolen waters are sweet, and hid bread is pleasant' (Bennett, p. 96).

88   ALL FOOLS   [ACT I

    Where you enjoy a husband, and may freely
    Perform all obsequies you desire to love.
Gazetta. Indeed I have a husband, and his love   20
    Is more than I desire, being vainly jealous.
    Extremes, though contrary, have the like effects:
    Extreme heat mortifies like extreme cold,
    Extreme love breeds satiety as well
    As extreme hatred, and too violent rigour   25
    Tempts chastity as much as too much licence.
    There's no man's eye fixed on me but doth pierce
    My husband's soul. If any ask my welfare,
    He straight doubts treason practised to his bed,
    Fancies but to himself all likelihoods   30
    Of my wrong to him, and lays all on me
    For certain truths. Yet seeks he with his best
    To put disguise on all his jealousy,
    Fearing, perhaps, lest it may teach me that
    Which otherwise I should not dream upon.   35
    Yet lives he still abroad at great expense,
    Turns merely gallant from his farmer's state,
    Uses all games and recreations,
    Runs races with the gallants of the court,

---

23. Extreme heat] *Reed;* Extreames heat *Q.*

---

19. *obsequies*] rites, rituals (cit. *OED* n.²).
21. *vainly*] foolishly, senselessly (*OED* adv. 2).
27–8. *no man ... soul*] As noted at 1.1.99, once a person's eye-beams have hit an object and return to the eye from whence they originated, they are carried to the soul by the spirit. Gazetta believes that Cornelio is so jealous that his soul receives the eye-beams of any man who looks at her.
29. *straight doubts*] immediately fears (*OED* straight adv. 2a; fear v. 2).
31–2. *lays ... truths*] blames me as if what he imagines were true.
32. *his best*] his best effort.
33–5.] In the twelfth-century poem *The Owl and the Nightingale*, Owl asserts that a husband's jealousy is sure to drive his wife to adultery: 'Behind locked doors their wives are shut / And that's how marriage bonds get cut. / For if they're held in this subjection / Their actions take a new direction' (ll. 1557–60).
36. *lives ... abroad*] He spends all his time away from home. The use of 'abroad' was not limited to 'overseas' (*OED* adv.)
37.] Cornelio is introduced not only as a jealous husband but also as a would-be gallant who should have stayed on the farm. 'Merely', in this sense, means 'totally', as in Hamlet's 'unweeded garden / That grows to seed, things rank and gross in nature / Possess it merely' (1.2.135–7).
39. *Runs races*] one of the more fashionable pastimes of a gallant or courtier. In 1586, George Manners, a well-to-do law student at the Inns of Court, wrote to his father that when he was not too busy studying, 'for exercises ... I use the dancing school, tennis, running, and leaping and such like in the fields' (Finkelpearl, p. 17).

  Feasts them at home, and entertains them costly,   40
  And then upbraids me with their company.
Enter CORNELIO.

  See, see, we shall be troubled with him now.
Cornelio. Now, ladies, what plots have we now in hand?
  They say when only one dame is alone
  She plots some mischief, but if three together,   45
  They plot three hundred. Wife, the air is sharp,
  You'd best to take the house lest you take cold.
Gazetta. Alas, this time of year yields no such danger.
Cornelio. Go in, I say. A friend of yours attends you.
Gazetta. He is of your bringing, and may stay.   50
Cornelio. Nay, stand not chopping logic. In, I pray.
Gazetta. Ye see, gentlewomen, what my happiness is.
  These humours reign in marriage. Humours, humours.
Exit [GAZETTA]. *He followeth.*

Gratiana. Now by my sooth, I am no fortune-teller,
  And would be loath to prove so, yet pronounce   55
  This at adventure, that 'twere indecorum

---

43. SP.] Reed; *Cor. Corn. Cornelio Q*.
53.1. SD. GAZETTA] Manley; *not in Q*.
54. SP.] Reed; *Gra. Grat. Q*.

---

40. *costly*] sumptuously (*OED* adv. 2b).
47. *take cold*] At this time, one could either 'take' or 'catch' cold; both expressions were in wide use.
50. *stay*] wait (*OED* v.¹ 9).
51. *chopping logic*] bandying words, splitting hairs, as in Capulet's anger over Juliet's refusal to marry Paris: 'How, how, chopp'd logic!' (3.5.149).
53. *humours*] Jealousy's status as a physical condition, caused by an imbalance in the body's humours, is an interesting question. Since Hippocrates, literature on this subject has been consistent only in its inconsistency—generally, a jealous disposition was not the direct result of one particular humour, but was seen as a branch of that all-purpose condition, melancholy, caused by an excess of black bile. In his massive compendium *The Anatomy of Melancholy* (1621), Robert Burton devotes more than sixty pages to jealousy, its taxonomy, causes, symptoms, prognostics, and prevention. He writes that some call jealousy the cause of melancholy, others call it a symptom, but 'for the latitude it hath, and that prerogative above other ordinary symptoms, it ought to be treated of as a species apart, being of so great and eminent note, so furious a passion, and almost of as great extent as love itself' (Bk. 3, p. 257).
54. *by my sooth*] in good truth, a mild oath.
56. *at adventure*] recklessly (*OED* adventure n. 3b).
 indecorum] an impropriety (*OED* n. 1).

This heifer should want horns.
Bellanora. Fie on this love!
I rather wish to want than purchase so.
Gratiana. Indeed, such love is like a smoky fire
In a cold morning. Though the fire be cheerful, 60
Yet is the smoke so sour and cumbersome,
'Twere better lose the fire than find the smoke.
Such an attendant then as smoke to fire
Is jealousy to love. Better want both
Than have both.

Enter VALERIO *and* FORTUNIO.

Valerio. Come, Fortunio, now take hold 65
On this occasion, as myself on this.
One couple more would make a barley-break.

---

57. *heifer ... horns*] The heifer is Gazetta, and Gratiana is speaking, rather archly, of her friend's self-admitted lack of a good sex life. Cuckoldry, as a theme, appears nowhere in Terence; for the subplot, Chapman relies heavily, and delightfully, on Ovid. In *The Art of Love*, we have the story of a woman who does indeed 'want' horns. Assuring his young male readers that most girls are so desperate for sex that picking them up is easy, Ovid offers the example of Pasiphaë, wife of King Minos. When Minos offends Neptune by refusing to sacrifice a prize bull in his honour, the god's revenge is to make Pasiphaë fall passionately in love with the very same animal, but she has no idea how to attract it. Ovid asks her, 'Why bother with mirrors when the company you're seeking / Is upland cattle? Why keep fixing your hair, you silly girl? You're no heifer (on *that* you can trust your mirror) / But oh, how you wish you could sprout horns' (1.305-8). Pasiphaë's frustration grows and grows, but nothing works until she climbs into a hollow wooden cow (presumably fitted with horns), designed by the architect Daedalus. At last she mates with the bull, the result being the Minotaur. Gazetta's remark is an example of the splendid comic ambiguity we find in Chapman, both in his comedies and in poems such as the delightful *Ovid's Banquet of Sense*. Gratiana is speaking 'at adventure', and the audience does not know, nor is it meant to know, if 'indecorum' would lie in Gazetta cuckolding her husband, or in her not doing so.

57-8. *Fie ... purchase so*] Bellanora puns on 'want', agreeing that it may be better to do without love if it involves what Gazetta is going through.

65-7. *take hold ... barley-break*] Valerio urges Fortunio to join hands with Bellanora, as he now does with Gratiana, like the participants of the popular country game of barley-break. It was played by three couples, one couple at each end of a field with the third couple in 'hell', the centre. The two free couples had to change partners by breaking hands and running to the other end, while the couple in hell had to intercept them without losing hold of one another's hands. A captured player took a turn in hell.

SC. 2]   ALL FOOLS   91

Gratiana. I fear, Valerio, we shall break too soon;
   Your father's jealous spial will displease us.
Valerio. Well, wench, the day will come his Argus eyes   70
   Will shut, and thou shalt open. 'Sfoot, I think
   Dame Nature's memory begins to fail her.
   If I write but my name in mercers' books,
   I am as sure to have at six months' end
   A rascal at my elbow with his mace   75
   As I am sure my father's not far hence.

---

68. SP.] *Parrott¹; For.* Q.
69. jealous spial] *Bradley (conj.) cit. Parrott²*; Jealosie Spy-all *Q;* jealous spy-all *Shepherd;* jealous espial *Parrott¹*.

---

68. SP] *Q* gives these lines to Fortunio, but, as Parrott notes (p. 727), in the next speech Valerio appears to be answering his wife's remark.
   break too soon] Gratiana continues the barley-break metaphor. She fears breaking (starting the game) prematurely, thereby risking capture. In Suckling's allegorical poem 'A Barley-Break', the couples are Love and Folly, Reason and Fancy, and Hate and Pride: 'it fell / That Love and Folly were in hell / They break, and Love would Reason meet / But Hate was nimbler on her feet' (5–8). Suckling describes three such breaks, but poor Love and Folly end up in hell where they began.
   69. *jealous spial*] Shepherd's emendation of *Q*'s 'jelosie' to 'jealous' seems apt, and has the advantage of restoring the metre. 'Spial', sometimes seen as 'spyall', is intense spying or observation (*OED* n. 1). Keeping a careful watch was important in barley-break; Sidney's *Arcadia* describes a game where the couple in hell 'Must strive with waiting foot, and watching eye' (p. 203).
   displease us] vex us, make us unhappy (*OED* v. 2a).
   70–1 *Argus eyes / Will shut*] In Ovid's *Metamorphoses,* Jupiter turned Io into a beautiful white heifer, in order to hide his affair with her from the jealous Juno. Suspecting something, Juno demanded the heifer as a gift, and placed it in the care of Argus, whose 'head had a hundred eyes, which rested in relays, / two at a time'. So Jupiter sent Mercury, disguised as a shepherd, to lull Argus to sleep with the music of his reed pipes and his long stories. When Mercury saw that Argus's eyes were closed, 'he stroked the sentry's / drooping lids with his magic wand', and cut off its head. Juno retrieved the eyes and placed them among the feathers of her bird, the peacock (1. 625–6, 715–16).
   71. *open*] *OED* offers no definition in an intransitive sense that suits the context. Valerio probably means 'thou shalt open thine'—Chapman is good at creating confusion by over-compression of a line.
   72–8.] Dame Nature seems to have forgotten that Gostanzo has lived long enough, and the 'debt' he owes her (l. 76) is overdue.
   73.] Mercers were dealers in fabrics, especially fine ones such as silk and velvet, often bought on credit. To be in a mercer's or tailor's book was a common metaphor for being in debt.
   75.] The rascal in question would be a sergeant, whose mace was an ornamental staff or sceptre carried as a badge of office (cf. 1.2.81 n.).

My father yet hath owed Dame Nature debt
These threescore years and ten, yet calls not on him.
But if she turn her debt-book over once
And, finding him her debtor, do but send 80
Her sergeant, John Death, to arrest his body,
Our souls shall rest, wench, then, and the free light
Shall triumph in our faces, where now night,
In imitation of my father's frowns,
Lours at our meeting.

Enter RINALDO.

See where the scholar comes. 85
Rinaldo. Down on your knees, poor lovers, reverence learning!

77–8.] 'Nature's debt' is a proverbial trope for death (Dent D168). The tradition of seventy years denoting a full life comes from Psalms, 90.10: 'The time of our life is threescore years and ten'.
78. *yet calls not*] yet Dame Nature calls not.
79. *turn*] turn the pages of, read. Sir John Davies asks, in *Nosce Teipsum*, 'When we have all the learned volumes turned / Which yield men's wits both help and ornament / What can we know? or what can we discern?' (ll. 55–7).
81. *sergeant, John Death*] Originally any servant or attendant, by early modern times a sergeant had become a relatively low-ranking soldier or civil official. The most famous association of a sergeant with death is, of course, Hamlet's 'this fell sergeant, Death / Is strict in his arrest' (5.2.336–70). John has always been England's favourite name for an otherwise unnamed male, e.g., John-a-Nokes and John-a-Styles, fictitious names used in law books to denote the parties in a civil action.
82. *Our souls shall rest*] a play on 'arrest' in the previous line, and on the different meanings of 'soul'. When death arrests Gostanzo, his (immortal) soul will be at rest, while the souls of Valerio and Gratiana may be taken in a far more comprehensive and common meaning, derived from the Latin *anima*. This soul is the mind in its many functions, the inner source of all thoughts, all desires, and all emotions.
82–3. *the free light ... faces*] Valerio is saying that everything will be fine once his father dies, which cannot be soon enough for him. We find a hint of this in Terence's *Brothers*, when Micio, the indulgent father, tells his more severe brother Demea that he would do better to let his son sow his wild oats now, rather than 'waiting till he's thrown your corpse out of door—which is what he's waiting for—and doing it later' (108–10). More explicitly, in Plautus's *The Ghost*, young Philolaches is in love with the courtesan/slave Philematium, and has bought her freedom. Now out of money, and concerned that she will lose interest in him if he is unable to shower her with gifts, he says, 'I'd like to get news of my father's death now, so that I could disinherit myself of my property and she could be the heir' (233–5).
85. *Lours*] looks angrily or threateningly (*OED* v. 1), as in *Richard III*, 'all the clouds that loured upon our house' (1.1.3).
the scholar] As noted at 1.1.316, Rinaldo is a student at the University of Padua.
86. *reverence*] greet with great respect by bowing or kneeling (*OED* v. 1a).

SC. 2]   ALL FOOLS   93

Fortunio. I pray thee, why, Rinaldo?
Rinaldo.   Mark what cause
   Flows from my depth of knowledge to your loves,
   To make you kneel and bless me while you live.
Valerio. I pray thee, good scholar, give us cause.   90
Rinaldo. Mark then, erect your ears. [*To Valerio*] You know what
      horror
   Would fly on your love from your father's frowns
   If he should know it. And your sister here,
   My brother's sweetheart, knows as well what rage
   Would seize his powers for her, if he should know   95
   My brother wooed her, or that she loved him.
   Is not this true? Speak all.
All.   All this is true.
Rinaldo. It is as true that now you meet by stealth
   In depth of midnight, kissing out at grates,
   Climb over walls. And all this I'll reform.   100
Valerio. By logic?
Rinaldo.   Well, sir, you shall have all means
   To live in one house, eat and drink together,
   Meet and kiss your fills.
Valerio.   All this by learning?
Rinaldo. Ay, and your frowning father know all this.
Valerio. Ay, marry, small learning may prove that.   105
Rinaldo. Nay, he shall know it, and desire it too,
   Welcome my brother to him, and your wife,
   Entreating both to come and dwell with him.
   Is not this strange?
Fortunio.   Ay, too strange to be true.

---

   90. scholar] *Reed;* Scholards *Q;* scholard *Parrott¹*.
   91. SD.] *This ed.; not in Q.*
   97. SP. *All*] *This ed.; Q has Omn. or Omnes throughout.*

   87–8. *what cause ... your loves*] Parrott's gloss is delightful: 'What good cause my profound sagacity gives for you all to love me'.
   91. *erect your ears*] This use of 'erect' precedes *OED*'s earliest citation of 1626. The much more common 'prick up your ears' is at 3.1.158.
   93. *know it*] know of it, your secret marraige.
   95. *for her*] against Bellanora.
   101. *logic*] Grammar, logic, and rhetoric were the three arts comprising the *trivium*, the core curriculum Rinaldo would be studying at the university. In *The Alchemist*, Subtle promises to teach Kastril 'the grammar and logic / And rhetoric of quarrelling' (4.2.64–5).
   104. *know*] 'could' or 'shall' know (cf. Abbott 365).
   105. *marry*] indeed.

94   ALL FOOLS   [ACT I

Rinaldo. 'Tis in this head shall work it. Therefore, hear.   110
   Brother, this lady you must call your wife,
   For I have told her sweetheart's father here
   That she is your wife. And because my father,
   Who now believes it, must be quieted
   Before you see him, you must live awhile   115
   As husband to her in his father's house.
   Valerio, here's a simple mean for you
   To lie at rack and manger with your wedlock,
   And, brother, for yourself to meet as freely
   With this your long-desired and barrèd love.   120
Fortunio. You make us wonder.
Rinaldo.   Peace, be ruled by me,
   And you shall see to what a perfect shape
   I'll bring this rude plot, which blind chance—the ape
   Of counsel and advice—hath brought forth blind.
   Valerio, can your heat of love forbear   125
   Before your father, and allow my brother
   To use some kindness to your wife before him?
Valerio. Ay, before him I do not greatly care,
   Nor anywhere indeed. My sister here

---

110. *'Tis ... work it*] When Rinaldo says 'this head' he means his own. 'Work' is to be taken in the sense of 'perform' or 'execute', as in 'work a miracle', which is what Rinaldo seems to think he can do.
   111. *this lady*] Gratiana. Lines such as this one are perfectly clear in the theatre, but can be confusing on the page.
   112. *her sweetheart's father*] Gostanzo, the father of Gratiana's 'sweetheart' Valerio.
   116. *his father's*] i.e., Gostanzo's.
   117. *mean*] means. Rinaldo uses the now archaic singular here, in contrast to the common plural form at 1.2.101.
   118. *rack and manger*] A rack is a vertical frame, perhaps attached to a barn wall, for holding fodder; a manger is a trough or box used for the same purpose. To 'lie at rack and manger' is proverbial for living in plenty (Dent R4).
   wedlock] wife (*OED* n. 3), a less common usage also found in *Eastward Ho*, as Security says to Winifred, 'How now, my coy wedlock?' (3.1.22).
   123. *rude*] rough, hastily assembled (*OED* adj. 17).
   blind chance] Dame Fortune, who is always blindfolded.
   123–4. *ape ... advice*] In saying that Dame Fortune mockingly mimics sober advice (*OED* ape n. 3), Rinaldo may be alluding to the proverb 'Fortune, not wisdom, governs our lives'. It probably originated with the tragedian Chaeremon (fourth century BC), and gained wide currency after being quoted by Theophrastus, who in turn was quoted by both Cicero in the *Tusculan Disputatons* and Plutarch in the *Moralia* (Cicero, p. 451; Plutarch 2: 75).
   124. *blind*] although blind.

SC. 2]   ALL FOOLS   95

    Shall be my spy. If she will wrong herself,   130
    And give her right to my wife, I am pleased.
Fortunio. [*To Bellanora*] My dearest life, I know will never fear
    Any such will or thought in all my powers.
    When I court her then, think I think 'tis thee.
    When I embrace her, hold thee in mine arms.   135
    Come, let us practise gainst we see your father.
                           [*He goes to embrace Gratiana.*]
Valerio. Soft, sir, I hope you need not do it yet;
    Let me take this time.
Rinaldo.   Come, you must not touch her.
Valerio. No, not before my father.
Rinaldo.   No, nor now,
    Because you are so soon to practise it,   140
    For I must bring them to him presently.
    Take her, Fortunio. Go hence, man and wife.
    We will attend you rarely with fixed faces.
    Valerio, keep your countenance, and conceive
    Your father in your forgèd sheepishness,   145
    Who thinks thou dar'st not look upon a wench,
    Nor knowst at which end to begin to kiss her.
                                      Exeunt.

---

132. SD.] *This ed.; not in* Q.   136.1 SD.] *This ed.; not in* Q.
147.2] Q *has* FINIS ACTUS PRIMI; *omitted Reed*.

  130–1. *If she ... pleased*] If Bellanora is willing to allow her beloved, Fortunio, to pretend to be married to Gratiana, then Valerio will not object to the plan.
  135. *hold thee*] I will imagine I hold thee.
  136. *let us practise*] Fortunio's eagerness to get started is a fine comic touch.
  gainst] in preparation for when (*OED* against adj. 19).
  137. *Soft*] Gently, take it easy.
  138. *Let me*] The metre instructs the actor to emphasise 'me'. Valerio wants to kiss Gratiana while he still can.
  140. *practise it*] put it into practice, actually begin. This dialogue is similar to the corresponding sequence in *The Self-Tormenter*, although the girl is off stage, and Clitipho, Valerio's counterpart, wants to run off for one last kiss, and is restrained by his slave Syrus (ll. 376–9).
  141. *them*] Fortunio and Gratiana.
  143. *rarely*] splendidly (*OED* adv. 3).

Act 2

ACT 2, SCENE I

[*Enter*] GOSTANZO, MARC ANTONIO.

Gostanzo. It is your own too simple lenity
  And doting indulgence shown to him still
  That thus hath taught your son to be no son.
  As you have used him, therefore, so you have him.
  Durst my son thus turn rebel to his duty, 5
  Steal up a match unsuiting his estate,
  Without all knowledge of or friend or father,
  And, to make that good with a worse offence,
  Resolve to run beyond sea to the wars?
  Durst my son serve me thus? Well, I have stayed him, 10
  Though much against my disposition,
  And this hour I have set for his repair
  With his young mistress and concealèd wife,
  And in my house here they shall sojourn both,
  Till your black anger's storm be overblown. 15
Marc Antonio. My anger's storm? Ah, poor Fortunio,
  One gentle word from thee would soon resolve
  The storm of my rage to a shower of tears.
Gostanzo. In that vein still? Well, Marc Antonio,
  Our old acquaintance and long neighbourhood 20
  Ties my affection to you and the good

---

0. Act 2, Scene 1] *Hudston (subst.);* Actus secundi, Scaena prima *Q.*
6. unsuiting] *Reed;* unshuting *Q.*   9. Resolve] *Q(c);* Adsolve *Q(u).*

---

0. *Act 2 Scene 1*] As the scene progresses, we learn that we are outdoors, near Gostanzo's house.
1. *lenity*] mildness (*OED* n.).
7. *or friend or father*] The repeated 'or', in place of 'either ... or', is a common locution (Abbott 136).
9. *beyond sea*] Omission of 'the' in such phrases is often seen in this period (Abbott 88).
10. *I have stayed him*] 'I have kept Fortunio from running away'. Only the first half of the line refers to Valerio.
12. *repair*] Chapman plays cleverly with two meanings of the word, 'lodging' and 'moral improvement' (*OED* n.[1] 2, n.[2] 3). Fortunio will receive both at Gostanzo's house.
13.] a line easily misunderstood. The mistress and wife are one person.
20. *neighbourhood*] warm feelings between neighbours (*OED* n. 6).

SC. I]   ALL FOOLS   97

    Of your whole house; in kind regard whereof
    I have advised you, for your credit sake
    And for the tender welfare of your son,
    To frown on him a little. If you do not,   25
    But at first parley take him to your favour,
    I protest utterly to renounce all care
    Of you and yours and all your amities.
    They say he's wretched that out of himself
    Cannot draw counsel to his proper weal.   30
    But he's thrice wretched that has neither counsel
    Within himself nor apprehension
    Of counsel for his own good from another.
Marc Antonio. Well, I will arm myself against this weakness
    The best I can. I long to see this Helen   35
    That hath enchanted my young Paris thus,
    And's like to set all our poor Troy on fire.

              Enter VALERIO *with* [CURIO].

Gostanzo. Here comes my son. Withdraw, take up your stand.
    You shall hear odds betwixt your son and mine.
                     Marc [*Antonio*] *retires himself.*

---

37. Troy] *Reed (subst.);* Trope *Q.*   37.1. CURIO] *This ed; a Page Q.*
39.1. SD. Antonio] *Reed; not in Q. This placement of SD Parrott¹; together with 37.1 SD Q.*

---

  23. *credit*] credit's. The omission of the final 's' before 'sake' was acceptable in Elizabethan usage (Hope, p. 38), and a help to the actor if he is not to slow his delivery. *An Humorous Day's Mirth* has both 'living sake' and 'honour sake' (2.77, 7.169).
  27. *protest*] vow, declare emphatically (*OED* v. 2,3).
  28. *amities*] amity, friendship, a now archaic plural form.
  29–33.] To be unable to find advice from within oneself is bad enough; to be unable to accept good advice from others is worse.
  29. *out of himself*] from himself (Abbott 183).
  30. *counsel*] advice (*OED* n. 2).
  proper weal] personal welfare (*OED proper* adj. 3b, *weal* n.¹ 2a).
  32. *apprehension*] acquisition, understanding (*OED* n. 4, 8). The two senses are, of course, closely related.
  35–6. *this Helen ... my young Paris*] It is amusing how Marc Antonio seems to assume that Fortunio was completely innocent until he was ensnared by the seductive Gratiana. In Apollodorus, Homer, and other sources, the relationship between Helen and Paris is far more complex.
  37. *And's like*] and is likely to.
  38. *stand*] hiding place, usually associated with hunting *(OED* n. 13). In *Love's Labour's Lost*, the Forester tells the Princess of France of 'A stand, where you may make the fairest shoot' (4.1.10).
  39. *odds*] differences, dissimilarities (*OED* n. 2.b).

98   ALL FOOLS   [ACT 2

Valerio. [*To Curio*] Tell him I cannot do't. Shall I be made   40
  A foolish novice, my purse set abroach
  By every cheating come-you-seven, to lend
  My money and be laughed at? Tell him plain
  I profess husbandry, and will not play
  The prodigal like him gainst my profession.   45
Gostanzo. [*Aside to Marc Antonio*] Here's a son.
Marc Antonio. [*Aside to Gostanzo*]   An admirable spark.
Curio. Well, sir, I'll tell him so.   *Exit.*
Valerio.   'Sfoot, let him lead
  A better husband's life, and live not idly,
  Spending his time, his coin, and self on wenches.
Gostanzo. Why, what's the matter, son?   50
Valerio. Cry mercy, sir! Why, there come messengers
  From this and that brave gallant, and such gallants
  As I protest I saw but through a grate.
Gostanzo. And what's this message?
Valerio.   Faith, sir, he's disappointed
  Of payments, and disfurnished of means present.   55

---

40. SD.] *This ed; not in Q.*   46. SD.] *Parrott²; not in Q.*
47. SP.] *This ed.; Pag. Page Q.*   47. SD.] *This ed.; Exit Page Q.*

---

41. *set abroach*] opened up, customarily in reference to a cask of liquor (OED set v.¹ phrasal verbs).
42. *come-you-seven*] roll of the dice, or perhaps a dice player. Seven was a 'main', or winning throw, in the game of hazard, and a player would often call out 'come-you-seven' or 'come-on-seven' when casting the dice (*OED* seven n. 3a).
44. *profess husbandry*] espouse and practise thrift (*OED* v. 3a).
44–5.] Chapman may be evoking the story of the prodigal son (Luke, 15.11–32; cf. Bennett, p. 960).
46. *spark*] gallant, elegant young man. In *All's Well*, Parolles addresses the French lords as 'good sparks and lustrous' (2.1.41).
48. *husband's life*] 'Husband' is now used in the sense of household and business manager (*OED* n. 5a).
49. *Spending*] Since 'wenches' are brought into the discussion, 'spending' carries both its usual sense and implies 'ejaculating'. We return to Parolles (2.1.46n.), who employs the same double meaning in urging the French lords off to war: 'He wears his honour in a box unseen / That hugs his kicky-wicky here at home, / Spending his manly marrow in her arms' (2.3.279–81; cf. Williams, pp. 1281–2).
51. *Cry mercy*] I ask your pardon.
53. *grate*] Valerio probably means the grate of a door or window, but Brereton's suggestion of reference to the well-known grating of the Counter, London's debtor's prison, is plausible (cit. Parrott, p. 715).
54–5. *disappointed / Of payments*] unable to pay his debts.
55. *disfurnished*] deprived (*OED* disfurnish v.).

If I would do him the kind office, therefore,	
To trust him but some seven-night with the keeping	
Of forty crowns for me, he deeply swears,	
As he's a gentleman, to discharge his trust;	
And that I shall eternally endear him	60
To my wished service, he protests and contests.	
Gostanzo. Good words, Valerio. But thou art too wise	
To be deceived by breath. I'll turn thee loose	
To the most cunning cheater of them all.	
Valerio. 'Sfoot, he's not ashamed besides to charge me	65
With a late promise. I must yield. Indeed,	
I did, to shift him with some contentment,	
Make such a frivol promise.	
Gostanzo. Ay, well done.	
Promises are no fetters. With that tongue	
Thy promise passed, unpromise it again.	70
Wherefore has man a tongue of power to speak,	
But to speak still to his own private purpose?	
Beasts utter but one sound, but men have change	
Of speech and reason, even by nature given them,	
Now to say one thing, and another now,	75
As best may serve their profitable ends.	
Marc Antonio. [*Aside*] By'r Lady, sound instructions to a son.	
Valerio. Nay, sir, he makes his claim by debt of friendship.	
Gostanzo. Tush, friendship's but a term, boy. The fond world	
Like to a doting mother glazes over	80
Her children's imperfections with fine terms.	

---

77. SD.] *Collier; not in Q.*

    60. *endear him*] bind him, by obligations of gratitude (*OED* v. 6b).
    61. *To my wished service*] in any way I desire.
    contests] testifies, vows solemnly (*OED* contest v. 1; cf. Prol.12n.).
    63. *deceived by breath*] probably an allusion to the proverbial 'words are but wind' (Dent W833). Longaville employs similar reasoning in *Love's Labour's Lost*: 'Vows are but breath, and breath a vapour is' (4.3.66).
    63-4. *Turn thee loose / To*] set you free to deal with. The bawd Primero of Middleton's *Your Five Gallants* uses the same expression when confirming that a newly employed prostitute is ready to ply her trade: 'I fear not now to turn her loose to any gentleman in Europe' (1.1.254-5).
    65. *charge*] burden (*OED* v. 11).
    67. *shift ... contentment*] satisfy him temporarily.
    68. *frivol*] an obsolete form of 'frivolous' (*OED* adj. 2).
    77. *By'r Lady*] a mild oath.
    79. *fond*] foolish, the most common definition at this time. *OED*'s first citation in the sense of 'affectionate towards' is Oberon's 'He may prove / More fond on her, than she upon her love' in *A Midsummer Night's Dream* (2.1.265-6).

       What she calls friendship and true humane kindness
       Is only want of true experience.
       Honesty is but a defect of wit;
       Respect but mere rusticity and clownery.   85
Marc Antonio. [*Aside*] Better and better!—Soft, here comes my son.
       Enter FORTUNIO, RINALDO, *and* GRATIANA.
Rinaldo. [*Aside*] Fortunio, keep your countenance. [*To Gostanzo*]
       See, sir, here
       The poor young married couple, which you pleased
       To send for to your house.
Gostanzo.   Fortunio, welcome,
       And in that welcome I imply your wife's,   90
       Who I am sure you count your second self.   *He kisses her.*
Fortunio. Sir, your right noble favours do exceed
       All power of worthy gratitude by words,
       That in your care supply my father's place.
Gostanzo. Fortunio, I cannot choose but love you.   95
       Being son to him who long time I have loved,
       From whose just anger my house shall protect you,
       Till I have made a calm way to your meetings.

---

86. SD.] *Collier; not in Q.*
87. SD. *Aside*] *Collier; not in Q.* To Gostanzo] *Manley; not in Q.*

---

82. *humane*] courteous, compassionate (*OED* adj. 1). The word appears frequently in early modern drama, and in blank verse the accent is nearly always on the first syllable. Hence there is little aural distinction to be made from 'human'.
    84.] Iago expresses similar sentiments to Othello with 'honesty's a fool / And loses that it works for' (3.3.382–3).
    85. *rusticity and clownery*] These two words are synonymous, denoting the lack of intelligence or manners customarily attributed to rural people.
    91. *count*] consider (*OED* v. 3).
    your second self] The proverbial saying, 'a friend is one's second self' goes back to Aristotle in the *Magna Moralia* (Dent F696). But since Gostanzo thinks he is talking about Fortunio's wife, not just a friend, he also invokes Genesis, 2.24: 'Therefore shall man leave his father and his mother, and shall cleave to his wife, and they shall be one flesh'.
    91. SD. *He kisses her*] The peculiarly English practice of kissing people when meeting them was often remarked upon by foreigners. Erasmus, visiting England in 1499, wrote to the poet Fausto Andrelini about 'one custom which can never be recommended too highly. When you arrive anywhere, you are received with kisses on all sides, and when you take your leave they speed you on your way with kisses. The kisses are renewed when you come back. When guests come to your house, their arrival is pledged with kisses; and when they leave, kisses are shared once again. If you should happen to meet, then kisses are given profusely. In a word, wherever you turn, the world is full of kisses' (*Correspondence*, p. 193).

Fortunio. I little thought, sir, that my father's love
    Would take so ill so slight a fault as this. 100
Gostanzo. Call you it slight? Nay, though his spirit take it
    In higher manner than for your loved sake
    I would have wished him, yet I make a doubt,
    Had my son done the like, if my affection
    Would not have turned to more spleen than your father's. 105
    And yet I qualify him all I can,
    And doubt not but that time and my persuasion
    Will work out your excuse, since youth and love
    Were th'unresisted organs to seduce you.
    But you must give him leave, for fathers must 110
    Be won by penitence and submission,
    And not by force or opposition.
Fortunio. Alas, sir, what advise you me to do?
    I know my father to be highly moved,
    And am not able to endure the breath 115
    Of his expressed displeasure, whose hot flames
    I think my absence soonest would have quenched.
Gostanzo. True, sir, as fire with oil, or else like them
    That quench the fire with pulling down the house.
    You shall remain here in my house concealed 120
    Till I have won your father to conceive
    Kinder opinion of your oversight.
    Valerio, entertain Fortunio
    And his fair wife, and give them conduct in.
Valerio. You're welcome, sir.
Gostanzo.   What, sirrah, is that all? 125
    No entertainment to the gentlewoman?
Valerio. Forsooth, you're welcome by my father's leave.

---

103. *make a doubt*] fear (*OED* doubt n.¹ 4).

105. *spleen*] Gostanzo's spleen would have been like 'the swelling spleen, and frenzy raging rife' attendant upon Wrath in *The Faerie Queene* (1.4.35.7; cf. Prol.16n., 24n.).

106. *qualify*] appease (*OED* v. 10).

109. *organs*] mental or spiritual faculties regarded as instruments of the mind or soul (*OED* n.¹), virtually synonymous with 'humours'.

110. *give him leave*] be tolerant of his attitude.

118. *as fire with oil*] proverbial (Dent F287).

121. *conceive*] form in the mind (*OED* v. 8).

122. *oversight*] recklessness (*OED* oversee v. 7). At this time the word carried more serious connotations than our usual sense of inadvertent error. In Peele's *The Battle of Alcazar*, the King of Morocco arrays his forces in preparation for the Portuguese attack, led by King Sebastian, with the exhortation to 'make him know and rue his oversight / That rashly seeks the ruin of this land' (4.1.72–3).

125. *sirrah*] a term of address often used for boys or inferiors (*OED* n. 1).

126. *entertainment*] polite reception (*OED* n. 11a).

Gostanzo. What, no more compliment? Kiss her, you sheep's head!
Why, when? Go, go, sir, call your sister hither.
                                                                    Exit Valerio.
Lady, you'll pardon our gross bringing up?   130
We dwell far off from court, you may perceive.
The sight of such a blazing star as you
Dazzles my rude son's wits.
Gratiana.   Not so, good sir.
The better husband the more courtly ever.
Rinaldo. Indeed a courtier makes his lips go far,   135
As he doth all things else.

       Enter VALERIO, BELLANORA.

Gostanzo. [*To Bellanora*]   Daughter, receive
This gentlewoman home, and use her kindly.
                                [*Bellanora*] *kisses* [*Gratiana*].
Bellanora. My father bids you kindly welcome, lady,
And therefore you must needs come well to me.
Gratiana. Thank you, forsooth.
Gostanzo.   Go, dame, conduct 'em in.   140
        Exeunt Rinaldo, Fortunio, Bellanora, Gratiana.
[*To Valerio*] Ah, errant sheep's head, hast thou lived thus long,
And dar'st not look a woman in the face?
Though I desire especially to see
My son a husband, shall I therefore have him
Turn absolute cullion? Let's see, kiss thy hand!   145

---

136. SD. *To Bellanora*] *This ed.; not in Q.*
137.1. SD.] *This ed.; She kisses her Q.*   141. SD.] *This ed.; not in Q.*

---

128. *sheep's head*] simpleton (cit. *OED* n. 2a).

129. *when*] expressing impatience (*OED* adv. 1 b).

134.] Gratiana, obviously enjoying her part in the ruse, may be implying that the husbandman Valerio is an excellent courtier—he has courted her so well he is now her husband.

135–6.] A true courtier must be prepared to kiss many people, so he needs to be adept at it. In *Every Man Out of His Humour*, Fallace says of Fastidious Brisk: 'O fine courtier! How comely he bows him in his curtsy! How full he hits a woman between the lips when he kisses!' (4.1.24–5).

139. *come well*] be welcome. In Jonson's *Sejanus*, Macro informs Laco, 'I bring you letters and a health from Caesar', and Laco's reply is 'Sir, both come well' (5.1.114–15).

145. *cullion*] In its earliest sense, a cullion was a testicle, as Chaucer's Host tells the Pardoner, 'I wolde I hadde thy coillons in myn hond' (952). By Chapman's time it was a general term of contempt.

kiss thy hand] To kiss one's own hand when greeting a lady was a typical courtier's gesture. Macilente instructs Sogliardo in *Every Man Out of His Humour*, 'be sure to kiss your hand often enough' (5.1.46).

SC. I]   ALL FOOLS   103

 Thou kiss thy hand? Thou wip'st thy mouth, by th' mass.
Fie on thee, clown! They say the world's grown finer,
But I for my part never saw young men
Worse fashioned and brought up than nowadays.
'Sfoot, when myself was young, was not I kept   150
As far from court as you? I think I was.
And yet my father on a time invited
The Duchess of his house. I, being then
About some five-and-twenty years of age,
Was thought the only man to entertain her.   155
I had my congé—plant myself of one leg,
Draw back the tother with a deep-fetched honour,
Then with a bel-regard advant mine eye
With boldness on her very visnomy.
Your dancers all were counterfeits to me.   160
And for discourse in my fair mistress' presence
I did not, as you barren gallants do,
Fill my discourses up drinking tobacco,

---

146. *by th' mass*] a common oath.

150–79.] With his grand description of youthful accomplishments, Gostanzo is similar to Chremes of *The Self-Tormenter*, whose self-praise is particularly galling to his son Ctesipho: 'I can't stand it! Think of the exploits he boasts about to me when he's had a bit too much to drink ... Little does he know what a deaf ear I turn to his tale-telling' (219–23).

150. *myself*] sometimes used as a subject (Abbott 20).

153. *of his house*] to his house. Gostanzo's father was entertaining the Grand Duchess of Tuscany, one of few references to the ostensibly Florentine setting.

156. *congé*] Originally a ceremonious bow at leave-taking, a congé might also be done in salutation.

of] on. Chapman is always liberal with his prepositions (cf. l. 153n.).

156–7 *plant ... Draw*] The shift to present tense may be intentional; Gostanzo is re-enacting and thus reliving a great moment.

157. *the tother*] a common form of 'the other'.

honour] bow (cit. *OED* n. 5b).

158. *bel-regard*] flirtatious gaze. Gostanzo is showing off his French, the language of courtliness.

advant] a variant of 'avaunt', in this sense 'advance'. Gostanzo cast his eye-beams on the Duchess.

159. *visnomy*] physiognomy, facial features (*OED* n.).

160. *Your*] A common colloquial term for 'typical'.

counterfeits to] poor imitations of.

162. *barren*] unintelligent (*OED* adj. 8), as in Hamlet's dismissal of actors 'that will themselves laugh to set on some quantity of barren spectators to laugh too' (3.2.40–2).

163. *drinking*] smoking. One always 'drank', rather than 'smoked', tobacco in the early days of the habit.

> But on the present furnished evermore
> With tales and practised speeches, as sometimes, 165
> 'What is't a clock?' 'What stuff's this petticoat?'
> 'What cost the making? What, the fringe and all?'
> And what she had under her petticoat,
> And such-like witty compliments. And for need,
> I could have written as good prose and verse 170
> As the most beggarly poet of 'em all,
> Either acrostic, exordium,
> Epithalamions, satires, epigrams,
> Sonnets in dozens, or your quatorzanies
> In any rhyme, masculine, feminine, 175

---

174. quatorzanies] *Q;* quatorzains *Shepherd.*

164. *on the present*] presently, without delay.
furnished] was furnished, supplied. The verb is elided (Abbott 403).
166. *What stuff's this petticoat*] What material is this petticoat made of? In early modern usage, a petticoat could be an under-coat or tunic worn on the upper body, an outer skirt, or a decorative under-skirt (*OED* n. 2). 'Fringe' in the following line implies that Gostanzo means a skirt.
168.] The bawdy innuendo is obvious; the joke lies in that we do not know whether or not Gostanzo realises he is making it.
172. *acrostic, exordium*] An acrostic is a short poem or other composition in which the first letter of each line spells out a word or phrase. The less familiar exordium is the introductory passage of a literary work.
173. *Epithalamions*] An epithalamion (or epithalamium) is a wedding ode in praise of the bride and groom, wishing them good fortune. Chapman's effort in this genre, *Andromeda Liberata* (1614), written in honour of the wedding of Frances Howard to Robert Carr, Earl of Somerset, had less than the desired effect. The marriage was delayed by the need to annul the bride's former marriage, and then interrupted by her imprisonment in the Tower of London for murder (cf. *DNB*, 'Frances Howard').
satires] usually poems, rather than plays or prose works, in which prevailing vices or follies were held up to ridicule (*OED* n. 1a). John Marston's *The Scourge of Villainy*, printed the year before *All Fools* was written, is a fine example.
epigrams] Originally inscriptions on a monument or statue, epigrams were short, witty statements, usually in verse. The Latin poet Martial was considered a master of the form.
174. *Sonnets in dozens*] Sonnets were occasionally written in twelve lines, such as Shakespeare's *Sonnet 126*, 'O thou, my lovely boy ...'. The phrase may also suggest 'sonnets by the dozens'.
quatorzanies] Gostanzo's silly malapropism for 'quatorzain', a sonnet or other poem of fourteen lines, from the French *quatorze*. In a dedicatory poem to Thomas Watson's *Passionate Century* (1582), the poet is praised as the heir of Petrarch, 'Who scaled the skies in lofty quatorzain'. Some editors emend *Q* to read 'quatorzains', but that is probably missing the joke.
175. *masculine, feminine*] Masculine rhymes are the most common in English verse, formed by the same sound on a final, stressed syllable. In feminine rhyme, the

Or sdrucciola, or couplets, blank verse.
You're but bench-whistlers nowadays to them
That were in our times. Well, about your husbandry.
Go, for, i'faith, thou'rt fit for nothing else.
       Exit Valerio. [*Marc Antonio comes forward.*]
Marc Antonio. By'r Lady, you have played the courtier rarely. 180
Gostanzo. But did you ever see so blank a fool,
When he should kiss a wench, as my son is?
Marc Antonio. Alas, 'tis but a little bashfulness.
You let him keep no company, nor allow him
Money to spend at fence and dancing-schools; 185
You're too severe, i'faith.
Gostanzo.   And you too supple.
Well, sir, for your sake I have stayed your son
From flying to the wars. Now see you rate him,

179.1. SD. *Marc Antonio comes forward*] This ed.; prodit Mar Q; Marc Antonio appears Reed.

penultimate stressed syllable does the work, while the final unstressed syllable is identical in sound. The first quatrain of Shakespeare's Sonnet 152 has alternating masculine and feminine rhyme: 'In loving thee thou know'st I am forsworn, / But thou art twice forsworn to me love swearing: / In act thy bed-vow broke, and new faith torn / In vowing new hate after new love bearing' (1–4).

176. *sdrucciola*] from the Italian *rima sdrucciola*, or 'slippery rhyme'. It comprises a stressed, rhymed syllable followed by two unstressed, identical syllables. In *A Defence of Poetry*, Sir Philip Sidney notes that Italian does not allow for masculine rhyme, and contains exclusively the feminine or sdrucciola: 'The example of the former is *buono-suono*, of the sdrucciola is *femina-semina*'. Sidney adds, 'the English hath all three, as dice-trice, father-rather, motion-potion' (p. 74). 'Motion-potion' may seem a weak example, but proper pronunciation involves all three syllables. For an astounding display of *rima sdrucciola*, see W. S. Gilbert's 'I Am the Very Model of a Modern Major-General', from *The Pirates of Penzance*.

177. *bench-whistlers*] proverbial for idlers, those who are all talk and no action (Dent B307).

178. *about your husbandry*] Go tend to the farm.

179.1 SD.] The reader might easily forget that Marc Antonio has been watching everything, while hidden, since l. 39.

181. *blank*] befuddled, devoid of expression (*OED* adj. 5), as in a blank stare.

185. *fence and dancing-schools*] Skill at fencing and dancing was obligatory for the young man who aspired to the courtly life. The conservative English fencing teachers, who favoured the traditional sword, resented the fashionable masters from Spain and Italy, with their long rapiers. Similarly, London's established dancing teachers discredited their competitors, saying they were disreputable people without qualifications, who encouraged all sorts of immoral behaviour at their schools (Anglin, pp. 407–10; Prest, p. 154; Brissenden, p. 6).

186. *supple*] compliant, easily persuaded (*OED* adj. 4).

                    To stay him yet from more expenseful courses,
                    Wherein your lenity will encourage him.   190
Marc Antonio. Let me alone; I thank you for this kindness.
                                                                                Exeunt.

                    Enter VALERIO *and* RINALDO.

Rinaldo. So, are they gone? Now tell me, brave Valerio,
            Have I not won the wreath from all your wits,
            Brought thee t'enjoy the most desired presence
            Of thy dear love at home, and with one labour   195
            My brother to enjoy thy sister, where
            It had been her undoing t'have him seen,
            And make thy father crave what he abhors:
            T'entreat my brother home t'enjoy his daughter,
            Command thee kiss thy wench, chide for not kissing,   200
            And work all this out of a Machiavel,
            A miserable politician?
            I think the like was never played before!
Valerio. Indeed, I must commend thy wit of force.
            And yet I know not whose deserves most praise,   205

---

196. to enjoy] *Shepherd;* t'enjoy *Q.*

---

189. *expenseful*] costly, possibly a Chapman coinage (1st cit. *OED* adj.). It precedes 'expensive' by some sixty years.

191. *Let me alone*] Leave everything to me, often seen in Elizabethan texts.

191.2 SD.] The scene does not change here. The ensuing dialogue shows that Valerio and Rinaldo have been right by the door, listening, and might even poke their heads in, from time to time.

193. *wreath*] the laurel wreath of Apollo, given to victors in various forms of competition. Apollo's identification with the laurel derives from Ovid's story of the god's love of the nymph Daphne. When seeing Cupid draw his bow, Apollo mocked the boy for practising a man's game; in revenge, Cupid shot Apollo with a golden arrow, and Daphne with one of lead, so she could never return his love. When the determined Apollo chased her through the forest, Daphne begged her father, the river-god Peneus, to save her, which he did by turning her into a laurel tree. Apollo then promised his lost love, 'Since you cannot be mine in wedlock, / You must at least be Apollo's tree … The generals of Rome shall be wreathed with you, when the jubilant paean / of triumph is raised and the long procession ascend the Capitol' (*Metam.* 1.557–61).

all your wits] all others in the imagined race to determine the quickest wit.

196. *to enjoy*] *Q* and most previous editions repeat the 't'enjoy' of l. 194, but the metre requires two separate words.

202. *politician*] schemer, hypocrite, as in Hotspur's estimation of 'this vile politician Bolingbroke' (*1H4* 1.3.241; cf. 1.1.401n.).

204.] I am obliged to commend your wit.

205–8. *I know not … true form*] These lines are strikingly similar to what Chaerea, the supposed Eunuch of Terence's play, says after his success: 'What should I mention

  Or thine or my wit: thine for plotting well,
  Mine that durst undertake and carry it
  With such true form.
Rinaldo.   Well, th'evening crowns the day.
  Persever to the end. My wit hath put
  Blind Fortune in a string into your hand.   210
  Use it discreetly, keep it from your father,
  Or you may bid all your good days good-night.
Valerio. Let me alone, boy!
Rinaldo.   Well, sir, now to vary
  The pleasures of our wits: thou knowst, Valerio,
  Here is the new-turned gentleman's fair wife,   215
  That keeps thy wife and sister company;
  With whom the amorous courtier Dariotto
  Is far in love, and of whom her sour husband
  Is passing jealous, puts on eagle's eyes

---

206. Or thine] *Evans;* Of thine *Q.*

---

first or praise most? Should I praise the man who advised me to do it, or me for having the courage to embark on it?' (1044–6).

 208. *th'evening crowns the day*] proverbial (Dent E190). Rinaldo's warning that final success is a long way from being achieved is similar to Revenge's admonition in *The Spanish Tragedy*, 'Thou talk'st of harvest when the corn is green / The end is crown of every work well done' (2.6.7–8).

 209. *Persever*] persevere. This spelling is often employed when the metre requires emphasis on the second syllable.

 210. *Blind Fortune in a string*] proverbial (Dent W886). In this period, Fortune, or more often the world, was held 'in' a string. *OED*'s first citation for the now familiar 'on' a string is 1894.

 213–21.] The scene moves to the play's second plot line now, as Rinaldo and Valerio plan to exploit Cornelio's extreme jealousy, solely for their own amusement.

 215. *Here is*] Rinaldo would indicate the stage door through which Gazetta and Cornelio are about to enter.

 new-turned] synonymous with 'start-up' (Actors.8). Gentlemanly status, with its requisite coat of arms, was awarded by a herald who was a member of the College of Arms, the body that ruled on all such matters. Officially, the applicant had to prove his noble lineage, but in Elizabeth's reign the system had become corrupt. In *De Republica Anglorum*, Sir Thomas Smith, who was Queen Elizabeth's ambassador to France, complains, 'as for gentlemen, they may be made good cheap in England'. He goes on to explain that for a price, the herald will give the applicant 'arms newly made and invented, the title whereof shall pretend to have been found by the said herald in perusing and viewing of old registers, where his ancestors in times past had been recorded to bear the same'. Another method was for the herald to forget about lineage, and simply 'write that for the merits of that man, and certain qualities which he doth see in him, and for sundry noble acts which he hath performed, he by the authority which he hath as king of heralds and arms, giveth to him and his heirs these and these arms' (pp. 71–2).

 219. *eagle's eyes*] proverbial (Dent E6).

108　　　　　　　　　ALL FOOLS　　　　　　　　　[ACT 2

  To pry into her carriage. Shall we see　　　　　　　　220
  If he be now from home, and visit her?
     Enter GAZETTA *sewing,* CORNELIO *following.*
  See, see, the prisoner comes.
Valerio.　　　　　　　But soft, sir, see
  Her jealous jailor follows at her heels.
  Come, we will watch some fitter time to board her,
  And in the meantime seek out our mad crew.　　　　　　225
  My spirit longs to swagger.
Rinaldo.　　　　　　　Go to, youth,
  Walk not too boldly. If the sergeants meet you,
  You may have swaggering work your bellyful.
Valerio. No better copesmates.
          Gazetta sits and sings, sewing.
  I'll go seek 'em out with this light in my hand.　　　　230
  The slaves grow proud with seeking out of us.
         Exeunt [VALERIO *and* RINALDO].
Cornelio. A pretty work. I pray what flowers are these?
Gazetta. The pansy this.
Cornelio.　　　　　　Oh, that's for lovers' thoughts.
  What's that, a columbine?
Gazetta.　　　　　　　No, that thankless flower

231.1. SD. VALERIO *and* RINALDO] *Parrott¹; not in Q.*

 220. *carriage*] conduct, behaviour (*OED* n. 15a).
 224. *board*] approach, as in Sir Toby's advice to Sir Andrew Aguecheek, 'board her, assail her, woo her' (1.3.47).
 228. *swaggering*] In his preface to *Achilles' Shield*, the eighteenth book of the *Iliad*, Chapman uses 'swaggering' as an example of the new and fashionable words then entering the language 'without etymology or derivation' (sig. B2r).
 229. *copesmates*] A copesmate can be either an adversary or its exact opposite, a comrade (*OED* n.). 'Adversaries' seems to be the sense here.
 230. *this light*] this sword (Parrott).
 231. *slaves*] frequently used derisively to indicate inferiority in a general sense (*OED* n¹. 1b).
 233. *pansy*] The first English translation of Flemish botanist Rembert Dodoens's *A New Herbal, or History of Plants* (1578) describes a flower 'of three diverse colours, whereof the highest leaves for the most part are of violet and purple colour, the others are bluish or yellow, with black and yellow streaks ... this flower is called in English pansy, love-in-idleness, and heart's-ease' (p. 149).
 234. *columbine ... thankless flower*] The columbine's association with cuckoldry appears to derive from its horn-shaped nectaries. In the English botanist John Gerard's revised edition of Dodoens (prev. n.), we learn that the blue columbine's stalk 'is a cubit and a half high, slender, reddish, and slightly haired, the slender sprigs whereof bring forth every one, one flower with five little hollow horns, as it were hanging forth' (p. 1093).

sc. 1] ALL FOOLS 109

    Fits not my garden.
Cornelio.   Hem! Yet it may mine.   235
    This were a pretty present for some friend,
    Some gallant courtier, as for Dariotto,
    One that adores you in his soul, I know.
Gazetta. Me? Why me more than yourself, I pray?
Cornelio. Oh, yes, he adores you, and adhorns me.   240
    I'faith, deal plainly, do not his kisses relish
    Much better than such peasants as I am?
Gazetta. Whose kisses?
Cornelio.   Dariotto's! Does he not
    The thing you wot on?
Gazetta.   What thing, good lord?
Cornelio. Why, lady, lie with you.
Gazetta.   Lie with me?   245
Cornelio. Ay, with you.
Gazetta.   You with me, indeed!
Cornelio. Nay, I am told that he lies with you too,
    And that he is the only whoremaster
    About the city.
Gazetta.   If he be so only,
    'Tis a good hearing that there are no more.   250

---

235. Hem!] *Reed;* Him? *Q.*

---

235. *Hem!*] *Q*'s 'Him?' is not without sense, but it would be unusual to refer to a flower by the masculine pronoun. 'Hem' is a popular early modern spelling for what *OED* describes, rather elegantly, as 'an interjectional utterance like a slight half cough, used to attract attention, give warning, or express doubt or hesitation' (*OED* hem int. a).

240. *adhorns*] cuckolds. Chapman might have invented this neat pun on adorns (1st cit. *OED* adhorn v.), which he uses again in *The Widow's Tears* (1.1.107).

241. *relish*] taste (*OED* v.¹ 1a).

244. *The thing you wot on*] the 'you-know-what', a phrase one typically uses when too embarrassed to be explicit about sex. We also find this archaic form, in a similar context, in Middleton and Rowley's *Wit at Several Weapons*. Sir Gregory Fop, the foolish suitor to Sir Perfidious Oldcraft's niece, says the exact same words in referring to her maidenhead (4.2.64).

246. *You with me, indeed*] Gazetta plays on Cornelio's 'ay', which is identical in sound to 'I'.

248. *only*] pre-eminent (*OED* adj. 3a).

249. *If he be so only*] If he be the only one. Gazetta responds again with a play on Cornelio's words.

250. *a good hearing*] a good thing to hear, as Vincentio says at the close of *The Taming of the Shrew*: ''tis a good hearing when children are toward' (5.2.182). Gazetta plays on Cornelio's 'only', using it in the sense of 'sole' or 'solitary'.

Cornelio. Well, mistress, well, I will not be abused.
Think not you dance in nets, for, though you do not
Make broad profession of your love to him,
Yet do I understand your darkest language,
Your treads o'th' toe, your secret jogs and wrings, 255
Your intercourse of glances. Every tittle
Of your close amorous rites I understand.
They speak as loud to me as if you said,
'My dearest Dariotto, I am thine'.
Gazetta. Jesus, what moods are these? Did ever husband 260
Follow his wife with jealousy so unjust?
That once I loved you, you yourself will swear.
And if I did, where did you lose my love?
Indeed, this strange and undeservèd usage
Hath power to shake a heart were ne'er so settled. 265
But I protest all your unkindness never
Had strength to make me wrong you but in thought.
Cornelio. No? Not with Dariotto?
Gazetta.   No, by heaven.
Cornelio. No letters passed, nor no designs for meeting?
Gazetta. No, by my hope of heaven.
Cornelio.   Well, no time past. 270
   Go, go, go in and sew.
Gazetta.   Well, be it so.   *Exit* GAZETTA.

---

252. *Think not ... in nets*] To dance in a net is a proverbial expression meaning to be unseen, or at least expecting to be so, even though barely hidden (Dent N130). Greene's *Pandosto* reads, 'Though kings' sons dance in nets, they may not be seen; but poor men's faults are spied at a little hole' (4: 293).

255. *treads o'th' toe*] playing footsy, a direct quote from the *Amores* (1.4.44), wherein Ovid tells Corinna what and what not to do at a dinner party (cf. Introduction, p. 28).
   jogs and wrings] nudges and squeezes (*OED* jog n.¹; wring n.²).

256. *intercourse of glances*] Ovid's instructions to Corinna are to 'Watch out for my nods and eye-talk, / Pick up my stealthy messages, send replies / I shall speak whole volumes with one raised eyebrow' (*Amores*, 1.4.17–19).

   tittle] originally a small stroke or punctuation mark in printing or writing, later any small or insignificant thing (*OED* n.). Its most familiar use is Matthew, 5.18: 'For truly I say unto you, till heaven and earth perish, one jot or one tittle of the law shall not scape, till all things be fulfilled'.

257. *close*] secret, hidden (*OED* adj. 4a).

265. *settled*] steady, confident.

270. *no time past*] there is still time, as Goldstone says to the Courtesan about her gold ring in *Your Five Gallants*: 'But yet there's no time past, you may redeem it' (2.1.184).

271–95.] Cornelio's soliloquy is quite different from the one delivered by the jealous husband Thorello in *Every Man In His Humour* (Q 1.4.142–70). Thorello offers a

Cornelio. Suspicion is, they say, the first degree
 Of deepest wisdom. And however others
 Inveigh against this mood of jealousy,
 For my part I suppose it the best curb   275
 To check the ranging appetites that reign
 In this weak sex. My neighbours point at me
 For this my jealousy. But should I do
 As most of them do, let my wife fly out
 To feasts and revels, and invite home gallants,   280
 Play Menelaus, give them time and place,
 While I sit like a well-taught waiting-woman,
 Turning her eyes upon some work or picture,
 Read in a book, or take a feignèd nap.
 While her kind lady takes one to her lap?   285
 No, let me still be pointed at, and thought
 A jealous ass and not a wittolly knave.
 I have a show of courtiers haunt my house,
 In show my friends, and for my profit too.
 But I perceive 'em, and will mock their aims   290
 With looking to their mark, I warrant 'em.
 I am content to ride abroad with them,
 To revel, dice, and fit their other sports,

---

tormented meditation on the pain of jealousy; Cornelio is more concerned with the need to ingratiate himself amongst the very courtiers who he thinks are cuckolding him (cf. Introduction, pp. 24–5).

272–3. *Suspicion ... wisdom*] proverbial (Dent F135).

281. *Menelaus*] King of Sparta and husband of Helen, hence the father of all cuckolds.

285. *takes one to her lap*] has sex with her lover. The lap as representation of the female genitalia is a common trope, as in Hamlet's question to Ophelia, 'Lady, shall I lie in your lap? ... Do you think I meant country matters?' (3.2.112–16; cf. Williams, pp. 784–5).

287. *wittolly*] willingly cuckolded. The noun 'wittol' is an old word meaning someone who is aware of, and complaisant with, his wife's adultery. Shakespeare may have coined this adjectival sense, the earliest recorded use being Falstaff's estimation of Master Ford: 'Hang him, poor cuckoldly knave, I know him not. Yet I wrong him to call him poor. They say the jealous wittolly knave hath masses of money' (2.2.270–2).

289. *In show*] in outward appearance, playing on 'show', in the sense of 'presentation' or 'exhibition', in the previous line.

290–1. *mock ... mark*] make them misfire by keeping close watch on their target (Hudston). If Cornelio were speaking literally, he need not worry, since Elizabethan soldiers usually closed their eyes when firing their muskets, and so were unlikely to hit anything (cf. Edelman, *Military*, p. 128).

292. *ride abroad*] go horseback riding.

293. *dice*] often used as a verb in this period.
 fit] fit in with, be suitable to.

112   ALL FOOLS   [ACT 2

    But by their leaves I'll have a vigilant eye
    To the main chance still. See, my brave comrades.   295

Enter DARIOTTO, [CURIO,] CLAUDIO *and* VALERIO, VALERIO *putting
up his sword.*

Dariotto. [*To Valerio*] Well, wag, well; wilt thou still deceive thy
    father,
    And being so simple a poor soul before him,
    Turn swaggerer in all companies besides?
Claudio. Hadst thou been rested, all would have come forth.
Valerio. Soft, sir, there lies the point; I do not doubt   300
    But t'have my pennyworths of these rascals one day.
    I'll smoke the buzzing hornets from their nests,
    Or else I'll make their leather jerkins stay,
    The whoreson hungry horseflies. Foot, a man
    Cannot so soon, for want of almanacs,   305
    Forget his day but three or four bare months,
    But straight he sees a sort of corporals
    To lie in ambuscado to surprise him.

295.1. SD. CURIO] *This ed.; and Page Parrott¹; not in Q.*
296. SP.] *Reed; Dar. Dari. Dario, Dariot. Q.* SD.] *Manley; not in Q.*
299. SP.] *Reed; Clau. Q.*

294–5. *I'll have … main chance*] proverbial (Dent E235). 'Main chance' may be defined as 'the prize' or 'the main objective'. As noted at 2.1.42, a 'main' is also a winning throw at dice.
    295. *brave*] either finely dressed, or worthy (meant ironically), or both (*OED* adj. 2, 3).
    298. *in all companies besides*] when with anyone except your father.
    299. *rested*] arrested (OED rest v.²).
    come forth] been revealed.
    301. *pennyworths*] revenge. Bartholomew Cokes vows to have his 'pennyworths out' on Justice Overdo in *Bartholomew Fair* (3.5.173).
    rascals] debt collectors, as at 1.2.75.
    303. *leather jerkins*] the buff coats of the sergeants who arrested debtors (Parrott).
    304. *Foot*] a shortening of 'Christ's foot' (cf. 1.1.150n.).
    305–6.] 'His day' is the due-date of a loan, which Valerio says he forgot because he had no almanac. In *Every Man In His Humour*, Cob complains about fasting days, when meat could not be consumed, 'but, I may curse none but these filthy almanacs, for, an 'twere not for them, these days of persecution would ne'er be known' (Q 3.1.167–9).
    307. *sort*] company (*OED* n.² 17a).
    corporals] Then, as now, a corporal was one rank below that of sergeant.
    308. *ambuscado*] Spanish for 'ambush'. As Mercutio says, sometimes Queen Mab 'driveth o'er a soldier's neck, / And then dreams he of cutting foreign throats / Of breaches, ambuscados, Spanish blades' (1.4.82–4).

Dariotto. Well, thou hadst happy fortune to escape 'em.
Valerio. But they thought theirs was happier to scape me. 310
   I, walking in the place where men's lawsuits
   Are heard and pleaded, not so much as dreaming
   Of any such encounter, steps me forth
   Their valiant foreman, with the word, 'I rest you'.
   I made no more ado, but laid these paws 315
   Close on his shoulders, tumbling him to earth.
   And there sat he on his posteriors
   Like a baboon, and, turning me about,
   I straight espied the whole troop issuing on me.
   I stepped me back, and, drawing my old friend here, 320
   Made to the midst of them, and, all unable
   T'endure the shock, all rudely fell in rout.
   And down the stairs they ran with such a fury
   As, meeting with a troop of lawyers there,
   Manned by their clients, some with ten, some with twenty, 325
   Some five, some three—he that had least, had one—
   Upon the stairs they bore them down afore them.
   But such a rattling then was there amongst them
   Of ravished declarations, replications.
   Rejoinders and petitions—all their books 330
   And writings torn and trod on, and some lost—
   That the poor lawyers coming to the bar
   Could say naught to the matter, but instead,

---

313. *steps me forth*] Valerio's use of the more elaborate reflexive form here and twice more within eight lines (318, 320) is a hint that he is dramatising his story as much as he can.
314. *rest*] arrest.
320. *old friend*] trusty sword. Valerio wants everyone to know he is an accomplished fencer.
322. *rout*] disorderly retreat (*OED* n.^{6} 2).
325. *Manned*] escorted (*OED* man v. 4).
328. *rattling*] chatter, prattling (*OED* rattle v.^{1} 3a).
329. *ravished*] spoiled, plundered. Valerio is describing the whole incident as if it were a military action.
329–30.] A declaration is a plaintiff's original statement or claim. The rejoinder, although third in Valerio's list, would come next—it is the defendant's answer to the plaintiff's claim. Finally we have the replication, the claimant's answer to the defendant's rejoinder. A petition was at that time much the same as a declaration, although nowadays normally restricted to matters such as bankruptcy or divorce (*OED* for all). Chapman would have been well acquainted with this terminology, and may have shared his character's disdain, since he was involved in a lawsuit at the time he was writing *All Fools* (cf. Introduction, p. 1).

                    Were fain to rail and talk besides their books
                    Without all order.
Claudio.   Faith, that same vein of railing   335
                    Became now most applausive. Your best poet is
                    He that rails grossest.
Dariotto.   True, and your best fool
                    Is your broad railing fool.
Valerio.   And why not, sir?
                    For, by the gods, to tell the naked truth,
                    What objects see men in this world but such   340
                    As would yield matter to a railing humour,
                    When he, that last year carried after one
                    An empty buckram bag, now fills a coach
                    And crowds the senate with such troops of clients

---

334. *besides their books*] extemporaneously. In Munday's *John a Kent and John a Cumber*, John a Kent plans to take part surreptitiously in the wedding masque that his rival magician, John a Cumber, is organising. He predicts, 'One of us Johns must play beside the book' (l. 1096).

335–8.] a contemporary reference to the craze for 'railing' verse satire, which was at its height in the summer of 1599, while Chapman was writing the play. London's authority figures had become increasingly alarmed and resentful over being subjected to criticism and ridicule in such works as Joseph Hall's *Virgidemiarum*, Sir John Davies's *Epigrams*, John Marston's *The Scourge of Villainy*, and Everard Guilpin's *Skialetheia*. On 1 June 1599, the day before Chapman received a progress payment of £1, all copies of these books and seven others were to 'be presently brought to the Bishop of London to be burnt', by order of John Whitgift, the Archbishop of Canterbury, and Richard Bancroft, the Bishop of London. The Bishops' ban, issued to the Stationers' Company, also stipulated that 'no satires or epigrams be printed hereafter'. The Bishops actually did the world a huge favour—although Marston might have turned to the theatre anyway, the ban made it inevitable, and not long afterwards he was working on *Antonio and Mellida* and *Antonio's Revenge* for Paul's Boys.

336. *applausive*] worthy of applause (1st cit. *OED* adj. 3).

338. *broad*] unrestrained, as Polonius tells Gertrude, 'Look you lay home to him. / Tell him his pranks have been too broad to bear with' (3.4.1–2).

339. *naked truth*] similar to the proverbial 'the truth shows best being naked' (Dent T589.)

342–3.] when a fellow who last year walked to court behind a single client, carrying his empty briefcase, now arrives in a coach. The 'buckram bag' that our offender carries is specifically a pettifogger's (disreputable lawyer's) briefcase, as seen in Marston's *The Malcontent*, where Passarello will be as recognisable in his velvet 'as a pettifogger by his buckram bag' (1.8.59), and Count Narcisso's complaint in Dekker's *If This Be Not a Good Play, The Devil Is in It*: 'We must all turn pettifoggers, and instead of gilt rapiers hang buckram-bags at our girdles' (1.2.97–8).

344. *senate*] This is one of the few moments when we are reminded that the setting is Florence. Early modern Italian writers sometimes refer to the *signoria*, the chief

SC. I]   ALL FOOLS   115

 And servile followers as would put a mad spleen   345
 Into a pigeon?
Dariotto.   Come, pray leave these cross-capers.
 Let's make some better use of precious time.
 See, here's Cornelio. Come, lad, shall we to dice?
Cornelio. Anything, I.
Claudio.   Well said. How does thy wife?
Cornelio. In health, God save her.
Valerio.   But where is she, man?   350
Cornelio. Abroad, about her business.
Valerio.   Why, not at home?

---

legislative and judicial assembly of Florence, as the *senato*; Castiglione advises that simple, unadorned language is best *se a qualsivoglia omo di bon giudicio occorresse far una orazione di cose gravi nel senato proprio di Fiorenza* ('if any man of good judgement needed to make a speech on serious matters before the very senate of Florence'). Even where *signoria* is used in the Italian, English translations of the time often have 'senate', as seen in Thomas Bedingfeld's version of Machiavelli's *Florentine History*, published in 1595 (Castiglione, p. 66; Machiavelli, *passim*).

 345–6. *mad spleen / Into a pigeon*] Valerio's ornithology is somewhat confused, although no more confused than the original 'science' upon which it is based. The proverbial mildness of the pigeon, due to its lack of a gall bladder, goes at least as far back as the *Problems of Aristotle with Other Philosophers and Physicians*, a book once thought to be by Aristotle, although scholars now attribute it to his 'school'. As the *Problems* made its way through medieval and Renaissance Europe in a variety of translations and commentaries, things were added, deleted, or changed. One addition, as found in an English translation of 1595, is '*Question.* Why are a sheep and a pigeon very mild beasts? *Answer.* Because they want gall, and it is the gall which stirreth unto anger' (sig. F5r–v). This gall is synonymous with yellow bile, or choler, the humour responsible for a 'choleric' disposition. Of course, literature's most famous gall-deprived pigeon is Hamlet: 'for I am pigeon-livered and lack gall' (2.2.577).

 346. *cross-capers*] an interesting expression with some ambiguity of meaning. Along with being a type of dance step and a metaphor for idle time-wasting, cross-capering is also associated with the mannerisms of tailors, especially French ones. Dekker's *News from Hell* satirises the English aping of French fashion by having French gentlemen assemble all their tailors together. With 'all the cross caperers being placed in strong ranks', on oration is delivered, encouraging them to create new fashions for Englishmen to spend all their money on (2: 114). Similarly, Dekker's masque *The Sun's Darling* has a French tailor promising, in phonetically spelled dialect, 'Wee, Monsieur, hey nimbla upon de cross caper, me take-a de measure of de body from de top of de noddle to de heel' (2.1.166–7).

 348. *See, here's Cornelio*] The gallants not having greeted Cornelio after being on stage for fifty-two lines could be due either to their studiously ignoring him, or his standing inconspicuously aside to observe them for a while. Either way, the wide Rose stage would have been helpful.

  Foot, my masters, take her to the court,
  And this rare lad, her husband. And—dost hear?—
  Play me no more the miserable farmer,
  But be advised by friends, sell all i'th' country,   355
  Be a flat courtier, follow some great man,
  Or bring thy wife there, and she'll make thee great.
Cornelio. What, to the court? Then take me for a gull.
Valerio. Nay, never shun it to be called a gull,
  For I see all the world is but a gull,   360
  One man gull to another in all kinds.
  A merchant to a courtier is a gull,
  A client to a lawyer is a gull,
  A married man to a bachelor a gull,
  A bachelor to a cuckold is a gull,   365
  All to a poet, or a poet to himself.
Cornelio. [*Aside*] Hark, Dariotto, shall we gull this guller?
Dariotto. [*Aside to Cornelio*] He gulls his father, man, we cannot gull
  him.
Cornelio. [*Aside to Dariotto*] Let me alone.—Of all men's wits alive
  I most admire Valerio's, that hath stol'n   370

---

367. SD.] *Parrott¹; not in Q.*   368. SD.] *This ed.; Aside Parrott¹; not in Q.*
369. SD.] *This ed.; Aside Parrott¹; not in Q.*

355–6. *sell all ... courtier*] Valerio's advice is similar to that given by Carlo Buffone to Sogliardo in *Every Man Out of His Humour*: ''twere good you turned four or five acres of your best land into two or three trunks of apparel' (1.2.35–6).

356. *flat*] absolute (*OED* adj. 6a)

356–7. *follow ... make thee great*] Valerio pointedly implies that Cornelio would be welcome to participate in the affairs of court if Gazetta had affairs with the courtiers. In Chapman's *Conspiracy of Charles Duke of Byron*, Roiseau speaks of 'a city dame / Brought by her jealous husband to the court, / Some elder courtiers entertaining him / While others snatch a favour from his wife' (2.2.1–4).

365–6.] How a bachelor might gull a married man is obvious; how a cuckold gulls a bachelor is not. One way he might do so is to be like John Allwit in *A Chaste Maid in Cheapside*, who lives off the bounty of Sir Walter Whorehound, in exchange for Sir Walter's enjoyment of Mistress Allwit's favours. For the first time in the play, the word 'cuckold' is spoken, and to say it in Cornelio's presence is, in itself, to mock him. 'Cuckold' is not a neutral word for the husband of an unfaithful wife. As an onomatopoeic term imitating the song of the cuckoo, which lays its eggs in another bird's nest, it is always derisive (cf. Introduction, pp. 29–30).

366.] The poet as the greatest of deceivers is a common image in early modern literature, most beautifully expressed by Theseus in *A Midsummer Night's Dream*: 'as imagination bodies forth / The forms of things unknown, the poet's pen / Turns them to shapes and gives to airy nothing / A local habitation and a name' (5.1.14–17).

369–80.] Cornelio decides that one who boasts of gulling others, and jokes about the state of his marriage to Gazetta, deserves some comeuppance.

SC. I]   ALL FOOLS   117

 By his mere industry, and that by spurts,
Such qualities as no wit else can match
With plodding at perfection every hour,
Which, if his father knew each gift he has,
Were like enough to make him give all from him. 375
I mean, besides his dicing and his wenching,
He has stol'n languages, th'Italian, Spanish,
And some spice of the French, besides his dancing,
Singing, playing on choice instruments.
These has he got, almost against the hair. 380
Claudio. But hast thou stol'n all these, Valerio?
Valerio. Toys, toys, a pox! And yet they be such toys
 As every gentleman would not be without.
Cornelio. Vainglory makes ye judge 'em light, i'faith.
Dariotto. Afore heaven, I was much deceived in him. 385
 But he's the man indeed that hides his gifts,
And sets them not to sale in every presence.
I would have sworn his soul were far from music,

---

384. 'em] *Deighton (conj.);* on *Q,* on't *Shepherd.*

371. *mere*] pure, undiluted (*OED* adj.² 1).
 spurts] brief efforts (*OED* n.¹ 2a).
375.] The 'him' of this line is Valerio, who would be forced to give up his life as a libertine should Gostanzo learn of his ways.
 377. *stol'n*] gained secretly (cit. *OED* steal v.¹ 4d).
 377–8. *th'Italian, Spanish ... French*] To include Italian in the list does seem odd, since Valerio and everyone else have supposedly been speaking Italian all along. Parrott justifies this to an extent by citing *The Courtier,* where we read, in Hoby's translation, that the quality of the true courtier is able 'to be seen in tongues, and specially in Italian, French and Spanish' (p. 369). However, this comes from Hoby's summary, and does not appear in Castiglione's text, where Federico Fregoso recommends that the courtier have 'the knowledge of sundry tongues ... and especially Spanish and French, because the intercourse of one nation and then the other is much haunted [habitually used] in Italy, and these two are more agreeable unto us than any of the rest' (Hoby, p. 147). In fact, Castiglione never refers to the 'Italian' language, but only to *questa nostra lingua, che noi chiamiano vulgare* ('this language of ours, that we call the vulgar tongue'), in a discussion of how much use should be made of the classical Tuscan dialect in everyday discourse (Castiglione, p. 70).
 380. *against the hair*] a proverbial expression similar to 'against the grain', i.e., contrary to the natural bent (Dent H18).
 382. *toys*] trifles, as at Prol.18.
 384. *'em light*] Parrott's emendation of *Q*'s 'on lyte' seems appropriate; Cornelio is accusing Valerio of false modesty in making so little of his talents. 'Light' was often used as an adverb in this period.
 385.] Dariotto's mock praise of Valerio for not boasting of his accomplishments is a fine touch, since we will soon see that Dariotto is equally vulnerable to flattery.

                    And that all his choice music was to hear
                    His fat beasts bellow.
Cornelio.   Sir, your ignorance   390
                    Shall eftsoon be confuted. Prithee, Val,
                    Take thy theorbo for my sake a little.
Valerio. By heaven, this month I touched not a theorbo.
Cornelio. Touched a theorbo! Mark the very word.
                    [*To Curio*] Sirrah, go fetch.   395
                                                    Exit [CURIO].
Valerio. If you will have it, I must needs confess
                    I am no husband of my qualities.
                                        He untrusses and capers.
Cornelio. See, what a caper there was!
Claudio.   See again!
Cornelio. The best that ever, and how it becomes him!
Dariotto. O that his father saw these qualities!   400

            Enter [CURIO] *with an instrument.*

Cornelio. Nay, that's the very wonder of his wit,
                    To carry all without his father's knowledge.
Dariotto. Why, we might tell him now.
Cornelio.   No, but we could not,
                    Although we think we could. His wit doth charm us.

---

395. SD.] *This ed.; not in Q.*   395.1. SD. CURIO] *This ed.; Page Q.*
400.1. SD. CURIO] *This ed.; a Page Q.*

391. *eftsoon*] very soon (*OED* adv. 3).
392. *theorbo*] a large lute with a double neck and two sets of tuning-pegs, the lower holding the melody strings and the upper the bass strings (1st cit. *OED* n.).
393. *touched*] At this time it was as common to say one 'touched' a stringed instrument as 'played' it. Jonson's *Ode in Celebration of Her Majesty's Birthday* has 'Let every lyre be strung / Harp, lute, theorbo sprung / With touch of learned thumbs' (16–18).
396–7.] In his false reluctance to show his musical talents, Valerio is attempting to display the courtly quality of *sprezzatura*, as described by Bernardo Dovizi da Bibbiena in the first book of *The Courtier* (Hoby, pp. 59–63). There is no satisfactory English synonym for *sprezzatura*; it might be described as the ability to perform difficult tasks with the appearance of unstudied ease. Hoby's 'recklessness' is misleading, since it depends on the less common sense of 'indifference', rather than the usual 'rash' or 'foolhardy' (*OED* reckless adj.). 'Nonchalance', used by other translators, is perhaps the closest, but no single word covers the various shades of meaning we find in Castiglione.
397. SD. *untrusses*] unties (*OED* truss v. 5a). Valerio loosens the points connecting his doublet and hose so that he can more easily dance about (Parrott).

    Come, sweet Val, touch and sing.
Dariotto. [*Aside*]   Foot, will you hear   405
    The worst voice in Italy?

Enter RINALDO.

Cornelio.   O God, sir! [*Valerio*] *sings.*
    Courtiers, how like you this?
Dariotto.   Believe it, excellent!
Cornelio. Is it not natural?
Valerio.   If my father heard me,
    Foot, he'd renounce me for his natural son.
Dariotto. By heaven, Valerio, an I were thy father,   410
    And loved good qualities as I do my life,
    I'd disinherit thee, for I never heard
    Dog howl with worse grace.
Cornelio.   Go to, Signor Courtier.
    You deal not courtly now to be so plain,
    Nor nobly, to discourage a young gentleman   415
    In virtuous qualities, that has but stol'n 'em.
Claudio. Call you this touching a theorbo?
All.   Ha, ha, ha!
            Exeunt all but Valerio and Rinaldo.
Valerio. How now, what's here?
Rinaldo.   Zounds, a plot laid to gull thee.
    Could thy wit think the voice was worth the hearing?
    This was the courtier's and the cuckold's project.   420
Valerio. And is't e'en so? 'Tis very well, Master Courtier

---

405. SD.] *This ed.; not in Q.*   406. SD. *Valerio*] *This ed.; He Q.*
421. Master] *Reed;* mast *Q.*   421–4] *verse Collier; prose Q.*

408–9.] Cornelio puns on 'natural' here, saying Valerio's singing talents are innate, but 'natural' was also a common word for 'fool'. In his reply, Valerio uses the word in the sense of 'real' or 'biological'.

410. *an*] if, a common form.

421–6.] These lines are a turning point in the play. Having been told that getting him to embarrass himself by singing in public was the work of Dariotto and Cornelio, Valerio must have his revenge. He will begin by encouraging Cornelio's belief that Dariotto is cuckolding him. In itself that would be a simple task, but the score will be even only when Cornelio makes a public fool of himself because of some ingenious provocation by Valerio (cf. Introduction, pp. 31–2).

421. *Master Courtier*] Q's 'mast Courtier' is probably an abbreviation, part of the compositor's crowding of four lines of verse into three lines of prose (sig. E3r), in an effort to finish the act on one page and start Act 3 at the top of the next. The actor would certainly say 'master'.

And Dan Cornuto. I'll cry quit with both,
And first, I'll cast a jar betwixt them both,
With firing the poor cuckold's jealousy.
I have a tale will make him mad, 425
And turn his wife divorced loose amongst us.
But first let's home, and entertain my wife.
O father, pardon, I was born to gull thee. *Exeunt.*

428.1] *Q has* FINIS ACTUS SECUNDI; *omitted Reed.*

422. *Dan Cornuto*] Lord Cuckold. 'Dan' is the old French form of *Dom*, synonymous with the Spanish *Don*; 'Cornuto' is Italian for 'horned'. In *The Faerie Queene*, Spenser writes of 'Dan Chaucer, well of English undefiled, / On Fame's eternal beadroll [pedigree] worthy to be filed' (4.1.32.8–9).

cry quit] short for 'cry quittance', meaning 'get even'.

423. *jar*] conlict, discord. The word is often, but not always, applied to musical sounds.

Act 3

ACT 3, SCENE I

Enter FORTUNIO, BELLANORA, GRATIANA, GOSTANZO
following closely.

Fortunio. [*To Bellanora*] How happy am I, that by this sweet means
　I gain access to your most lovèd sight,
　And therewithal to utter my full love,
　Which but for vent would burn my entrails up.
Gostanzo. [*Aside*] By th' mass, they talk too softly.
Bellanora.　　　　　　　　　　　　　　Little thinks　　　5
　The austere mind my thrifty father bears
　That I am vowed to you, and so am bound
　From him who for more riches he would force

---

0. Act 3, Scene 1] *Hudston (subst.);* Actus III, Scena I *Q.*
5. SD.] *Parrott¹; not in Q.*

---

　0. Act 3, Scene 1] The scene begins in Gostanzo's house, and gradually moves to the exterior setting during the dialogue between Rinaldo and Gostanzo (3.1.31–112). We learn at 3.1.27 that one night has passed.
　0.1 SD. closely] secretly (*OED* adv. 3).
　4.] This is the only time in the play Fortunio expresses his love for Bellanora. He does so by likening it to a hot gas that must be expelled from his intestines.
　6. *thrifty*] frugal, miserly (*OED* adj. 4 a).
　7. *vowed to you*] Under English matrimonial law, if Bellanora and Fortunio have exchanged vows, even if done privately, they are now married. This type of wedding was known as a spousal *de præsenti*, as defined in Henry Swinburne's *Treatise of Spousals of Matrimonial Contracts*, written about 1600, although not published until 1686. He writes, 'Spousals *de præsenti* are mutual promise or contract of present matrimony, as when the man doth say to the woman, I do take thee to my wife', and she then answereth, "I do take thee to my husband".' Furthermore, 'that woman, and that man, which have contracted spousals *de præsenti* ... cannot by any agreement dissolve those spousals, but are reputed for very husband and wife in respect of the substance and indissoluble knot of matrimony'. This and other marriage laws were controversial, since church courts often had a different view of the matter (Swinburne, pp. 8, 13; Sokol, pp. 1–19).
　bound] constrained, forbidden. Because she has already exchanged vows, Bellanora cannot marry some other man whom Gostanzo, 'for more riches', would force upon her. He is presumably the unnamed suitor mentioned at 1.2.14.

On my disliking fancy.
Fortunio. 'Tis no fault
With just deeds to defraud an injury. 10
Gostanzo. [*Aside*] My daughter is persuading him to yield
In dutiful submission to his father.

Enter VALERIO.

Valerio. Do I not dream? Do I behold this sight
With waking eyes? Or from the ivory gate
Hath Morpheus sent a vision to delude me? 15
Is't possible that I, a mortal man,
Should shrine within mine arms so bright a goddess,
The fair Gratiana, beauty's little world?
Gostanzo. [*Aside*] What have we here?
Valerio. My dearest mine of gold,
All this that thy white arms enfold, 20
Account it as thine own freehold.
Gostanzo. [*Aside*] God's my dear soul, what sudden change is here?
I smell how this gear will fall out, i'faith.
Valerio. Fortunio, sister, come, let's to the garden.
Exeunt [*all except* GOSTANZO].
Gostanzo. Sits the wind there, i'faith? See what example 25
Will work upon the dullest appetite.
My son, last day so bashful that he durst not

---

11. SD.] Parrott¹; not in Q.   19. SD.] Parrott¹; not in Q.
22. SD.] Parrott²; not in Q.   24. SD. all except GOSTANZO] This ed.; not in Q.

---

9. *disliking fancy*] This expression is something of an oxymoron, since 'fancy', in this sense, usually implies favourable inclination.
10. *defraud*] cheat, deny, a figurative sense of the word.
14–15. *Or from ... delude me*] In Chapman's translation of the *Odyssey*, Penelope tells her guest, the disguised Ulysses, that dreams come from 'Two two-leaved gates, the one of ivory / The other horn. These dreams that fantasy / Takes from polished ivory port delude / The dreamer ever, and no truth include' (19.772–5). Morpheus was one of the god of sleep's thousand sons; Ovid tells us he 'can only imitate human beings' (*Metam.* 11.636).
17. *shrine*] enshrine, literally to enclose in a sanctuary or other holy place (*OED* v. 3c).
21. *freehold*] permanent and absolute ownership of property. Valerio's imagery is more financial than poetic; Parrott notes that these rhyming lines might be part of an old song.
23. *gear*] affair, business (*OED* n. 11 c)
27. *last day*] yesterday, a common phrase. Having a night pass between Acts 2 and 3 probably comes from *The Self-Tormenter*, where Chremes begins Act 3 with the words 'I see it's dawn already' (410). This is rare in Roman comedy, where the action usually takes place within a single day.

SC. I]   ALL FOOLS   123

    Look on a wench, now courts her, and, by'r Lady,
    Will make his friend Fortunio wear his head
    Of the right modern fashion.

                    Enter RINALDO

                      What, Rinaldo.   30
Rinaldo. I fear I interrupt your privacy.
Gostanzo. Welcome, Rinaldo. Would 't had been your hap
    To come a little sooner, that you might
    Have seen a handsome sight. But let that pass.
    The short is that your sister Gratiana   35
    Shall stay no longer here.
Rinaldo.   No longer, sir?
    Repent you then so soon your favour to her
    And to my brother?
Gostanzo.   Not so, good Rinaldo,
    But to prevent a mischief that I see
    Hangs over your abusèd brother's head.   40
    In brief, my son has learned but too much courtship.
    It was my chance even now to cast mine eye
    Into a place where to your sister entered
    My metamorphosed son. I must conceal
    What I saw there, but to be plain, I saw   45
    More than I would see. I had thought to make
    My house a kind receipt for your kind brother,
    But I'd be loath his wife should find more kindness
    Than she had cause to like of.
Rinaldo.   What's the matter?
    Perhaps a little compliment or so?   50
Gostanzo. Well, sir, such compliment perhaps may cost
    Married Fortunio the setting on.

  29–30. *Will make ... fashion*] Fortunio will wear cuckold's horns on his head.
  32. *hap*] chance, fortune (*OED* n.¹).
  35. *short*] result, upshot (*OED* n.). The expression can appear by itself or as part of 'the short and the long', as in Nick Bottom's great news, 'for the short and the long is, our play is preferred' (4.2.38–9).
    sister] sister-in-law, since Gratiana is supposed to be married to Fortunio. The suffix 'in-law' was occasionally used in this period, but usually the simple 'sister' or 'brother' served to indicate a relationship by marriage as well as immediate family.
  44. *metamorphosed*] At this time the precise definition would be 'changed in form, by supernatural means'.
  47. *receipt*] refuge (*OED* n. 8).
  51–2. *may cost ... setting on*] 'Fortunio will pay for this'. The 'setting on' is the required payment, often for a round of drinks, as Stellio promises his friends when leaving a tavern in Lyly's *Mother Bombie*, 'I cannot stay, but this good fellowship shall cost me the setting on at our next meeting' (2.5.907–8).

                    Nor can I keep my knowledge. He that lately
                    Before my face I could not get to look
                    Upon your sister, by this light, now kissed her,   55
                    Embraced and courted with as good a grace
                    As any courtier could. And I can tell you—
                    Not to disgrace her—I perceived the dame
                    Was as far forward as himself, by th' mass.
Rinaldo. You should have schooled him for't.
Gostanzo.   No, I'll not see't,   60
                    For shame once found is lost. I'll have him think
                    That my opinion of him is the same
                    That it was ever. It will be a mean
                    To bridle this fresh humour bred in him.
Rinaldo. Let me then school him. Foot, I'll rattle him up.   65
Gostanzo. No, no, Rinaldo, th'only remedy
                    Is to remove the cause, carry the object
                    From his late-tempted eyes.
Rinaldo.   Alas, sir, whither?
                    You know my father is incensed so much
                    He'll not receive her.
Gostanzo.   Place her with some friend   70
                    But for a time, till I reclaim your father.
                    Meantime your brother shall remain with me.
Rinaldo. (*To himself*) The care's the less, then. He has still his
                    longing

---

53. *keep*] keep to myself.
58. *disgrace*] disparage, speak ill of (*OED* v. 6).
60. *schooled*] admonished (*OED* school v.¹ 3).
I'll not see it] I'll pretend not to have seen it.
61. *shame … lost*] a variation on the proverb 'past shame is past amendment' (Dent S271). Tharsalio offers the same sentiment in *The Widow's Tears* (3.1.147).
65. *rattle him up*] scold him. In Nicholas Udall's translation of the *Apothegms* (1542), Erasmus says of Diogenes, 'covetous persons he rattled and shook up, for yet in words they disprised money, whereas in their hearts they loved the same of life' (Udall, p. 77).
68. *late-tempted*] recently tempted, another example of the early modern practice of using adjectives as adverbs (Abbott 1).
71. *reclaim*] win back, restore the affections of, as at 1.1.375.
73. *The care's the less*] 'There is nothing to worry about'. When Queen Elinor of Peele's *Edward I* begs the King to ensure that their son's christening be a great occasion, he replies, 'My lovely lady let that care be less / For my young son the country will I feast' (ll. 1481–2).
73–4. *He has still … daughter*] Fortunio's desire to be with Bellanora is still accommodated.

   To be with this gull's daughter.
Gostanzo.   What resolve you?
   I am resolved she lodges here no more.   75
   My friend's son shall not be abused by mine.
Rinaldo. Troth, sir, I'll tell you what a sudden toy
   Comes in my head. What think you if I brought her
   Home to my father's house?
Gostanzo.   Ay, marry, sir.
   Would he receive her?
Rinaldo.   Nay, you hear not all: 80
   I mean with use of some device or other.
Gostanzo. As how, Rinaldo?
Rinaldo.   Marry, sir, to say
   She is your son's wife, married past your knowledge.
Gostanzo. I doubt last day he saw her, and will know her
   To be Fortunio's wife.
Rinaldo.   Nay, as for that,   85
   I will pretend she was even then your son's wife,
   But feigned by me to be Fortunio's,
   Only to try how he would take the matter.
Gostanzo. 'Fore heaven, 'twere pretty!
Rinaldo.   Would it not do well?
Gostanzo. Exceeding well, in sadness.
Rinaldo.   Nay, good sir,   90
   Tell me unfeignedly, do ye like't indeed?
Gostanzo. The best that e'er I heard.
Rinaldo.   And do you think
   He'll swallow down the gudgeon?
Gostanzo.   A my life,
   It were a gross gob would not down with him,

77–8. *toy ... head*] a proverbial expression for having an 'idle fancy' or 'silly idea' (Dent T456.1).

84. *doubt*] fear.

86.] Rinaldo fools Gostanzo in exactly the same way Syrus fools Chremes in *The Self-Tormenter*, by telling him the truth (766–81).

90. *in sadness*] seriously (*OED* sadness n.2).

93. *gudgeon*] a small European fresh-water fish, much used for bait (*OED* n.[1]). To swallow one was to believe a tall story. In *The Famous History of the Life and Death of Captain Thomas Stukeley*, King Philip of Spain asks, 'Are not these English like their country fish / Called gudgeons, that will bite at every bait? / How easily the credulous fools believe / The thing they fancy' (16.153–6).

A] on (cf. Abbott 140).

94. *gob*] a lump of raw meat or other food (*OED* n.[1] 3a).

down] go down, be swallowed easily. The sense is supported by what Gostanzo says of Marc Antonio in the following lines.

	An honest knight, but simple, not acquainted	95
	With the fine sleights and policies of the world.	
	As I myself am.	
Rinaldo.	I'll go fetch her straight;	
	An this jest thrive, 'twill make us princely sport.	
	But you must keep our counsel, second all,	
	Which to make likely, you must needs sometimes	100
	Give your son leave—as if you knew it not—	
	To steal and see her at my father's house.	
Gostanzo.	Ay, but see you, then, that you keep good guard	
	Over his forward, new-begun affections,	
	For, by the Lord, he'll teach your brother else	105
	To sing the cuckoo's note. Spirit will break out,	
	Though never so suppressed and pinionèd.	
Rinaldo.	Especially your son's. What would he be,	
	If you should not restrain him by good counsel?	
Gostanzo.	I'll have an eye on him, I warrant thee!	110
	I'll in and warn the gentlewoman to make ready.	
Rinaldo.	Well, sir, and I'll not be long after you.	

Exit Gostanzo.

Heaven, heaven, I see these politicians,
Out of blind Fortune's hands, are our most fools.
'Tis she that gives the lustre to their wits, 115
Still plodding at traditional devices.
But take 'em out of them to present actions,
A man may grope and tickle 'em like a trout,

---

96. *sleights and policies*] cunning tricks.
97. *her*] Gratiana.
99. *keep our counsel*] keep our secret (*OED* counsel n. 5a).
second] support, help with (*OED* v.¹).
106. *sing the cuckoo's note*] proverbial for cuckoldry (Dent C892.11).
Spirit] natural inclination, essential character (*OED* n. 8).
108–10.] These lines are similar to those of the slave Syrus in *The Self-Tormenter*: 'What do you suppose he'll do later on, Chremes, if you don't keep your eye on him, tick him off, and advise him with all the power the gods have given you? (591–2).
114. *Out of blind Fortune's hands*] whether favoured by Dame Fortune or not, perhaps a play on the proverbial 'fortune favours fools' (Dent F600).
115–18.] Fortune lets the wits of foolish schemers shine so long as they keep to their usual tricks. Confront them with something different, and they are easily gulled.
118.] A traditional method of catching trout was to calm them by tickling their gills, and then seize them by hand. In *Twelfth Night*, when placing the forged letter that will gull Malvolio, Maria says 'Lie thou there, for here comes the trout that must be caught by tickling' (2.5.21–2).

SC. I]   ALL FOOLS   127

    And take 'em from their close dear holes, as fat
    As a physician, and as giddy-headed   120
    As if by miracle heaven had taken from them
    Even that which commonly belongs to fools.
    Well, now let's note what black ball of debate
    Valerio's wit hath cast betwixt Cornelio
    And the enamoured courtier. I believe   125
    His wife and he will part. His jealousy
    Hath ever watched occasion of divorce,
    And now Valerio's villainy will present it.
    See, here comes the twin-courtier, his companion.

                     Enter CLAUDIO.

Claudio. Rinaldo, well encountered!
Rinaldo.   Why, what news?   130
Claudio. Most sudden and infortunate, Rinaldo.
    Cornelio is incensed so 'gainst his wife
    That no man can procure her quiet with him.

---

121. by] *Reed;* be *Q.*

  119. *take them ... holes*] In his *Four Books of Husbandry* (1577), Conrad Heresbach advises that when digging a fish pond, 'in the banks and sides ... you must have bushes and creek holes, for the fish to hide them in from the heat of the sun' (p. 173).
  119–20. *as fat / As a physician*] The two principal old men of the *Commedia dell'Arte* were the Pantaloon and the Doctor. The Venetian *Pantalone*, as we know from Jaques in *As You Like It*, was 'lean and slippered' (2.7.158), but the *Dottore* was corpulent, since it was at the University of Bologna, a city famous for its trenchermen, where one studied to enter the learned professions. Often speaking in Bolognese dialect, the Doctor was usually a lawyer, but sometimes a physician, hence the appropriateness of Chapman's alliterative phrase (Oreglia, pp. 84–91).
  122.] even the minimal intelligence that fools possess.
  123. *black ball of debate*] The tradition of casting an unfavourable vote by means of a black ball derives from classical Athens, when jurors would place a white pebble or bean in an urn to vote for acquittal, or a black one for conviction. Plutarch tells how Alcibiades, after defecting from Athens to the Spartan side, hid at Thurii in southern Italy. When someone recognised him and asked if he did not trust his own countrymen, he replied, 'Yes, in other things, if you like. But where my life is at stake, I wouldn't trust my own mother not to mistake a black pebble for a white one when she casts her vote' (p. 265). Here the expression is used figuratively, in the sense of a mischievous accusation made to cause disruption.
  125. *the enamoured courtier*] Dariotto.
  127. *watched occasion*] looked for grounds. Chapman now introduces the theme that dominates the latter part of the play, Cornelio's determination to divorce Gazetta for adultery.
  128. *villainy*] Rinaldo goes along with Valerio's plan to embarrass Cornelio, but he is not happy with the idea of driving him to divorce (cf. Introduction, pp. 40–1).
  133. *procure her quiet*] make her peace (Parrott).

I have assayed him, and made Marc Antonio,
With all his gentle rhetoric, second me. 135
Yet all, I fear me, will be cast away.
See, see, they come. Join thy wit, good Rinaldo,
And help to pacify his yellow fury.
Rinaldo. With all my heart, I consecrate my wit
To the wished comfort of distressèd ladies. 140

Enter CORNELIO, MARC ANTONIO, VALERIO, [CURIO].

Cornelio. Will any man assure me of her good behaviour?
Valerio. Who can assure a jealous spirit? You may be afraid of the shadow of your ears, and imagine them to be horns. If you will assure yourself, appoint keepers to watch her.
Cornelio. And who shall watch the keepers? 145
Marc Antonio. To be sure of that, be you her keeper.
Valerio. Well said, and share the horns yourself, for that's the keeper's fee.
Cornelio. But say I am gone out of town, and must trust others. How shall I know if those I trust be trusty to me? 150
Rinaldo. Marry, sir, by a singular instinct, given naturally to all you married men, that if your wives play leger-de-heel, though you be a hundred miles off, yet you shall be sure instantly to find it in your foreheads.

140.1. SD. CURIO] *This ed.; Page Q.*

---

134. *assayed*] approached, spoken to (*OED* assay v. 15).
138. *yellow fury*] Yellow has long been associated with jealousy. In Herrick's poem, *How Marigolds Came Yellow*, 'Jealous girls these sometimes were / While they lived, or lasted here; / Turned to flowers, still they be / Yellow, marked for jealousy' (ll. 1–4). Since 'fury' is involved, there is also an allusion to yellow choler, or bile, the humour that causes it.
140. *wished*] To elide 'for' in 'wished for' was common at this time.
145.] Chapman returns to Juvenal's sixth *Satire*, where the cuckolded man complains, 'I know the advice my old friends give—"Lock her up / And bar the doors"—But who is to guard / Over the guards themselves?' (6.344–5).
147–8. *share ... keeper's fee*] Gamekeepers were customarily given a deer's head, including the horns, as part of their fee. In his *Description of England*, William Harrison observes that some keepers did especially well: 'parts of the deer given unto the keeper by a custom, who beside three shillings four pence or five shillings in money, hath the skin, head, umbles, chine, and shoulders' (p. 305).
150. *trusty*] trustworthy (*OED* adj. 1).
152. *leger-de-heel*] light-heel, harlot. When the Duke in Dekker's *Honest Whore, Part Two* gives an order to arrest all prostitutes, the disbelieving courtier Carolo asks, 'attach all the light heels i'th city, and clap em up?' (4.2.105),
153–4. *instantly ... foreheads*] In *Every Man In His Humour* (*Q*), Thorello asks Giuliani, 'is my forehead anything rougher than it was wont to be?' (5.3.332–3).

Cornelio. Sound doctrine, I warrant you; I am resolved, i'faith. 155
Curio. Then give me leave to speak, sir, that hath all this while been
　silent. I have heard you with extreme patience. Now, therefore,
　prick up your ears, and vouchsafe me audience.
Claudio. Good boy, a mine honour!
Cornelio. [*To Curio*] Pray, what are you, sir? 160
Curio. I am here, for default of better, of counsel with the fair Gazetta.
　And though herself had been best able to defend herself, if she
　had been here and would have pleased to put forth the buckler
　which nature hath given all women, I mean her tongue—
Valerio. Excellent good boy. 165
Curio. Yet, since she either vouchsafes it not, or thinks her innocence
　a sufficient shield against your jealous accusations, I will presume
　to undertake the defence of that absent and honourable lady,
　whose sworn knight I am, and in her of all that name—for 'lady'
　is grown a common name to their whole sex—which sex I have 170
　ever loved from my youth, and shall never cease to love till I
　want wit to admire.
Marc Antonio. An excellent spoken boy.
Valerio. Give ear, Cornelio, here is a young Mercurio sent to persuade
　thee. 175
Cornelio. Well, sir, let him say on.

---

160. SD.] *This ed.; not in Q.*

161. *of counsel with*] as counsellor, advisor to (*OED* n. 6).

163–4. *buckler ... tongue*] A buckler is a small, round shield, frequently used in Elizabethan swordplay, here equated with the woman's tongue, along with an indecent pun on the female pudenda. In the word play between Benedick and Margaret in *Much Ado*, Benedick offers, 'I give thee the bucklers', and Margaret replies 'Give us the swords, we have bucklers of our own' (5.2.17–19). Curio makes the obvious innuendo, and then pretends to deny it with a variation of the proverbial 'A woman's strength is in her tongue' (Dent W675).

166. *vouchsafes it not*] makes no denial.

169–70. *for 'lady' ... sex*] a jibe at the Earl of Essex. In 1599, he was in command of the army in Ireland, indulging his habit of granting knighthoods to all and sundry, and hence ladyships to the wives of these 'Essex knights'. The matter is raised again at 3.1.330 (cf. Introduction, pp. 33–4; Edelman, 'Knights, Pigeons, and Chapman's *All Fools*', *NQ* 59 (2012): 553–7).

171. *from my youth*] a pointer to the absurdity of the whole speech, since Curio is a boy.

174. *Mercurio*] Italian for Mercury. As herald and messenger of the gods, Mercury was also known as the god of eloquence.

Curio. It is a heavy case to see how this light sex is tumbled and tossed from post to pillar under the unsavoury breath of every humorous peasant. Gazetta, you said, is unchaste, disloyal, and I wot not what. Alas, is it her fault? Is she not a woman? Did she not suck it—as others of her sex do—from her mother's breast? And will you condemn that as her fault which is her nature? Alas! Sir, you must consider a woman is an unfinished creature, delivered hastily to the world before nature had set to that seal which 180

---

177. *heavy case*] sad situation, as Marcus Andronicus, Titus's brother, says to his son Publius, 'is not this a heavy case, / To see thy noble uncle thus distraught?' (*Tit.* 4.3.25–6).

light] Chapman is cleverly ambiguous here. Curio may mean 'wanton' or 'unchaste', but as he is speaking in Gazetta's defence, he might say that women are 'shining' and 'pure', or indeed 'not heavy', since they are 'tumbled and tossed' in the next line (*OED* light adj.[1] 1, 4b; adj.[2] 1a, 1c).

178. *post to pillar*] proverbial (Dent P328), nowadays more common in reverse order.

humorous] here, irrational, or capricious.

183–4. *unfinished ... hastily*] The word 'hastily', along with a description of women as inherently 'unchaste, disloyal', calls on Hesiod's story of Pandora, the first woman, in *Works and Days*. Zeus, angry with Prometheus's gift of fire to men, takes revenge by giving them 'an evil thing in which they may all be glad of heart while they embrace their own destruction ... he bade famous Hephaestus make haste and mix earth with water and to put in it the voice and strength of human kind, and fashion a sweet, lovely maiden-shape, like to the immortal goddesses in face'. Aphrodite added 'cruel longing and cares that weary the limbs', and Hermes supplied 'a shameless mind and a deceitful nature'. Zeus 'called this woman Pandora, because all they who dwelt on Olympus gave each a gift, a plague to men who eat bread' (ll. 61–82).

184–5. *seal ... perfect*] A number of allusions are (perhaps too) densely packed into this short phrase. Curio's seal is the stamp or impression made upon metal or another substance to guarantee its value. It serves here as metaphor for sexual love, or more specifically the loss of a woman's virginity, which, contrary to many cultural traditions, makes her more, not less perfect. The same construct occurs in in the first sestiad of Marlowe's *Hero and Leander*. Although they have just met, Leander tries to convince Hero that 'virginity, albeit some highly prize it', is overrated: 'Base bullion for the stamp's sake we allow; / Even so for men's impression do we you, / By which alone, our reverend fathers say, / Women receive perfection every way' (1.262, 265–8). Marston offers the identical thought, and identifies its source, in *Antonio's Revenge*, when the old nurse Nutriche tells Maria, the night before her wedding, 'I have read Aristotle's *Problems*, which saith that woman receiveth perfection by the man' (3.4.11–12). The passage Nutriche would have read is one of the many that made their way into the *Problems* (cf. 2.1.345–6n.), as medieval scholars added commentary and additional material: '*Question.* Why doth the matrix or womb of a woman draw greedily the seed of man? for as Averroes doth say, there was a maid in a bath, where some seed had been, the which the maid drawing, did conceive with child, and was delivered? *Answer.* Averroes doth say, that the womb and nature do draw the seed as the lodestone doth iron, and the agate steel: but she doth draw it for the perfection of her self' (sig. E3r).

should have made them perfect. Faults they have, no doubt, but 185
are we free? Turn your eye into yourself, good Signor Cornelio,
and weigh your own imperfections with hers. If she be wanton
abroad, are not you wanting at home? If she be amorous, are
not you jealous? If she be high set, are not you taken down? If
she be a courtesan, are not you a cuckold? 190
Cornelio. Out, you rogue!
Rinaldo. On with thy speech, boy.
Marc Antonio. You do not well, Cornelio, to discourage the bashful
youth.
Claudio. Forth, boy, I warrant thee. 195
Curio. But if our own imperfections will not teach us to bear with
theirs, yet let their virtues persuade us. Let us endure their bad
qualities for their good; allow the prickle for the rose, the brack
for the velvet, the paring for the cheese, and so forth. If you say
they range abroad, consider it is nothing but to avoid idleness 200
at home. Their nature is still to be doing; keep 'em a-doing at
home. Let them practise one good quality or other, either
sewing, singing, playing, chiding, dancing, or so, and these will
put such idle toys out of their heads into yours. But if you cannot
find them variety of business within doors, yet at least imitate 205
the ancient wise citizens of this city, who used carefully to
provide their wives gardens near the town to plant, to graft in,
as occasion served, only to keep 'em from idleness.

187–90. *If she ... cuckold*] a parody of John Lyly's prose style, known as euphuism (cf. Introduction, p. 34).

188. *wanting*] unable to perform sexually.

189. *high set ... taken down*] Apart from the literal definition of 'placed in a high position', 'high set' has a variety of figurative uses, including intoxicated, musically set in a high key, or sensuously excited. In this instance, Curio implies that, whenever Gazetta is sexually aroused, Cornelio becomes impotent.

193. *bashful*] This word has always meant 'shy', so Marc Antonio is clearly enjoying himself.

198–9. *allow the prickle ... cheese*] Curio quotes the initial paragraph of Lyly's *Euphues: The Anatomy of Wit*.

198. *brack*] flaw (*OED* n.¹ 3).

203. *playing*] playing a musical instrument.

chiding] To include chiding (scolding, complaining) amongst this list of positive activities is a nice touch.

207. *gardens ... to graft in*] Any planting or grafting women did in their gardens often had more to do with sex than horticulture. According to Stubbes in *The Anatomy of Abuses*, 'for that their gardens are locked, some of them have three or four keys apiece, whereof one they keep for themselves, the other their paramours have to go in before them ... Then to these gardens, they repair when they list with a basket and a boy, where they, meeting their sweethearts, receive their wished desires' (pp. 136–7).

132   ALL FOOLS   [ACT 3

Valerio. Everlasting good boy.
Cornelio. I perceive your knavery, sir, and will yet have patience.   210
Rinaldo. Forth, my brave Curio.
Curio. As to her unquietness—which some have rudely termed
shrewishness—though the fault be in her, yet the cause is in you.
What so calm as the sea of it own nature? Art was never able to
equal it. Your dicing tables, nor your bowling alleys, are not   215
comparable to it. Yet if a blast of wind do but cross it, not so
turbulent and violent an element in the world. So—nature, in
lieu of women's scarcity of wit, having indued them with a large
portion of will—if they may, without impeach, enjoy their wills,
no quieter creatures under heaven. But if the breath of their   220
husbands' mouths once cross their wills, nothing more

John Florio offers a similar observation in an oft-quoted passage from *Second Fruits*: 'Women are in churches saints, abroad angels, at home devils, at windows sirens, at doors pies [magpies], and in gardens, goats' (2nd ed., p. 175). Grafting had a particular association with cuckoldry, due to the custom of amputating a cock's spurs and grafting them to its comb, where they resembled horns (cf. Introduction, pp. 44–5).

210.] Cornelio may be saying this to himself, the 'sir' being Valerio.

214. *it own*] its own, as in Horatio's description of the Ghost, 'It lifted up it head' (1.2.216; cf. Abbott 228).

215–16. *Your ... to it*] The 'nor' before 'bowling' may be construed as 'and' (Abbott 408). Dice and bowls need an absolutely flat surface; an 'alley' was any long narrow enclosure where bowls was played, not the large building with numerous 'lanes' of the modern variety.

216. *cross it*] pass across the calm sea, leading to wordplay on 'cross' at l. 229.

217. *element*] water, one of the four basic elements, the others being earth, air, and fire.

218. *women's scarcity of wit*] Erasmus has an answer to this traditional sentiment in his colloquy, 'The Abbot and the Learned Lady'. The absurdly ignorant abbot cannot understand why a lady would even try to gain wisdom, and remarks, 'I've often heard the common saying "A wise woman is twice foolish."' The lady, who is based on Sir Thomas More's very learned daughter Margaret Roper, replies, 'That's commonly said, yes, but by fools. A woman truly wise is not wise in her own conceit. On the other hand, one who thinks herself wise when she knows nothing is indeed twice foolish.' Erasmus presents a different approach to the same question in *The Praise of Folly*, where Folly says 'the Greek proverb is "an ape is still an ape, even if it is dressed up in royal purple"; just so, a woman is still a woman—that is, a fool—no matter what role she may try to play'. But Folly is a woman, and speaks words of wisdom throughout her discourse (*Colloquies*, p. 504, *Folly*, p. 29).

218–19. *indued ... will*] a version of the proverbial 'women will have their wills' (Dent W723). In his *Breviary of Health* (1552), Andrew Boorde adds a Latin tag, and directly relates the proverb to the subject under discussion here: '*ut homo non cantet cum cuculo* [so that a man may not sing with the cuckold], let every man please his wife in all matters' (sig. Bb4r).

219. *impeach*] hindrance (*OED* n. 1).

tempestuous. Why, then, sir, should you husbands cross your wives' wills thus, considering the law allows them no wills at all at their deaths, because it intended they should have their wills while they lived? 225

Valerio. Answer him but that, Cornelio.

Cornelio. All shall not serve her turn. I am thinking of other matters.

Marc Antonio. [*Aside*] Thou hast half won him, wag. Ply him yet a little further.

Curio. Now, sir, for these cuckooish songs of yours, of cuckolds, horns, 230 grafting, and such-like, what are they but mere imaginary toys, bred out of your own heads as your own, and so by tradition delivered from man to man, like scarecrows to terrify fools from this earthly paradise of wedlock, coined at first by some spent poets, superannuated bachelors, or some that were scarce men of 235 their hands; who, like the fox, having lost his tail, would persuade others to lose theirs for company? Again, for your cuckold, what is it but a mere fiction? Show me any such creature in nature. If there be, I could never see it. Neither could I ever find any sensible difference betwixt a cuckold and a Christian creature. 240 To conclude, let poets coin, or fools credit, what they list. For mine own part, I am clear of this opinion, that your cuckold is

---

228. SD.] *This ed.; not in Q.*

222. *cross*] thwart, oppose (*OED* v. 14).

223–5. *the law ... while they lived*] Under English law, a married woman could not make a will without her husband's consent; there was no real point, since she did not own any property independently (Sokol, p. 171). Taken in its entirety, this witty play on 'women will have their wills', spoken several lines above, has the sound of an established proverb, but no example before Sir John Manningham's *Diary* is to be found in any of the standard references. As noted in the Introduction (pp. 4–5), Manningham could well have recorded what he heard at the theatre, a clue to the date of the Blackfriars performance (cf. Edelman, 'John Manningham at the Blackfriars Theatre', *NQ* 60 (2013): 445–7).

234. *wedlock*] *OED*'s definition for 'wedlock' in this context, different from its use at 1.2.118, is 'matrimonial union' (n. 3).

spent] tired, worn out (*OED* adj. 3), with the sexual quibble on 'spend' (cf. 2.1.49n.).

235. *superannated*] incapacitated by age (1st cit. *OED* adj.).

235–6. *men of their hands*] valiant men, a common phrase.

236–7. *fox ... company*] This repetition of the story used at 1.1.92–3 may be a pointer to revision of the original text at some time, or simply Chapman's haste in composition.

241. *coin*] invent words or phrases. To 'coin' money by the stamping of metal was a Middle English term; the figurative application to language was quite recent in Chapman's time.

credit] believe (*OED* v. 1).

list] like, choose (*OED* v.¹ 2b).

a mere chimera, and that there are no cuckolds in the world but those that have wives, and so I will leave them.

Cornelio. 'Tis excellent good, sir. I do take you, sir, d'ye see, to be, as it were, bastard to the saucy courtier that would have me father more of your fraternity, d'ye see, and so are instructed—as we hear—to second that villain with your tongue, which he has acted with his tenure piece, d'ye see? 245

Curio. No such matter, a my credit, sir. 250

Cornelio. Well, sir, be as be may, I scorn to set my head against yours, d'ye see, when in the meantime I will firk your father, whether you see or no.

Exit, drawing his rapier.

Rinaldo. God's my life, Cornelio! *Exit.*

Valerio. Have at your father, i'faith, boy, if he can find him. 255

Marc Antonio. See, he comes here; he has missed him.

Enter DARIOTTO.

Dariotto. How now, my hearts, what, not a wench amongst you?
'Tis a sign you're not in the grace of wenches
That they will let you be thus long alone.

Valerio. Well, Dariotto, glory not too much 260
That, for thy brisk attire and lips perfumed,

---

243. *chimera*] In Chapman's *Iliad*, 'Chimera the invincible' has 'a lion's shape before, / Behind, a dragon's. In the midst a goat's shagged form she bore, / And flames of deadly fervency flew from her breath and eyes' (6.183–5). Here, we find the ordinary modern sense of any mythical creature or figment of the imagination.

243–4. *no cuckolds ... wives*] This sensible observation is also made by Chaucer's Miller in the prologue to his tale: 'Who hath no wyf, he is no cokewold' (3152).

245, 247, 249. *d'ye see*] Heard nowhere else in the play, this vocal tic is Chapman's hint to the actor that Cornelio has become completely unhinged.

246. *bastard ... courtier*] The angry Cornelio accuses Curio, perhaps not literally, of being Dariotto's bastard son.

249. *tenure piece*] Gazetta. Williams sees this as a quibble equating an adulteress with a piece of property under tenure, i.e., long-term occupation, held by her lover (Williams, pp. 1374–5; *OED* tenure n. 1).

250. *credit*] good name, reputation (*OED* n. 5).

251. *scorn to set ... yours*] Cornelio remembers the proverb, 'do not set your wit against a fool's' (Dent W547).

252. *firk*] beat up (*OED* v. 4a). The word 'father', here and in the next line, continues the idea of Curio being, at least in Cornelio's mind, Dariotto's son.

255. *Have at*] He'll have at. The omission of a subject pronoun is common (Abbott 400). 'Have at', either literally or in a host of figurative senses, means to challenge or attack, e.g., the swordfighting term, 'have at you', similar to *en garde*.

261.] 'Brisk' is synonymous with 'spruce' or 'fashionable'. The smell on Dariotto's lips would probably come from kissing his hand (cf. 2.1.145n.), since the hands or gloves of a courtier were often perfumed. In *1 Henry IV*, when the 'certain lord, neat and trimly dressed' approached Hotspur to demand his prisoners, Hotspur was enraged 'to see him shine so brisk, and smell so sweet' (1.3.33, 54).

Thou playest the stallion ever where thou com'st,
And, like the husband of the flock, runnst through
The whole town herd, and no man's bed secure,
No woman's honour unattempted by thee. 265
Think not to be thus fortunate for ever,
But in thy amorous conquests at the last
Some wound will slice your mazer. Mars himself
Fell into Vulcan's snare, and so may you.
Dariotto. Alas, alas, faith, I have but the name. 270
I love to court and win, and the consent,
Without the act obtained, is all I seek.
I love the victory that draws no blood.
Claudio. Oh, 'tis a high desert in any man
To be a secret lecher. I know some 275

262–4.] Jonson uses a similar trope in *Epicene*, when Dauphine says he loves all the collegiate ladies, and Clerimont replies, 'We'll keep you at home, believe it, i'the stable, an you be such a stallion' (4.1.103–4).

268. *mazer*] noggin. Mazer is maple or a similar hardwood; figuratively, it is the chief component of the human head. In Dekker's *That Wonderful Year*, a sleeping drunk is hit on the head, and 'thinking the cans had flown about, cried 'Zounds! What, do you mean to crack my mazer?' (1: 137).

268–9. *Mars ... snare*] The tale of Vulcan, his wife Venus, and her lover Mars is the original model for countless stories of a husband pretending to go away on a business trip in order to catch his wife in the act. In Chapman's *Odyssey*, Vulcan 'forged a net that none could loose or cut', secretly installed it above and around Venus's bed, and 'feign'd as if he went / To well-built Lemnos, his most loved town'. The moment she thought her husband was gone, Venus summoned Mars, and 'Down they went; and straight / About them cling'd the artificial sleight / Of most wise Vulcan; and were so ensnar'd, / That neither they could stir their course prepar'd / In any limb about them, nor arise' (8.387, 399–400, 412–16). Ovid's version is in *The Art of Love* (2.577–81).

270. *I have but the name*] I am only such by reputation, not in fact.

271–2. *the consent ... all I seek*] Dariotto says that all the fun is in the getting there, and that he has no interest in actually having sex with his conquests.

273.] Parrott is surely correct in noting that this line comes from the episode in the *Amores* when Ovid succeeds in bedding Corinna, 'Despite the united efforts of husband, door, and porter / That unholy trinity ... This bloodless conquest / Demands a super triumph' (2.12.3–6). The situations do not exactly correspond, since Ovid has indeed completed the seduction, while Dariotto claims that this is unimportant.

274. *desert*] excellence, behaviour deserving of reward (*OED* n.[1] 1).

275. *secret lecher*] Claudio, suspecting that Dariotto is all talk, adds to the flattery by praising him for being a 'secret lecher' and not boasting of his amatory deeds. In the *Art of Love*, Ovid advises, 'Have fun, but play it discreetly, / Don't broadcast your intrigues / As a boost for your ego' (2.389–91). Later, he deplores the disappearance of traditional Roman reticence in sexual matters: 'But now we flaunt our prowess / At such nocturnal pursuits, pay a high price / Just for the kick of bragging. Will you give every girl in town the / Treatment, just to be able to tell your friends / "I had her, too"?' (2.625–9). This is an amazing thing for Ovid to say, since the entire poem is one long boast.

That, like thyself, are true in nothing else.
Marc Antonio. And, methinks, it is nothing if not told.
At least the joy is never full before.
Valerio. Well, Dariotto, th'hadst as good confess.
The sun shines broad upon your practices; 280
Vulcan will wake and intercept you one day.
Dariotto. Why, the more jealous knave and coxcomb he.
What, shall the shaking of his bed a little
Put him in motion? It becomes him not.
Let him be dulled and staled, and then be quiet. 285
The way to draw my custom to his house
Is to be mad and jealous; 'tis the sauce
That whets my appetite.
Valerio. Or any man's.
Sine periculo friget lusus.
They that are jealous, use it still of purpose 290
To draw you to their houses.
Dariotto. Ay, by heaven,
I am of that opinion. Who would steal
Out of a common orchard? Let me gain
My love with labour, and enjoy't with fear,
Or I am gone.

Enter RINALDO.

Rinaldo. What, Dariotto here? 295
Foot, dar'st thou come near Cornelio's house?

---

278. *never full before.*] never complete until you've told everyone.
279. *th'hadst as good*] you might as well.
282. *coxcomb*] A coxcomb was the traditional fool's cap, so named for its similarity to the comb of feathers on a cock's head, and, by extension, the fool himself.
284–8. *It becomes ... appetite*] Dariotto's attitude derives from a particularly delightful passage in the *Amores*, when Ovid begs Corinna's husband to guard her jealously, in order to present a worthwhile challenge: '*You* may not feel any need (and more fool you) to guard that / Girl of yours—but it sharpens my desire, / So would you oblige? What's allowed is a bore, it's what isn't / That turns me on' (2.19.1–4).
289. Sine periculo friget lusus] literally 'without danger, the game goes cold'. Valerio is egging Dariotto on by humouring his pretensions. Two quotations from Terence are at work here. The first is spoken by the slave Syrus to his young master Clitipho in *The Self-Tormenter*, as he reveals the plan to place Clitipho's mistress in his father's house: *Non fit sine periclo facinus magnum nec memorabile*: 'No one achieves anything great or memorable without taking risks' (314). The word *friget*, however, is prominent in the often quoted *sine Cerere et Libero friget Venus* ('without Ceres and Bacchus, Venus grows cold'), spoken by the tipsy young man Chremes in *The Eunuch* (732). Modern translators of *The Eunuch* have enjoyed a figurative approach, e.g., Peter Brown, 'No arousal without carousal', and Betty Radice, 'Love needs a bite and a sup to warm things up'.

SC. I]   ALL FOOLS   137

Dariotto. Why, is the bull run mad? What ails he, trow?
Rinaldo. I know not what he ails, but I would wish you
     To keep out of the reach of his sharp horns,
     For, by this hand, he'll gore you.
Dariotto.   And why me   300
     More than thyself, or these two other whelps?
     You all have basted him as well as I.
     I wonder what's the cause.
Rinaldo.   Nay, that he knows,
     And swears withal that wheresoe'er he meets you,
     He'll mark you for a marker of men's wives.   305
Valerio. Pray heaven he be not jealous by some tale
     That have been told him lately. Did you never
     Attempt his wife? Hath no love's harbinger,
     No looks, no letters, passed 'twixt you and her?
Dariotto. For looks I cannot answer. I bestow them   310
     At large and carelessly, much like the sun.

---

310. looks] *Shepherd (subst.);* looke Q.

   298. *what he ails*] what ails him.
   301. *these two other whelps*] Valerio and Claudio.
   302. *basted*] Dariotto may mean 'beaten' or 'thrashed' in a figurative sense, but in the next speech Rinaldo puns on 'mark' and 'marker'. Therefore 'basted' could be employed in the rare usage of marking, in the sense of branding, a sheep, or here by extension, the 'bull' Cornelio (*OED* baste v.^{2} 4, v.^{3}; cf. Halliwell, *Dictionary*, baste).
   305. *mark you*] give you a scar. In Chapman's *Iliad*, the goddess Athena, siding with the Greeks, encourages Diomed to make a fresh assault on Troy. This should be done even if Aphrodite, whom Athena blames for starting the war, takes arms on behalf of the Trojans: 'But if that goddess be so bold (since she first stirred this war) / Assault and mark her from the rest with some infamous scar' (5.136–37).
   marker] pilferer, shoplifter. As we learn in Greene's *Second Part of Conny-catching*, shoplifting requires a team of three: the lift, the marker, and the santar. First, the lift, 'attired in the form of a civil country gentleman, comes with the marker into some mercer's shop, haberdasher's, goldsmith's, or any such place where any particular parcels of worth are to be conveyed'. After inspecting several samples, the lift asks the shopkeeper to fetch some more, and while his back is turned, the lift 'commits his garbage [stolen goods] to the marker, for note the lift is without his cloak, in his doublet and hose, to avoid suspicion'. At that point the santar walks by the shop, and the marker calls out to him under the pretence of having an important message to deliver. He leaves the shop, hands over the message (i.e., the 'garbage'), and the santar walks away with it (10: 118, 119; cf. Edelman, 'Chapman's "All Fools", *Explicator* 72 (2014): 49–51).
   308. *harbinger*] herald, forerunner (*OED* n. 3).
   311. *At large*] freely, and over a large area (*OED* large adj. phr. 5a, I); cf. 4.1.333.
   much like the sun] The impartiality of the sun, which distributes its rays everywhere, is noted in many proverbial expressions, from 'He maketh his sun to arise on the evil,

  If any be so foolish to apply them
  To any private fancy of their own—
  As many do—it's not my fault, thou knowest.
Valerio. Well, Dariotto, this set face of thine—   315
  If thou be guilty of offence to him—
  Comes out of very want of wit and feeling
  What danger haunts thee. For Cornelio
  Is a tall man, I tell you, and 'twere best
  You shunned his sight awhile, till we might get   320
  His patience, or his pardon. For past doubt
  Thou diest, if he but see thee.

      Enter CORNELIO.

Rinaldo.   Foot, he comes.
Dariotto. Is this the cockatrice that kills with sight?
  How dost thou, boy? Ha?
Cornelio.   Well.
Dariotto.   What, lingering still
  About this paltry town? Hadst thou been ruled   325
  By my advice, thou hadst by this time been
  A gallant courtier, and at least a knight.
  I would have got thee dubbed by this time, certain.
Cornelio. And why then did you not yourself that honour?
Dariotto. Tush, 'tis more honour still to make a knight   330
  Than 'tis to be a knight, to make a cuckold

---

and the good, and sendeth rain on the just and unjust' (Matthew, 5.45) to the Chorus's description of Henry V: 'a largess universal, like the sun, / His liberal eye doth give to everyone' (4.Cho.43–4).

 315. *set face*] predetermined facial expression. The Elizabethans made a science of adopting a particular 'set face' to suit the situation. In John Cooke's splendid play, *Greene's Tu Quoque*, the servingman-turned-gentleman Bubble asks his former master Staines for help in this regard: 'See, yonder's the company that I look for; therefore if you will set my face of any fashion, pray do it quickly' (ll. 2284–6).

 316. *him*] Cornelio.

 319. *tall*] valiant at arms, as Bardolph says of Falstaff, 'a tall gentleman, by heaven, and a most gallant leader' (*2H4* 3.2.61–2).

 323.] The cockatrice, or basilisk, is a serpent whose look is fatal, as we know from the Duchess of York, who does not think highly of her son, Richard III: 'O my accursed womb, the bed of death! / A cockatrice hast thou hatched to the world, / Whose unavoided eye is murderous' (4.1.53–5).

 330–1. *'tis more honour ... be a knight*] another dig at the Earl of Essex's penchant for handing out knighthoods (cf. 3.1.169–70n.; Introduction, pp. 33–4).

SC. I]   ALL FOOLS   139

 Than 'tis to be a cuckold.
Cornelio.   You're a villain.
Dariotto. God shield, man! Villain?
Cornelio.   Ay, I'll prove thee one.
Dariotto. What, wilt thou prove a villain? By this light thou deceiv'st
 me, then.   335
Cornelio. Well, sir, thus I prove it.   *Draws.*
All. Hold, hold! Raise the streets!
Claudio. Cornelio!   [*Dariotto draws.*]
Rinaldo. Hold, Dariotto, hold! [*Cornelio wounds Dariotto.*]
Valerio. What, art thou hurt?   340
Dariotto. A scratch, a scratch.
Valerio. [*To Curio*] Go, sirrah, fetch a surgeon.
              [*Exit* CURIO.]
Cornelio. You'll set a badge on the jealous fool's head, sir? Now set a
 coxcomb on your own.
Valerio. What's the cause of these wars, Dariotto?   345
Dariotto. Foot, I know not.

---

338. SD.] *This ed.; not in* Q. 339. SD.] *This ed.; not in* Q.
342. SD.] *This ed.; not in* Q. 342.1. SD.] Parrott[1] (*subst.*); *not in* Q.

---

332. *Y'are a villain*] Under the code known as the *duello*, calling someone a villain was the first step in a challenge to a duel. The Italian fencing master Vincentio Saviolo writes in the second book of his *Practise* that the challenger is not 'he that is called a traitor or villain, or by some other injurious name ... for the challenge shall ever fall on him that offereth the injury' (sig. 1r). Cornelio is demanding that Dariotto deny he is a villain by saying 'thou liest'; at that point Cornelio would respond to the 'lie certain', and the challenge would be official.
 333. *God shield*] God forbid, a mild oath.
 I'll prove thee one] I will prove you are a villain by defeating you in a duel.
 334–5.] Dariotto denigrates Cornelio's ability in the courtly art of fencing by pretending to be astonished that he would be looking to have a duel. Wanting no part of a swordfight himself, Dariotto does not say 'thou liest', but his hope of avoiding combat is thwarted when Cornelio abandons the niceties of the *duello* and draws his sword.
 337. *Raise the streets*] arouse the citizens with a 'hue and cry'.
 339–42.] Chapman is having some fun at Shakespeare's expense. The sequence is too close to Mercutio's untimely death in *Romeo and Juliet* to be accidental.
 343. *badge*] The cuckold's horns were proverbially called his badge (Dent B27.11). In *The Bugbears*, a play of uncertain authorship written about 1565, the servant Squartacantino tells his foolish old master Catalupo, who thinks he is about to marry a young woman, 'I doubt your young wife will mark you I wot how / With Saint Cornelius' badge' (1.3.11–12).

140　　　　　　　　　ALL FOOLS　　　　　　　　　[ACT 3

Cornelio. Well, sir, know and spare not. I will presently be divorced,
　　and then take her amongst ye.
Rinaldo. Divorced? Nay, good Cornelio.
Cornelio. By this sword, I will. The world shall not dissuade me.　　350
　　　　　　　　　　　　　　　　　　　　　　Exit.
Valerio. Why, this has been your fault now, Dariotto.
　　You youths have fashions, when you have obtained
　　A lady's favour, straight your hat must wear it,
　　Like a jackdaw that, when he lights upon
　　A dainty morsel, caws and makes his brags,　　　　　　　　　　355
　　And then some kite doth scoop it from him straight,
　　Where, if he fed without his dawish noise,
　　He might fare better, and have less disturbance.
　　Forbear it in this case, and when you prove
　　Victorious over fair Gazetta's fort,　　　　　　　　　　　　　360
　　Do not, for pity, sound your trump for joy,
　　But keep your valour close, and 'tis your honour.

　　　　　　　　　　Enter [CURIO] *and* POCK.

Pock. God save you, Signor Dariotto.
Dariotto. I know you not, sir. Your name, I pray?
Pock. My name is Pock, sir, a practitioner in surgery.　　　　　365

362.1. SD. CURIO] *This ed.; Page Q.*　　363. SP.] *Collier; Poc. Pock Q.*

---

347. *know and spare not*] You will soon know, with no detail left out, as Gloucester says to Queen Elizabeth in *Richard III*: 'What? Threat you me with telling of the King? / Tell him, and spare not' (1.3.112–13).
353. *your hat must wear it*] A courtier would wear a lady's glove, ribbon, or other token in his hat. Fastidius Brisk of *Every Man Out of His Humour* says 'this feather grew in her sweet fan, sometimes, though now, it be my poor fortune to wear it' (2.2.242–3).
354–5.] In his *Etymologies*, Isidore of Seville (ca. 560–636) writes, 'the jackdaw (*graculus*) is named for its garrulity (*garrulitas*), not, as some people would have it, because they fly "in flocks" (*gregatim*), since it is quite clear they are named for their call, for it is the most talkative species and importunate in its calls' (p. 267). Brags can be boasts, as we normally use the word today, or simply loud noises, often associated with trumpet calls (*OED* n.[1]).
356. *kite*] like 'hawk', a member of the falcon family.
357. *dawish*] like a daw, a rare word (*OED* n.).
361–2.] 'Trump' is an archaic form of 'trumpet'. Castiglione's Count Ludovico advises that the true courtier avoids 'above all things bragging and unshameful praising himself, for therewith a man always purchaseth himself the hatred and ill will of the hearers' (Hoby, p. 49).
362. *close*] secret, as at 2.1.257.

SC. 1] ALL FOOLS 141

Dariotto. Pock, the surgeon, you're welcome, sir. I know a doctor of
    your name, Master Pock.
Pock. My name has made many doctors, sir.
Rinaldo. Indeed, 'tis a worshipful name.
Valerio. Marry is it, and of an ancient descent. 370
Pock. Faith, sir, I could fetch my pedigree far, if I were so disposed.
Rinaldo. Out of France, at least.
Pock. And if I stood on my arms, as others do—
Dariotto. No, do not, Pock. Let other stand a' their arms, and thou o'
    thy legs, as long as thou canst. 375
Pock. Though I live by my bare practice, yet I could show good cards
    for my gentility.

---

367. *Master*] The professions of surgeon and physician were distinct in Elizabethan times, and since surgery was considered a craft, Pock is 'Master', not 'Doctor'. Under the Statute of Artificers and Apprentices, passed in 1563, Pock would have had to serve an apprenticeship of seven years, and be at least twenty-four years old, before being eligible to join the Company of Barber-Surgeons. The amalgamation of the two companies in 1520 gave rise to the myth that the same person practised both crafts, but they were always kept strictly apart (Keevil, p. 167; Pelling & Webster, pp. 173–4).

368.] Pock's name is, of course, a play on 'pox', or venereal disease, which has indeed kept many doctors in work. There may be some self-advertisement involved—although physicians, not surgeons, were meant to treat disease, the English surgeon William Clowes wrote a book, *Morbus Gallicus* (1579), on the causes, symptoms, and treatment of syphilis, and claimed to have cured more than a thousand men of during a five-year residency at London's St Bartholomew's Hospital (sig. B2r).

372. *Out of France*] Syphilis was known, at least to the English, as a French disease, hence the title of Clowes's book (prev. n.) and Ancient Pistol's news that his wife has died of 'a malady of France' (*H5* 5.1.82). The association began with Europe's first major outbreak, which took place amongst French soldiers at the siege of Naples in 1494. Therefore, to the French it was an Italian disease, but the Italians blamed it all on the Spaniards. In Geoffrey Fenton's translation of Guicciardini's *History* (1599) we read, 'it is known ... that such a disease was transported out of Spain to Naples, and yet not proper or natural to that nation, but brought thither from the Isles [West Indies], which ... in those seasons began to be known to our regions by the navigation of Christopher Columbus' (p. 99).

373. *stood on my arms*] asserted my gentlemanly status.

374–5. *Let other ... thou canst*] Sir Petronel Flash makes the same pun when deriding Golding's quality in *Eastward Ho* (3.2.127–9). 'Other' (*Q*), as a form of 'others', is sometimes seen in this era (Abbott 12).

376. *by my bare practice*] by my meagre practice, or perhaps 'only by my practice' (*OED* adj. 10, 11).

show good cards] Pock offers to provide evidence of his gentility, as a card player does when showing his winning hand. In his *Diary*, John Manningham relates an anecdote about a lawyer who presented a case before William Fleetwood, the very popular recorder (a type of magistrate) of London: ' "We have good cards to show for it", said a lawyer to the old recorder Fleetwood. "Well", said he, "I am sure we have

Valerio. Tush, thou canst not shake off thy gentry, Pock, 'tis bred i'th' bone. But to the main, Pock. What thinkest thou of this gentleman's wound, Pock? Canst thou cure it, Pock? 380
Pock. [*Examining Dariotto's head*] The incision is not deep, nor the orifice exorbitant. The pericranion is not dislocated. I warrant his life for forty crowns without perishing of any joint.
Dariotto. Faith, Pock, 'tis a joint I would be loath to lose for the best joint of mutton in Italy. 385
Rinaldo. Would such a scratch as this hazard a man's head?
Pock. Ay, by'r Lady, sir, I have known some have lost their heads for a less matter, I can tell you. Therefore, sir, you must keep good diet. If you please to come home to my house till you be perfectly cured, I shall have the more care on you. 390

381. SD.] *This ed.; not in Q.*
386. hazard] *Reed;* hazards *Q.*

---

kings and queens for us, and then you can have but a company of knaves on your side"' (p. 160).

378–9. *'tis bred i'th' bone*] a play on the proverb spoken by Downright in *Every Man In His Humour* (F), 'It will never out o'the flesh that's bred i'the bone' (2.1.66–7). For Pock, the particular 'bone' would be the penis. In *Troilus and Cressida*, Thersites wishes syphilis, or, as he calls it, the 'incurable bone-ache', on Patroclus, and the 'Neapolitan bone-ache' on the entire Greek army (5.1.22, 2.3.18–19).

382. *exorbitant*] abnormal, unusual (*OED* adj. 2).

pericranion] either the membrane enveloping the skull, or the skull itself (*OED* n.).

dislocated] pulled out of joint (1st cit. *OED* adj.). Ridiculous as it sounds, Pock's terminology is little different from actual practice. In Thomas Gale's *Enchiridion of Chirurgerie* (1563), the 'Master' recommends treating wounds with his 'artificial balm' that 'hath in him the virtue attractive, conglutinative, and dessicative; his description you shall find in the antidotarie' (sig. C1r).

warrant] guarantee (*OED* v.).

384–5. *'tis a joint ... Italy*] Dariotto puns on both 'joint' and 'mutton'. 'Joint' is yet another common word for penis, while 'mutton' is often used as a synonym for prostitute. In *The Roaring Girl*, Mistress Openwork complains that her husband 'feeds upon stale mutton abroad, having better and fresher at home' (6.186–8; cf. Williams, pp. 745, 926).

386. *hazard*] put at risk, as in a game of chance (*OED* v. 1).

388–9. *good diet*] In Franciscus Arcaeus's surgical manual, *A Most Excellent and Compendious Method of Curing Wounds* (1588), we are advised, 'In the very beginning of any cure, we do feed them which are diseased of any wound in the head raisins and a little bread both at dinner and supper ... and we use this diet until the seventh day ... But if the party be of a choleric complexion to suffer him once a day to eat the flesh of a pullet or cockerel, until he hath passed the seventh day' (sig. E4r).

389. *come home ... house*] It would be important to Dariotto's cure that Pock place him in the right room. The *Compendious Method* (prev. n.) advises, 'If it shall be in the winter season, let his chamber be in the upper part of the house ... but in summer season a lower chamber is best. Lest the patient be hurt by heat, let the chamber door be always kept shut, and hang a cloth before the door to keep off the air that cometh into the chamber' (sig. E3v).

Valerio. That's your only course to have it well quickly.
Pock. By what time would he have it well, sir?
Dariotto. A very necessary question. Canst thou limit the time?
Pock. Oh, sir, cures are like causes in law, which may be lengthened or shortened at the discretion of the lawyer. He can either keep 395
it green with replications or rejoinders, or sometimes skin it fair a'th' outside for fashion sake, but so he may be sure 'twill break out again by a writ of error, and then has he his suit new to begin. But I will covenant with you that by such a time I'll make your head as sound as a bell. I will bring it to suppuration, and 400
after I will make it coagulate and grow to a perfect cicatrice, and all within these ten days, so you keep a good diet.
Dariotto. Well, come, Pock. We'll talk farther on't within. It draws near dinner time. What's o'clock, boy?
Curio. By your clock, sir, it should be almost one, for your head rung 405
noon some half hour ago.
Dariotto. Is't true, sir?
Valerio. Away, let him alone. Though he came in at the window he sets the gates of your honour open, I can tell you.
Dariotto. Come in, Pock, come, apply; and for this deed 410

---

396. *green*] the most common way of referring to a fresh or unhealed wound (*OED* adj. 7b).

396-8. *skin it fair ... break out again*] Although he is speaking metaphorically about Gertrude's soul rather than a physical wound, this is precisely what Hamlet says will happen if she applies an 'unction' to it: 'It will but skin and film the ulcerous place / Whilst rank corruption, mining all within, / Infects unseen' (3.4.145, 147-9).

398. *writ of error*] a writ instructing a court to submit its record to a court of review, in order to see if an error has been committed. As John Cowell says in his legal dictionary *The Interpreter* (1607), 'a writ of error is that properly which lieth to redress false judgement given in any court of record' (sig. Cc1r).

399. *covenant*] often used as a verb in Chapman's time.

400. *suppuration*] Astonishingly, the standard treatment of wounds was the one most likely to kill the patient. Surgeons and physicians, having misunderstood the ideas of Galen and Hippocrates, believed that healing was promoted by packing the wound with foul mixtures to bring on corruption and suppuration, producing *pus bonum et laudabile* or 'laudable pus' (Forrest, p. 269, Gabriel & Metz, 1: 54-6).

405-6. *head rung noon*] proverbial for receiving a good blow to the head (Dent N210). Thomas Heywood, in his account of Queen Elizabeth's early years, *England's Elizabeth* (1631), describes the princess's journey from London to Woodstock, under the charge of Sir Henry Bedingfeld, in 1555. Although for all intents and purposes a prisoner, Elizabeth was greeted enthusiastically along the way, 'with the loud acclamations of people, and the sound of bells'. The angry Sir Henry 'called them rebels and traitors, beating them back with his truncheon; as for the ringers he made their pates ring noon, before they were released out of the stocks' (pp. 155-6).

408. *in at the window*] To come in at the window, or over the hatch, was proverbial for being conceived illegitimately (Dent W456).

144 ALL FOOLS [ACT 3

    I'll give the knave a wound shall never bleed.
                            Exeunt all but RINALDO *and* VALERIO.
Valerio. So, sir, I think this knock rings loud acquittance
    For my ridicules.
Rinaldo. Well, sir, to turn our heads to salve your licence,
    Since you have used the matter so unwisely   415
    That now your father has discerned your humour
    In your too careless usage in his house,
    Your wife must come from his house to Antonio's
    And he, to entertain her, must be told
    She is not wife to his son, but to you,   420
    Which news will make his simple wit triumph
    Over your father. And your father, thinking
    He still is gulled, will still account him simple.
    Come, sir, prepare your villainous wit to feign
    A kind submission to your father's fury,   425
    And we shall see what hearty policy
    He will discover, in his feignèd anger,

411.1. SD.] *This placement Parrott¹; after l. 413 Q.*
412. SP.] *Parrott¹; not in Q.*
413. ridicules] *This ed.;* riciduouse *Q;* ridiculous *Reed.*

411.] I'll cuckold him. Dariotto quotes the *Amores* again (cf. 3.1.275n.), this time promising the same total victory Ovid achieved.

412 SP.] No new speaker is indicated in *Q*, these lines forming part of Dariotto's exit speech, with the last line reading 'For my ridiculouse', followed by an exit direction at the right margin. Parrott must be correct in giving the line to Valerio, who thinks that the knock on the head Dariotto received is 'loud acquittance', i.e., payment in full, for having mocked him earlier. For Dariotto to exit on a couplet, as the lines are printed in *Q*, is apt.

413. *ridicules*] All modern-spelling editions have *Q*'s 'ridiculouse' as 'ridiculous', ending the sentence on an adjective with no noun to modify. Parrott has Rinaldo interrupt Valerio before he could finish his thought—if this is what Chapman intended, it is Chapman at his clumsiest, and we are left with no idea what the ridiculous thing is. I offer a second possibility, which is that Dariotto has been repaid for the 'ridicules' he inflicted on Valerio about his musical talents. Although *OED* gives no citation for ridicule as a noun before 1658, 'ridicle', an archaic form derived from Latin and French, meaning 'mockery', appears several times in Foxe's *Acts and Monuments* (1583, pp. 146, 169, 236). Given his predilection for latinate forms, Chapman could well have drawn on the same word here. Taken together, ll. 412–13 are then made perfectly metrical.

414. *salve your licence*] put a balm or healing unguent on your impropriety in embracing Gratiana (*OED* salve v. 1, licence n. 3b).

417. *usage*] conduct, as at 2.1.264.

426. *hearty policy*] bold and spirited deception. Rinaldo describes Gostanzo as 'politic', in the sense of 'scheming', at 1.1.401.

427. *discover*] reveal, the most common definition at this time.

SC. I]   ALL FOOLS   145

  To blind Antonio's eyes and make him think
  He thinks her heartily to be your wife.
Valerio. Oh, I will gull him rarely, with my wench   430
  Low-kneeling at my heels before his fury,
  And injury shall be salved with injury.   [*Exeunt.*]

---

432. SD.] *Evans; not in Q.*
432.1] *Q has Finis Actus 3; omitted Reed.*

Act 4

ACT 4, SCENE I

[*Enter*] MARC ANTONIO, GOSTANZO.

Marc Antonio. You see how too much wisdom evermore
Outshoots the truth. You were so forwards still
To tax my ignorance, my green experience
In these grey hairs, for giving such advantage
To my son's spirit that he durst undertake 5
A secret match so far short of his worth;
Your son so seasoned with obedience,
Even from his youth, that all his actions relish
Nothing but duty and your anger's fear.
What shall I say to you, if it fall out 10
That this most precious son of yours has played
A part as bad as this, and as rebellious,
Nay, more, has grossly gulled your wit withal?
What if my son has undergone the blame
That appertained to yours, and that this wench 15
With which my son is charged, may call you father?
Shall I then say you want experience,
You're green, you're credulous, easy to be blinded?
Gostanzo. Ha, ha, ha!
Good Marc Antonio, when't comes to that, 20
Laugh at me, call me fool, proclaim me so.
Let all the world take knowledge I am an ass.

---

0. Act 4, Scene 1] *Hudston (subst.);* Actus 4 Scena I *Q.*
0.1. SD. *Enter*] *Reed; not in Q.*

---

0. Act 4, Scene 1] The outdoor setting continues.

1–2. *too much wisdom ... truth*] The 'too much wisdom' is Gostanzo's supposed superior knowledge in bringing up a son; to 'outshoot' or 'overshoot' a target is a common metaphor for being mistaken. Since we last saw the two fathers, Rinaldo, Valerio, and Fortunio have 'confessed' to Marc Antonio that Valerio is the real husband of Gratiana, and that they only pretended otherwise as a prank. Now Marc Antonio, with a good deal of smugness, is about to reveal the truth to Gostanzo.

4. *advantage*] favourable opportunity (*OED* n. 2d), as in Shakespeare's Venus asking Adonis for a kiss, 'let not advantage slip' (l. 129).

9. *your anger's fear*] fear of your anger.

10–18.] Marc Antonio is stating all this as a hypothetical, to set Gostanzo up for what he believes will be a bigger fall when he reveals it to be true.

SC. I]   ALL FOOLS   147

Marc Antonio.   Oh, the good God of gods,
   How blind is pride! What eagles we are still
   In matters that belong to other men,   25
   What beetles in our own. I tell you, knight,
   It is confessed to be as I have told you,
   And Gratiana is by young Rinaldo
   And your white son brought to me as his wife.
   How think you now, sir?
Gostanzo.   Even just as before,   30
   And have more cause to think honest credulity
   Is a true lodestone to draw on decrepity.
   You have a heart too open to embrace
   All that your ear receives. Alas, good man.
   All this is but a plot for entertainment,   35
   Within your house, for your poor son's young wife
   My house, without huge danger, cannot hold.
Marc Antonio.   Is't possible? What danger, sir, I pray?
Gostanzo.   I'll tell you, sir. 'Twas time to take her thence.
   My son, that last day you saw could not frame   40
   His looks to entertain her, now, by'r Lady,
   Is grown a courtier. For myself, unseen,
   Saw when he courted her, embraced and kissed her,
   And, I can tell you, left not much undone
   That was the proper office of your son.   45

---

23. *God of gods*] This sounds pagan, but see Psalms, 136.2: 'Praise ye the God of gods: for his mercy endureth forever'.

26. *What beetles in our own*] how blind we are to our own pridefulness. The blindness of the beetle, like the sharp vision of the eagle (l. 24), is proverbial (Dent B219). In his *World of Wonders* (1607), Henri Estienne sarcastically praises the Italian critical fashion for disparaging Latin poets: 'if it were true, he only among all the students of poets and poetry for these divers hundred years, was sharp sighted and eagle eyed, the rest as blind as moles and beetles' (sig. B1r). Marc Antonio's lines are close to those of Menedemus in *The Self-Tormenter*: 'Ye gods, it's obviously a law of human nature that men are better at seeing and deciding about other people's affairs than their own' (502–5).

29. *white son*] proverbial for a beloved or favourite son (Dent B579).

31–2. *honest ... decripity*] Parrott's eloquent gloss is 'credulity hastens the coming of imbecile decrepitude as the magnet draws iron'.

32. *lodestone*] magnetic oxide of iron, figuratively anything that attracts (*OED* n.).

35–7. Gostanzo now turns the tables on Marc Antonio, or so he thinks, by revealing that Gratiana is still Fortunio's wife, and that Valerio and Rinaldo pretended otherwise to get her into Marc Antonio's house. Fortunio is to remain with Gostanzo in order to get more schooling in being an obedient son.

36–7. *wife / My house*] The word 'whom' after 'wife' is implied (cf. Abbott 244).

Marc Antonio. What world is this?
Gostanzo.   I told this to Rinaldo,
　　Advising him to fetch her from my house.
　　And his young wit, not knowing where to lodge her
　　Unless with you, and saw that could not be
　　Without some wile, I presently suggested　　　　　　　　　50
　　This quaint device, to say she was my son's.
　　And all this plot, good Marc Antonio,
　　Flowed from this fount only to blind your eyes.
Marc Antonio. Out of how sweet a dream have you awaked me!
　　By heaven, I durst have laid my part in heaven　　　　　55
　　All had been true, it was so lively handled,
　　And drawn with such a seeming face of truth.
　　Your son had cast a perfect veil of grief
　　Over his face, for his so rash offence
　　To seal his love with act of marriage　　　　　　　　　　60
　　Before his father had subscribed his choice.
　　My son—my circumstance lessening the fact—
　　Entreating me to break the matter to you,
　　And, joining my effectual persuasions
　　With your son's penitent submission,　　　　　　　　　　65
　　Appease your fury, I at first assented,
　　And now expect their coming to that purpose.
Gostanzo. 'Twas well, 'twas well. Seem to believe it still.
　　Let art end what credulity began;
　　When they come, suit your words and looks to theirs,　70
　　Second my sad son's feigned submission.
　　And see in all points how my brain will answer
　　His disguised grief with a set countenance

---

53. your] *Reed;* our *Q.*

50–1. *I presently ... quaint device*] Of course, Gostanzo takes credit for Rinaldo's idea.
53. *this fount*] Gostanzo might touch his head as he speaks (Parrott).
55. *laid my part in heaven*] wagered my soul (*OED* lay v.¹ 12a).
56. *lively*] in a lifelike manner, vividly (*OED* adv. 2a).
59–63.] At 3.1.97, Rinaldo told Gostanzo that he would 'fetch' Gratiana before approaching Marc Antonio with the new ruse, and we now see that Valerio and Fortunio participated in the gulling as well.
62. *my circumstance ... fact*] Marc Antonio's original 'circumstance' was his belief that Fortunio married without permission. His forgiving reaction lessens the seriousness of the offence ('the fact'), so he would be in the right frame of mind to appeal to Gostanzo on Valerio's behalf.
64. *effectual*] powerful (*OED* adj.).
66. *Appease*] to appease. Omission of 'to' in the infinitive is common in early modern texts (Abbott 349).

Of rage and choler. Now observe and learn
To school your son by me.
  [*Enter*] RINALDO, VALERIO, GRATIANA.
Marc Antonio.   On with your mask.   75
  Here come the other maskers, sir.
Rinaldo. [*To Valerio*]   Come on, I say,
  Your father with submission will be calmed;
  Come on; down o' your knees.
Gostanzo. [*To Valerio*]   Villain, durst thou
  Presume to gull thy father? Dost thou not
  Tremble to see my bent and cloudy brows   80
  Ready to thunder on thy graceless head,
  And with the bolt of my displeasure cut
  The thread of all my living from thy life
  For taking thus a beggar to thy wife?
Valerio. Father, if that part I have in your blood,   85
  If tears, which so abundantly distil
  Out of my inward eyes, and for a need
  Can drown these outward—[*Aside to Rinaldo*] Lend me thy
     handkercher—
  And being indeed as many drops of blood
  Issuing from the creator of my heart,   90
  Be able to beget so much compassion,
  Not on my life, but on this lovely dame.
  Whom I hold dearer!
Gostanzo.   Out upon thee, villain!
Marc Antonio. Nay, good Gostanzo, think you are a father.
Gostanzo. I will not hear a word. Out, out upon thee!   95

74.1. SD. *Enter*] Reed; *Intrant* Q.   76. SD.] *This ed.; not in* Q.
78. SD.] *This ed.; not in* Q.   88. SD.] *Parrott¹; not in* Q.

---

83. *living*] estate and possessions (*OED* n. 4).

85–92.] The crux of this difficult speech lies in the word 'creator'. Parrott persuasively argues that Valerio is pretending to appeal to Gostanzo by ties of blood that have their origin in 'the creator (i.e., begetter) of his heart, that is, from his father himself' (p. 720). Chapman, as he does in Curio's speech, might be parodying Lyly. An augmentation of outward tears with inner tears of blood is found in *Mother Bombie*, although there the situation is reversed. The father Prisius tells his daughter Livia that one day she will know the pain of ungrateful children: 'With tears trickling down thy cheeks and drops of blood falling from thy heart, thou wilt in uttering of thy mind wish them rather unborn than unnatural' (1.3.402–5).

92. *Not on ... but on*] Compassion was often given 'on' someone, as in Epicene's appeal to Morose, 'Good sir, have some compassion on me' (5.4.157).

Wed without my advice, my love, my knowledge,
Ay, and a beggar, too, a trull, a blowze!
Rinaldo. [*Aside to Gostanzo*] You thought not so last day, when you
   offered her
A twelvemonths' board for one night's lodging with her.
Gostanzo. [*Aside to Rinaldo*] Go to, no more of that. Peace, good
   Rinaldo.   100
It is a fault that only she and you know.
Rinaldo. [*Aside to Gostanzo*] Well, sir, go on, I pray.
Gostanzo. [*To Valerio*]   Have I, fond wretch,
With utmost care and labour brought thee up,
Ever instructing thee, omitting never
The office of a kind and careful father,   105
To make thee wise and virtuous like thy father,
And hast thou in one act everted all,
Proclaimed thyself to all the world a fool,
To wed a beggar?
Valerio.   Father, say not so.
Gostanzo. Nay, she's thy own. Here, rise, fool. Take her to thee,   110
Live with her still. I know thou countst thyself
Happy in soul only in winning her.
Be happy still. Here, take her hand, enjoy her.
Would not a son hazard his father's wrath.
His reputation in the world, his birthright,   115
To have but such a mess of broth as this?
Marc Antonio. Be not so violent, I pray you, good Gostanzo.
Take truce with passion, license your sad son

---

98. SD.] *Parrott*[1]; *not in Q.*   100. SD.] *Parrott*[1]; *not in Q.*
102. SD. *Aside to Gostanzo*] *Parrott*[1]; *not in Q. To Valerio*] *This ed.; not in Q.*

---

97. *a trull, a blowze*] Both words are common epithets for a low-born or sluttish woman.

98–101.] Gostanzo's supposed attempt to buy a night's enjoyment with Gratiana seems shocking, although in Roman comedy there is nothing unusual in a father competing with his son for the same girl, especially when the son is looking to finance his relationship with a *meretrix*, rather than marry a girl from a good family. In Plautus's *Comedy of Asses*, the young Argyrippus has no objection to father Demaenetus (who put up the money) being with his love, Philaeneum, as part of the deal (830–5).

107. *everted*] overthrown, turned upside down (*OED* evert v.)

115–16. *birthright ... mess of broth*] The story of Esau's sale of his birthright for 'bread and pottage of lentils' is told in Genesis, 25.29–34. The familiar phrase 'mess of pottage' appears in the headnote to Genesis, 25 in the *Geneva Bible.*

118. *Take truce*] One often 'takes' truce in early modern texts, e.g., Hieronimo in *The Spanish Tragedy*, 'I will to ease the grief that I sustain, / Take truce with sorrow while I read on this' (3.7.30–1).

To speak in his excuse.
Gostanzo.   What! What excuse?
    Can any orator in this case excuse him?   120
    What can he say? What can be said of any?
Valerio. Alas, sir, hear me. All that I can say
    In my excuse is but to show love's warrant.
Gostanzo. [*Aside*] Notable wag!
Valerio.   I know I have committed
    A great impiety, not to move you first   125
    Before the dame I meant to make my wife.
    Consider what I am, yet young and green.
    Behold what she is. Is there not in her,
    Ay, in her very eye, a power to conquer
    Even age itself and wisdom? Call to mind,   130
    Sweet father, what yourself being young have been.
    Think what you may be, for I do not think
    The world so far spent with you but you may
    Look back on such a beauty, and I hope
    To see you young again, and to live long   135
    With young affections. Wisdom makes a man
    Live young forever, and where is this wisdom
    If not in you? Alas, I know not what
    Rests in your wisdom to subdue affections,
    But I protest it wrought with me so strongly   140
    That I had quite been drowned in seas of tears
    Had I not taken hold in happy time
    Of this sweet hand. My heart had been consumed
    T'a heap of ashes with the flames of love
    Had it not sweetly been assuaged and cooled   145
    With the moist kisses of these sugared lips.
Gostanzo. [*Aside to Marc Antonio*] O puissant wag, what huge large
    thongs he cuts

---

147. SD.] *Parrott¹ (subst.); not in Q.*

121. *of any*] by anyone (Parrott).

124. *Notable*] Gostanzo's delight in the act Valerio is putting on brings Theseus's approval of *Pyramus and Thisbe* to mind: 'and so it is, truly, very notably discharged' (5.1.360–1).

125. *move*] approach, appeal to (*OED* v. 31a).

140. *wrought*] raged (*OED* work v. 34).

147. *puissant*] mighty, powerful. Gostanzo's enthusiastic playing along with what he thinks is Valerio's tall story is richly ironic.

147–8. *what huge ... leather*] a Dutch proverb, explained by Erasmus as one 'in circulation among the common people of my native country, by which they mean that everybody is less economical of other people's property than his own' (*Adages*, 33: 123). Gostanzo is admiring Valerio's enthusiasm in turning the raw material of Fortunio's supposed marriage to Gratiana into high drama.

      Out of his friend Fortunio's stretching leather.
Marc Antonio. [*Aside to Gostanzo*] He knows he does it but to blind
      my eyes.
Gostanzo. [*Aside*] O excellent! These men will put up anything.   150
Valerio. Had I not had her, I had lost my life,
      Which life indeed I would have lost before
      I had displeased you, had I not received it
      From such a kind, a wise, and honoured father.
Gostanzo. [*Aside*] Notable boy!
Valerio.   Yet do I here renounce   155
      Love, life, and all, rather than one hour longer
      Endure to have your love eclipsed from me.
Gratiana. O I can hold no longer! If thy words
      Be used in earnest, my Valerio,
      Thou woundst my heart, but I know 'tis in jest.   160
Gostanzo. [*Aside*] No, I'll be sworn she has her liripoop too.
Gratiana. [*To Valerio*] Didst thou not swear to love me, spite of
      father
      And all the world, that nought should sever us
      But death itself?
Valerio.   I did, but if my father
      Will have his son forsworn, upon his soul   165
      The blood of my black perjury shall lie,
      For I will seek his favour though I die.
Gostanzo. No, no, live still, my son. Thou well shalt know
      I have a father's heart. Come, join your hands.
      Still keep thy vows, and live together still,   170

---

149. SD.] *Parrott¹ (subst.); not in Q.*   150. SD.] *Parrott¹; not in Q.*
155. SD.] *Parrott¹; not in Q.*   161. SD.] *Parrott¹; not in Q.*
162. SD.] *This ed.; not in Q.*

149] The first 'he' is Fortunio, the second Valerio.

150. *These men will put up with anything*] Gullible men like Marc Antonio would believe anything. The irony here is delicious, since what Mark Antonio believes is actually the truth.

161. *she has her liripoop*] she has learned her part. A 'liripoop', from the Latin *liripipium*, is the hood worn with an academic gown. In idiomatic use, it is something to be learned or spoken, one's role or lesson (*OED* n. 2a). Lyly is fond of the word: it is found in *Sappho and Phao, Mother Bombie*, and his anti-Martinist tract *Pap with an Hatchet* (Bevington, ed., *Sappho*, p. 215).

162. *spite*] in spite. The preposition was often omitted in this period.

164–71.] This is a key moment in the play. Valerio brings his portrayal of the penitent, dutiful son to a new level in telling Gratiana he would rather die than displease his father. Enjoying the performance so much that he cannot resist joining in, Gostanzo decides to play the kindly father, and gives his blessing to Valerio's marriage.

  Till cruel death set foot betwixt you both.
Valerio. Oh, speak you this in earnest?
Gostanzo.   Ay, by heaven.
Valerio. And never to recall it?
Gostanzo.   Not till death.
Rinaldo. Excellent sir, you have done like yourself.
  What would you more, Valerio?
Valerio.   Worshipful father!   175
Rinaldo. [*To Valerio*] Come, sir, come you in, and celebrate your
  joys.
          Exeunt all save the old men.
Gostanzo. O Marc Antonio,
  Had I not armed you with an expectation,
  Would not this make you pawn your very soul,
  The wench had been my son's wife?
Marc Antonio.   Yes, by heaven!   180
  A knavery thus effected might deceive
  A wiser man than I, for I, alas,
  Am no good politician. Plain believing,
  Simple honesty, is my policy still.
Gostanzo. The visible marks of folly, honesty   185
  And quick credulity his younger brother.
  I tell you, Marc Antonio, there is much
  In that young boy, my son.
Marc Antonio.   Not much honesty,
  If I may speak without offence to his father.
Gostanzo. Oh, God, you cannot please me better, sir.   190
  H'as honesty enough to serve his turn.
  The less honesty ever the more wit.
  But go you home, and use your daughter kindly.
  Meantime I'll school your son, and do you still

---

176. SD.] *This ed.; not in Q.*

---

172. *Oh, speak ... in earnest?*] The actor playing Valerio might do a double-take upon hearing what Gostanzo his just said, instantly drop the histrionic antics of his previous speeches, and ask this question in a calm, offhand manner. Chapman gives his actors wonderful opportunities, not always apparent when reading the play.
  174. *you have ... yourself*] Naturally, Gostanzo would take this as a compliment, not realising Rinaldo means 'like yourself' as 'like the perfect fool you are'.
  178. *an expectation*] foreknowledge of what to expect.
  181. *effected*] carried out, accomplished (*OED* effect v. 1).
  185–6.] Gostanzo believes that honesty and credulity are the visible characteristics of folly. Autolycus delivers this proverb more clearly in *The Winter's Tale*: 'What a fool honesty is, and trust his sworn brother' (4.4.595–6; Dent H539.1).
  193. *your daughter*] your daughter-in-law, Gratiana. As noted above about 'sister' (3.1.35n.), the suffix 'in-law' was used in this period, but normally 'daughter' sufficed.

  Dissemble what you know. Keep off your son. 195
  The wench at home must still be my son's wife.
  Remember that, and be you blinded still.
Marc Antonio. You must remember, too, to let your son
  Use his accustomed visitations,
  Only to blind my eyes.
Gostanzo.   He shall not fail. 200
  But still take you heed, have a vigilant eye
  On that sly child of mine, for, by this light,
  He'll be too bold with your son's forehead else.
Marc Antonio. Well, sir, let me alone. I'll bear a brain.
               Exeunt.

      Enter VALERIO, RINALDO.

Valerio. Come, they are gone.
Rinaldo.   Gone? They were far gone here. 205
Valerio. Gulled I my father, or gulled he himself?
  Thou toldst him Gratiana was my wife,
  I have confessed it, he has pardoned it.
Rinaldo. Nothing more true, enough can witness it.
  And therefore when he comes to learn the truth— 210
  As certainly, for all these sly disguises,
  Time will strip truth into her nakedness—
  Thou hast good plea against him to confess

---

195. *Keep off your son*] keep Fortunio away from Gratiana.
197. *be you blinded still*] carry on the pretence.
203.] He will place horns on your son's head.
204. *I'll bear a brain*] I'll keep my wits about me. This proverbial phrase (Dent B596) often refers specifically to a good memory, as it does here and in the Nurse's recollection of the day Juliet was weaned, 'Nay, I do bear a brain' (1.3.29). At about the time Chapman was writing *All Fools*, Dekker was working on a play for the Admiral's Men called *Bear a Brain*, which, like much of Dekker's work, is lost (Foakes, p. 123).
204.2 SD.] Although the stage might be cleared momentarily, there is no scene change. The dialogue between Valerio and Rinaldo shows that they have been listening by the door, and could even have poked their heads in from time to time.
205. *far gone*] Rinaldo plays on 'far gone' in the sense of 'mad' or 'befuddled', as Polonius says of Hamlet, 'a said I was a fishmonger. 'A is far gone' (2.2.188–9).
209. *enough can witness it*] Enough people saw what happened and would be able to attest to it.
212.] Rinaldo's description of truth calls to mind Matthew, 10.16: 'there is nothing covered, that shall not be disclosed, nor hid, that shall not be known'. In Greene's *Mamillia*, we read, 'he that loves, casts beyond the moon, and especially he that dissembles: and craft had need of cloaking, where truth is ever naked' (2: 94).

SC. I]   ALL FOOLS   155

  The honoured action, and to claim his pardon.
Valerio. 'Tis true, for all was done, he deeply swore,   215
  Out of his heart.
Rinaldo.   He has much faith the whiles
  That swore a thing so quite against his heart.
Valerio. Why, this is policy.
Rinaldo.   Well, see you repair
  To Gratiana daily, and enjoy her
  In her true kind. And now we must expect   220
  The resolute and ridiculous divorce
  Cornelio hath sued against his wedlock.
Valerio. I think it be not so; the ass dotes on her.
Rinaldo. It is too true, and thou shalt answer it
  For setting such debate 'twixt man and wife.   225
  See, we shall see the solemn manner of it.

   Enter CORNELIO, CLAUDIO, NOTARY, [CURIO,] GAZETTA,
      BELLANORA, GRATIANA.

Bellanora. Good Signor Cornelio, let us poor gentlewomen entreat you
  to forbear.
Cornelio. Talk no more to me, I'll not be made cuckold in my own
  house. Notary, read me the divorce.   230
Gazetta. My dear Cornelio, examine the cause better before you
  condemn me.
Cornelio. Sing to me no more, siren, for I will hear thee no more. I will
  take no compassion on thee.

226.1. SD. CURIO] *This ed.; Page* Q.

 214. *The honoured action*] his marriage.
 216. *the whiles*] an archaic form of 'meanwhile', as Bianca says to Hortensio in *The Taming of the Shrew*, 'Take you your instrument, play you the whiles' (3.1.22).
 218. *repair*] return, make your way (*OED* v.1 1).
 220. *In her true kind*] as your wife.
 222. *wedlock*] wife, as at 1.2.118.
 230. *Notary*] a person officially authorised to perform certain legal formalities, such as drawing up or certifying contracts and deeds (*OED* n. 1a; cf. Introduction, pp. 37–8).
  divorce] the legal document Cornelio will submit giving the grounds for divorce.
 233. *siren*] a mythical enchantress, usually described as part bird and part woman, whose song lured sailors to their destruction. In Chapman's *Odyssey*, Circe warns Ulysses, 'First to the sirens you shall come, that taint / The minds of all men whom they can acquaint / With their attractions' (12.56–8). Forewarned, Ulysses has himself lashed to the mast of his ship to hear their song, but fills his sailors' ears with wax, so they sail safely by.

Curio. Good Signor Cornelio, be not too mankind against your wife. 235
    Say you're a cuckold—as the best that is may be so at a time—
    will you make a trumpet of your own horns?
Cornelio. Go to, sir, you're a rascal. I'll give you a fee for pleading for
    her one day. Notary, do you your office.
Valerio. Go to, signor, look better to your wife and be better advised, 240
    before you grow to this extremity.
Cornelio. Extremity? Go to, I deal but too mercifully with her. If I
    should use extremity with her, I might hang her and her copes-
    mate, my drudge here. How say you. Master Notary, might I
    not do it by law? 245
Notary. Not hang 'em, but you may bring them both to a white sheet.
Cornelio. Nay, by the mass, they have had too much of the sheet
    already.
Notary. And besides, you may set capital letters on their foreheads.
Cornelio. What's that to the capital letter that's written on mine? I say, 250
    for all your law, Master Notary, that I may hang 'em. May I not
    hang him that robs me of mine honour, as well as he that robs
    me of my horse?
Notary. No, sir, your horse is a chattel.

246. SP.] *Reed; Not. Nota. Notary Q.*
250. on mine] *Collier;* in minde *Q,* in mine *Reed.*

---

235. *mankind*] fierce, infuriated (*OED* adj.²).
237. *trumpet ... horns*] similar to the proverbial 'better to put one's horns into one's pocket than blow them' (Dent H623).
243–4. *copesmate*] companion (cf. 2.1.229n.). In *Greene's Groatsworth of Wit,* a jealous rival warns a bridegroom that his new wife is about to cuckold him, and tells him where she plans to meet 'her adulterous copesmate' (12: 123).
246. *white sheet*] Sanctions for adultery were usually a matter for church courts to administer. One common penalty was for the offender to stand before the congregation wearing a white sheet. A Cambridgeshire adulterer of 1570 had to 'stand three several Sundays or half days in the church porch ... from the second peal to morning prayer until the reading of the second lesson, be clothed in a white sheet down to the ground, a white wand in his hand and two papers with great letters of abominable adultery, the one upon his back and the other upon his breast' (Greaves, p. 234).
247. *too much of the sheet*] too much time in bed, a good pun on 'sheet' in the previous line.
249. *on their foreheads*] As seen above (246n.), the guilty party may be required to wear a sign on the front and back emblazoned with letters. In a London case of 1586, an adulterer had to stand before the preacher at St Paul's in the customary white sheet, but the paper inscribed with his offence was worn on his head (Greaves, p. 235).
250. *on mine*] *Q* has 'in minde'. Some editors emend to 'in mine', but Collier's 'on mine' makes more sense. Cornelio is obviously talking about horns, shaped like a large capital C.
254. *a chattel*] a movable possession, usually defined as any property except land (*OED* n. 4a).

SC. I]   ALL FOOLS   157

Cornelio. So is honour. A man may buy it with his penny, and if I may   255
hang a man for stealing my horse, as I say, much more for
robbing me of my honour. For why? If my horse be stolen, it
may be my own fault. For why? Either the stable is not strong
enough, or the pasture not well fenced, or watched, or so forth.
But for your wife that keeps the stable of your honour, let her   260
be locked in a brazen tower, let Argus himself keep her, yet can
you never be secure of your honour. For why? She can run
through all with her serpent noddle. Besides, you may hang a
lock upon your horse, and so can you not upon your wife.

Rinaldo. But I pray you, sir, what are the presumptions on which you   265
would build this divorce?

Cornelio. Presumption enough, sir. For besides their intercourse, or
commerce of glances, that passed betwixt this cockerel-drone

---

255. *A man ... penny*] another allusion to the ease with which one could purchase social status (cf. 2.1.215n.).

261. *locked ... tower*] The woman so imprisoned was Danae, daughter of Acrisius, King of Argos. An oracle warned Acrisius that Danae's son would one day kill him, so to keep her a virgin, he put her in a tower made of brass. As one might expect, Zeus was attracted to her and paid a visit in the form of a shower of gold; the fruit of this liaison was Perseus, who did indeed kill Acrisius. Chapman is alluding to Terence's most notorious 'naughty bit' from *The Eunuch*. Chaerea, who pretends to be a eunuch in order to get access to the girl he loves, ends up being assigned to help prepare her bath. He later relates, 'the girl sat in her room, looking up at a picture. The picture showed how Jupiter once sent down a shower of gold into Danae's lap, as the story goes. I began to look at the picture myself, too, and because he got up much the same trick once upon a time, my spirit rejoiced within me all the more, to think that a god had turned himself into a man and climbed secretly over another man's roof to seduce a woman through the skylight ... was I, a mere man, not to do the same?' (ll. 584–90; cf. Introduction, p. 8).

261. *keep*] guard.

263. *serpent noddle*] serpent's head, probably a reference to Mercury's 'magic wand', or caduceus. To escape from Argus as Io did (cf. 1.2.70–1n.), the adulteress can borrow Mercury's weapon and 'run through' (stab) her captor's hundred eyes. Originally, as the emblem of Asklepios, god of medicine, this staff had a single serpent coiled around it, but later, with two serpents, it became Mercury's (Arikha, pp. 17–18).

265. *presumptions*] legal grounds for belief, presumptive evidence (*OED* n. 4). Under English law and custom, Cornelio would need to provide witnesses to testify that his wife had committed adultery.

268. *cockerel-drone*] young layabout. A cockerel is a common metaphor for young man. Although the drone has the same function in the beehive, impregnating the female, as does the cock in the barnyard, ancient and early modern references always allude to its apparent laziness. In fact, Fitzherbert's *Book of Husbandry* does not even recognise the drone as a male: 'And also there is a bee called a drone, and she is greater than any other bee, and they will eat the honey, and gather nothing: and therefore they would be killed, and it is a saying, that she hath lost her sting, and then she will not labour as the other do' (p. 52).

158   ALL FOOLS   [ACT 4

and her, at my table the last Sunday night at supper, their winks, their becks—*Dieu garde!*— their treads a' the toe—as, by heaven, I swear she trod once upon my toe instead of his—this is chiefly to be noted, the same night she would needs lie alone, and the same night her dog barked. Did not you hear him, Valerio? 270
Valerio. And understand him too, I'll be sworn of a book.
Cornelio. Why, very good; if these be not manifest presumptions now, let the world be judge. Therefore, without more ceremony, Master Notary, pluck out your instrument. 275
Notary. I will, sir, if there be no remedy.
Cornelio. Have you made it strong in law, Master Notary? Have you put in words enough? 280
Notary. I hope so, sir; it has taken me a whole skin of parchment, you see.
Cornelio. Very good; and is egress and regress in?
Notary. I'll warrant you, sir, it is *forma juris.*
Cornelio. Is there no hole to be found in the orthography? 285
Notary. None in the world, sir.

---

270. *becks*] beckoning gestures (*OED* n.²)
Dieu garde!] God preserve us!
treads ... toe] a repeat of the line used earlier (cf. 2.1.255n).
271. *she trod ... my toe*] Without a witness, Cornelio's testimony, that Gazetta mistakenly stepped on his toe while playing footsy with her lover, will not be acceptable as grounds for a divorce (cf. Introduction, pp. 38–9).
272. *lie alone*] sleep in a separate room.
273. *her dog barked*] Ovid's appeal to Corinna's husband must have been one of Chapman's favourite passages in the *Amores* (cf. 3.1.284-8n.). Another suggestion for keeping watch on her, in order to make things more challenging, is 'Why not start locking up at night? / Why not ask who it is comes tapping, ever so softly, / On your front door—or why it is the dogs / Start barking at midnight' (2.19.38–41).
274. *sworn of a book*] In taking an oath, one would kiss the Bible. Lipsalve, Purge, and Gudgeon must 'kiss the book' (l. 1995) as they testify to Mistress Purge's supposed adultery in *The Family of Love*, and of course Shakespeare plays on the expression in *The Tempest*, the book being Stephano's bottle of sack.
277. *instrument*] in law, a formal document whereby a right is created or confirmed, or a fact recorded (*OED* n. 4). The pun on 'penis' is also found in Hortensio's hilarious attempt to teach Bianca the lute: 'Madam, before you touch the instrument / To learn the order of my fingering, / I must begin with rudiments of art' (*Shrew* 3.1.64–6).
283. *egress and regress*] The bawdy punning on legal terms continues. The phrase 'ingress, egress, and regress' comes from property law, and refers to the right to enter, leave, and return.
284. *forma juris*] according to law. In Dekker and Webster's *Northward Ho*, Mayberry asks 'if a man be ... divorced *forma juris*, whether he may have an action or no, 'gainst those that make horns at him' (1.1.170-2).

SC. I] ALL FOOLS 159

Cornelio. You have written s*unt* with an *s*, have you not?
Notary. Yes, that I have.
Cornelio. You have done the better for quietness' sake. And are none
  of the authentical dashes over the head left out? If there be.   290
  Master Notary, an error will lie out.
Notary. Not for a dash over head, sir, I warrant you, if I should oversee.
  I have seen that tried in *Butiro et Caseo*, in Butler and Cason's
  case, *decimo sexto* of Duke Anonimo.
Rinaldo. You've gotten a learned notary, Signor Cornelio.   295
Cornelio. He's a shrewd fellow indeed. I had as lief have his head in a
  matter of felony or treason as any notary in Florence. Read out,
  Master Notary. Hearken you, mistress. Gentlemen, mark, I
  beseech you.
All. We will all mark you, sir, I warrant you.   300
Notary. I think it would be something tedious to read all, and therefore,
  gentlemen, the sum is this. That you, Signor Cornelio, gentleman, for divers and sundry weighty and mature considerations
  you especially moving, specifying all the particulars of your

---

290. out] *Q;* on't *Parrott¹ (conj. Gilchrist).*   293. *et*] *Evans;* & *Q;* and *Reed.*

287. sunt *with an s*] *Sunt* is part of a basic precept of Roman law, *pacta sunt servanda*, 'all contracts must be kept'. Cornelio wants to make sure *sunt* is spelled with an 's' and not a 'c', which would indeed put a 'hole' in the orthography. The same joke occurs in Fletcher and Massinger's *The Spanish Curate*, when Diego, a sexton, is dictating a fake will as part of a swindle, and makes a bequest for the promotion of 'true orthography … They write s*unt* with a *c*, which is abominable' (4.5.97–8).

290. *authentical … head*] 'Authentical' is a variant form of authentic, in this context meaning 'legally valid' (*OED* adj. 2a). Parrott surmises that 'dashes' is a reference to the diacritical mark ~, known as a tilde, placed above ('over the head') of a vowel to indicate contraction of a following m or n. Cornelio fears that if just one ~ is missing, it could render the document invalid.

291. *lie out*] stand out visibly. Parrott emends this to 'lie on't', but Q's 'out' makes sufficient sense.

292. *Not for … should oversee*] No court will invalidate the bill for a missing dash if I am pleading the case.

293. Butiro et Caseo] Butter and Cheese, which the Notary takes to mean Butler and Cason. Parrott notes that this could be a variant on an old joke ascribed to the possibly fictional court jester John Scoggin, who once referred to *Brutum et Cassium* (Brutus and Cassius) as 'Butyrum et Caseum'.

294. decimo sexto *of Duke Anonimo*] in the sixteenth year of Duke Anonimo's reign.

296. *I had as lief*] I had rather, an archaic form from Old English found frequently in early modern drama.

297. *Florence*] The city is explicitly named as the setting twice, here and at 5.2.186.

300. *We … mark you*] another play on 'mark'. We will listen to you, and mark (brand) you for a fool (cf. 3.1.305).

wife's enormities in a schedule hereunto annexed, the transcript 305
whereof is in your own tenure, custody, occupation, and keeping:
That for these, the aforesaid premises, I say, you renounce,
disclaim, and discharge Gazetta from being your leeful or your
lawful wife, and that you eftsoons divide, disjoin, separate,
remove, and finally eloign, sequester, and divorce her, from your 310
bed and your board. That you forbid her all access, repair, egress
or regress, to your person or persons, mansion or mansions,
dwellings, habitations, remanences, or abodes, or to any shop,
cellar, sollar, easement's chamber, dormer, and so forth, now
in the tenure, custody, occupation, or keeping of the said Cor- 315
nelio, notwithstanding all former contracts, covenants, bargains,
conditions, agreements, compacts, promises, vows, affiances,
assurances, bonds, bills, indentures, poll deeds, deeds of gift,
defeasances, feoffments, endowments, vouchers, double vouchers, privy entries, actions, declarations, explications, rejoinders, 320

308–9. *leeful or your lawful*] 'Leeful' is an obsolete form of 'lawful' (*OED* adj.). This comical repetition also appears in Lording's *Ram Alley*, with Throat's 'She is my leeful lawfull, and my true / Married wife' (ll. 2389–90).

309. *eftsoons*] moreover, likewise (*OED* adv.).

310. *eloign*] as a legal term, to remove, send away (*OED* v. 3).

sequester] set aside, separate (*OED* v.1).

310–11. *your bed and your board*] divorce *a mensa et thoro* (from table and bed). This was more of a legal separation than a divorce as we know it, since the husband and wife could not remarry (cf. Introduction, p. 38).

313. *remanences*] matters that remain (*OED* n.).

314. *sollar*] upper room, attic (*OED* n.¹).

easement's chamber] the privy, with a quibble on easement as the legal right to the use of another's property. A fifteenth-century will gives 'the said Jenete ... easement of the kitchen to make in her meat, and easement of the well in the yard' (Tymms, p. 23).

dormer] sleeping chamber, dormitory (1st cit. *OED* n.).

317. *affiances*] pledges of faith, most often marriage contracts (*OED* n.).

318. *poll deeds*] usually written as 'deed poll'. Deeds were written on paper or parchment which was either 'indented' (cut to a serrated edge) or 'polled' (cut to a straight edge). A deed or declaration made and executed by only one party was usually written on polled paper; agreements between two parties were usually on indented paper.

319. *defeasances*] documents rendering a former act, existing condition, or right null and void (*OED* n. 2).

foeffments] complete transfers of property to a new owner, who had the right to sell it or pass it on to his, or rarely her, heirs.

320. *explications*] detailed explanations, as in today's most common sense, so probably something like 'legal opinions' here.

320–1. *rejoinders, surrejoinders*] For 'rejoinders', see ll. 229–30 n.; a surrejoinder is the plaintiff's answer to the defendant's rejoinder.

surrejoinders, rights, interests, demands, claims, or titles whatsoever, heretofore betwixt the one and the other party, or parties,
being had, made, passed, covenanted, and agreed, from the
beginning of the world till the day of the date hereof. Given the
seventeenth of November, fifteen hundred and so forth. Here, 325
sir, you must set to your hand.
Cornelio. What else, Master Notary? I am resolute, i'faith.
Gazetta. Sweet husband, forbear.
Cornelio. Avoid, I charge thee in name of this divorce! Thou mightst
have looked to it in time, yet this I will do for thee. If thou canst 330
spy out any other man that thou wouldest cuckold, thou shalt
have my letter to him. I can do no more. More ink. Master
Notary, I write my name at large.
Notary. Here is more, sir.
Cornelio. Ah, ass, that thou could not know thy happiness till thou 335
hadst lost it! How now? My nose bleed? Shall I write in blood?
What, only three drops? 'Sfoot, this is ominous. I will not set
my hand to't now, certain. Master Notary, I like not this abodement, I will defer the setting to of my hand till the next court
day. Keep the divorce, I pray you, and the woman in your house 340
together.
All. Burn the divorce, burn the divorce!

---

337. this is] *Reed;* thi's *Q;* 'tis *Shepherd;* this's *Parrott².*
338. to't] *Reed;* toot *Q.*

---

325. *and so forth*] The document would also need to include the year of the Duke's rule (cf. 4.1.294n.) or another such formality.

327. *What else*] Of course, what else would I do? (Parrott).

329. *Avoid*] Away with you! A strong dismissal such as one would say to a witch or evil spirit, as does Ananais in *The Alchemist*, 'Avoid, Satan! / Thou art not of the light' (4.7.50–1).

333. *at large*] in large letters (*OED* large adj. phr. 5d).

335–6. *Ah, ass ... lost it*] Cornelio could be thinking of his bachelor days here, as does Thorello of *Every Man In His Humour* (*Q*) when asking himself, 'what meant I to marry? / I that before that was ranked in such content, / My mind attired in smooth silken peace, / Being free master of mine own free thoughts' (3.3.15–18). Alternatively, this might be the moment he suddenly decides he does not want a divorce after all. The nosebleed that follows may be self-inflicted with the quill pen he is holding.

336. *My nose bleed?*] A nosebleed was considered an omen of bad luck. Antonio remarks, in *The Duchess of Malfi*, 'My nose bleeds. / One that were superstitious would count / This ominous' (2.3.41–3).

338–9. *abodement*] foreboding (*OED* n.¹). In *3 Henry VI*, King Edward tells his brother Richard, 'Tush, man, abodements must not now affright us' (4.7.13).

162   ALL FOOLS   [ACT 4

Cornelio. Not so, sir, it shall not serve her turn. Master Notary,
 keep it at your peril, and, gentlemen, you may be gone, a God's
 name. What have you to do to flock about me thus? I am neither 345
 howlet nor cuckoo. Gentlewomen, for God's sake, meddle with
 your own cases; it is not fit you should haunt these public
 assemblies.
All. Well, farewell, Cornelio.
Valerio. Use the gentlewoman kindly, Master Notary. 350
Notary. As mine own wife, I assure you, sir.
       Exeunt [all but CLAUDIO *and* CORNELIO].
Claudio. Signor Cornelio, I cannot but in kindness tell you that Valerio,
 by counsel of Rinaldo, hath whispered all this jealousy into your
 ears. Not that he knew any just cause in your wife, but only to
 be revenged on you for the gull you put upon him when you 355
 drew him with his glory to touch the theorbo.
Cornelio. May I believe this?
Claudio. As I am a gentleman. And if this accident of your nose had
 not fallen out, I would have told you this before you set to your
 hand. 360
Cornelio. It may well be, yet have I cause enough
 To perfect my divorce. But it shall rest
 Till I conclude it with a counterbuff
 Given to these noble rascals. Claudio, thanks.
 What comes of this, watch but my brain a little, 365

351.1. SD.] *This ed.; Exeunt Q.*
352. Valerio] *Collier;* Balerio *Q;* Bellanora *Reed.*

345–6. *neither howlet nor cuckoo*] A howlet (often owlet) is a small or young owl, and, according to John Swan in *Speculum Mundi* (1635), 'the hate and scorn of all the birds beside'. Cornelio alludes to what modern ornithologists call 'mobbing', the flocking together of small birds to drive off predators, and believes cuckoos receive, or should receive, the same treatment. Swan says of the cuckoo, 'this is a fowl hated of every other bird ... for she doth not build any nest, but layeth her egg in the nest of another, which hatcheth it up as her own' (pp. 402, 405; cf. Introduction, pp. 22–3).
 346. *Gentlewomen*] Bellanora and Gratiana.
 353. *by counsel of Rinaldo*] Claudio is mistaken; Valerio came up with the plan on his own (cf. Introduction, pp. 39–40).
 356. *drew*] lured.
 glory] vanity, desire for honour (*OED* n.), the original meaning of the word.
 362. *perfect*] complete, carry through, often used in legal contexts (*OED* v. 1). Our usual sense of 'make perfect' is similar but not identical. The actor would emphasise the first syllable here.
 363. *counterbuff*] return blow (*OED* n.).

    And ye shall see if, like two parts in one,
    I leave not both these gullers' wits imbriered.
    Now I perceive well where the wild wind sits.
    Here's gull for gull, and wits at war with wits.   *Exeunt.*

---

366. one] *Loane (conj.);* me Q.

    366. *like two parts in one*] like two men singing the same tune. Q has 'two parts in me', but the emendation suggested by George G. Loane in 1943 offers a superior reading. Early modern music masters such as Thomas Morley give various ways of 'breaking the plainsong' to create a canon, in which 'one singeth every note and rest in the same length and order which the leading part did sing before' (Loane, p. 341; Morley, p. 96).
    367. *imbriered*] entangled in briers (1st cit. *OED* imbrier v.).

Act 5

ACT 5, SCENE 1

[*Enter* RINALDO.]

Rinaldo. Fortune, the great commandress of the world,
Hath divers ways to advance her followers.
To some she gives honour without deserving.
To other some, deserving without honour,
Some wit, some wealth, and some wit without wealth,   5
Some wealth without wit, some nor wit nor wealth
But good smock-faces, or some qualities
By nature without judgement, with the which
They live in sensual acceptation,
And make show only, without touch of substance.   10
My fortune is to win renown by gulling.
Gostanzo, Dariotto, and Cornelio,
All which suppose, in all their different kinds,

---

0. Act 5, Scene 1] Hudston (subst.); *Actus Quinti: Scena Prima* Q.
0.1. SD.] *This ed.; Rinaldo solus* Q.   1. SP.] *Parrott¹; not in* Q.

---

0. *Act 5, Scene 1*] The scene moves to a street in front of the Half Moon tavern (cf. 5.1.64).

7. *smock-faces*] smooth, effeminate faces (1st cit. *OED* n.). A smock is a woman's undergarment, and early modern playwrights delighted in using it as a syllable to create new expressions. Along with 'smock-faces', Chapman alone has given us 'smocktearers', frequenters of brothels (*Mirth*, 8.83), and 'free smockage', permanent right of tenure to run a bawdy-house (*Widow's Tears*, 1.3.184).

7–8. *some qualities ... judgement*] some seemingly attractive qualities unaccompanied by a good mind.

9. *sensual acceptation*] Here, 'sensual' implies indifference to intellectual or moral interests (*OED* adj. 4a). 'Acceptation' is synonymous with 'acceptance' (*OED* n. 2), probably chosen for metrical purposes. The idea is that others accept our smock-faced man only on the basis of his appearance, as he has nothing else to offer.

11. *gulling.*] By replacing Q's comma after 'gulling' with a full stop, Parrott clarifies the difficult syntax of the passage. Rinaldo's pride in gulling is general, not specific to his current victims. 'Gostanzo, Dariotto, and Cornelio' are the direct object of the following sentence; the subject, down at line 16, is 'I'.

13. *kinds*] ways, natures.

    Their wits entire, and in themselves one piece,
    All at one blow, my helmet yet unbruised, 15
    I have unhorsed, laid flat on earth for gulls.
    Now in what taking poor Cornelio is
    Betwixt his large divorce and no divorce,
    I long to see, and what he will resolve.
    I lay my life he cannot chew his meat, 20
    And looks much like an ape had swallowed pills,
    And all this comes of bootless jealousy.
    And see, where bootless jealousy appears.

    Enter CORNELIO.

    I'll bourd him straight.—How now, Cornelio,
    Are you resolved on the divorce, or no? 25
Cornelio. What's that to you? Look to your own affairs.
    The time requires it. Are not you engaged
    In some bonds forfeit for Valerio?
Rinaldo. Yes, what of that?
Cornelio.   Why, so am I myself,
    And both our dangers great. He is arrested 30
    On a recognisance by a usuring slave.
Rinaldo. Arrested? I am sorry with my heart.
    It is a matter may import me much.
    May not our bail suffice to free him, think you?

---

14. one] *Parrott*² *(conj.);* no *Q.*

---

    14. *one piece*] *Q* has 'no piece', but I believe Parrott's conjecture, that it was meant to read 'one piece', to be correct. Rinaldo goes on to say, figuratively, that he has 'unhorsed' Gostanzo, Dariotto, and Cornelio 'at one blow' in a joust, without any damage to his own helmet. This feat was accomplished even though they 'suppose' (l. 13) that their wits are so armed and securely mounted to be 'at one piece' with their horses. We find a nearly identical phrase in William Heminge's description of a knight in *The Fatal Contract* (1639): 'centaur-like he's anchored to his seat / As he had twinned with the proud steed he rides on, / He grows unto his saddle all one piece' (5.2.291–3).
    17. *taking*] plight (*OED* n. 4a).
    18. *large*] comprehensive, complete (*OED* adj. 6a)
    20–1. *cannot chew ... pills*] A pill can be any unpalatable substance; the lines instruct the actor playing Cornelio to have a tortured expression, as if he has a sour taste in his mouth. In *Skialetheia* (1598), Everard Guilpin describes jealousy as a 'peevish disease which all food distate' (4.41).
    22. *bootless*] incurable (*OED* adj.¹ 2).
    24. *bourd*] mock, jest with (*OED* v.¹ 2). Gabriel Harvey pays this grudging tribute to one of his nemeses, Cambridge University Vice-Chancellor Andrew Perne, in *Pierce's Supererogation*: 'no man could bear a heavy injury more lightly, or forbear a learned adversary more cunningly, or bourd a wilful friend more dryly' (p. 194).
    31. *a recognisance*] a bond requiring payment of a debt (*OED* n. 1).

Cornelio. I think it may, but I must not be seen in't, 35
Nor would I wish you, for we both are parties,
And liker far to bring ourselves in trouble
Than bear him out. I have already made
Means to the officers to sequester him
In private for a time, till some in secret 40
Might make his father understand his state,
Who would perhaps take present order for him
Rather than suffer him t'endure the shame
Of his imprisonment. Now, would you but go
And break the matter closely to his father— 45
As you can wisely do't—and bring him to him.
This were the only way to save his credit,
And to keep off a shrewd blow from ourselves.
Rinaldo. I know his father will be moved past measure.
Cornelio. Nay, if you stand on such nice ceremonies, 50
Farewell our substance. Extreme diseases
Ask extreme remedies. Better he should storm
Some little time than we be beat for ever
Under the horrid shelter of a prison.
Rinaldo. Where is the place?
Cornelio.   'Tis at the Half Moon tavern. 55
Haste, for the matter will abide no stay.

37–8. *liker far... bear him out*] far more likely to get ourselves in trouble than to get Valerio out of it.

39. *Means*] approaches, efforts (*OED* n. 3b).

41. *state*] present circumstances (*OED* n. 1).

42. *present order*] immediate steps (*OED* order n. 18).

45. *closely*] privately, confidentially (cf. 3.1.0.1 SDn.).

46. *bring him to him*] bring Gostanzo to Valerio.

47. *his credit*] Valerio's reputation (*OED* n. 2).

48. *shrewd*] harsh, as in the 'shrewd days and nights' endured by Duke Senior and his courtiers in *As You Like It* (5.4.173).

50. *nice*] silly (*OED* adj. 1b). This word had an amazing number of meanings in early use, not one of them similar to today's all-purpose word for 'good' or 'pleasant'.

51. *substance*] possessions, goods (*OED* n. 16).

52. *he*] Gostanzo.

53–4. *beat ... prison*] The image, as Parrott notes, is one of a storm beating ships into a 'horrid' harbour, i.e., one bristling with rocks.

55. *Half Moon*] Chapman's London had four Half Moon taverns: in the Strand at the lower end of Bedford Street, in Cheapside by Gutter Lane, in Aldersgate Street, and in Milk Street (Sugden).

Rinaldo. Heaven send my speed be equal with my haste! *Exit.*
Cornelio. Go, shallow scholar, you that make all gulls,
 You that can out-see clear-eyed jealousy,
 Yet make this sleight a millstone, where your brain   60
 Sticks in the midst amazed. This gull to him
 And to his fellow guller shall become
 More bitter than their baiting of my humour.
 Here at this tavern shall Gostanzo find
 Fortunio, Dariotto, Claudio,   65
 And amongst them, the ringleader, his son,
 His husband and his saint, Valerio—
 That knows not of what fashion dice are made,
 Nor ever yet looked towards a red lattice,
 Thinks his blind sire—at drinking and at dice   70
 With all their wenches, and at full discover
 His own gross folly and his son's distempers.
 And both shall know, although I be no scholar,
 Yet I have thus much Latin, as to say
 Iam sumus ergo pares.   *Exit.*   75

60–1. *Yet make... amazed*] To be able to see into, or through, a millstone was a proverbial claim to acuity (Dent M965). Cornelio's 'sleight', i.e., his trickery (*OED* n.¹), will create a millstone that even Rinaldo's brain cannot penetrate.

61. *This gull*] this trick.

64. *Here at this tavern*] Chapman continues with the technique, established in *An Humorous Day's Mirth*, of bringing everyone to an ordinary, or tavern, to settle all the different strands of the plot. Jonson does the same thing in concluding *Every Man Out of His Humour* at the Mitre.

68–70. *That knows ... blind sire*] These lines are all parenthetical comments about Valerio.

69. *red lattice*] A red lattice window was a common sign for a tavern, as Balurdo informs us in Marston's *Antonio and Mellida*: 'I am not as well known by my wit as an alehouse by a red lattice' (5.2.124–5).

70–1. *at drinking ... wenches*] meaning Fortunio, Dariotto, and Claudio, as well as Valerio.

71. *at full discover*] will fully discover. The subject of this sentence, Gostanzo, is way back at l. 64.

72. *distempers*] disturbances in the complexion, or personality, caused by an uneven mix of humours in the body.

75.] 'So now we're even.' Parrott observes that the phrase occurs three times in one of Martial's epigrams (Bk. 2, Epigram 18).

168   ALL FOOLS   [ACT 5

[ACT 5, SCENE 2]

Enter VALERIO, FORTUNIO, CLAUDIO, GRATIANA, GAZETTA, BELLANORA. *A* [Page *and a*] Drawer *or two, setting a table.*

Valerio. Set me the table here. We will shift rooms
To see if Fortune will shift chances with us.
Sit, ladies, sit. Fortunio, place thy wench,
And Claudio, place you Dariotto's mistress.
I wonder where that neat spruce slave becomes.   5
I think he was some barber's son, by th' mass.
'Tis such a pickèd fellow, not a hair
About his whole bulk but it stands in print.
Each pin hath his due place, not any point
But hath his perfect tie, fashion, and grace.   10
A thing whose soul is specially employed
In knowing where best gloves, best stockings, waistcoats
Curiously wrought, are sold, sacks milliners' shops
For all new tires and fashions, and can tell ye
What new devices of all sorts there are,   15
And that there is not in the whole Rialto
But one new-fashion'd waistcoat, or one nightcap.

---

0. Act 5, Scene 2] *Parrott¹ (subst.); no scene break in Q.*
0.1. SD.] *This ed.; Enter Valerio, Fortunio, Claudio, Page, Grat., Gazetta, Bellanora. A Drawer or two, setting a table Q.*

---

0. *Act 5, Scene 2*] Q does not start a new scene here, but the stage would be clear with Cornelio's exit, and the action moves inside the tavern.

0.2 SD *Page*] a scullery-page (*OED* page n.¹ 2b), not the boy who gives the elaborate speech in Act 3 (cf. 5.2.43n.). Q's entry direction has 'Page' following 'Claudio', but he would enter with the other employees of the Half Moon.

2. *shift chances with us*] change our luck. Valerio must have been gambling, and losing, in another room, and hopes that moving here will improve things.

5. *where ... becomes*] what's become of Dariotto? In *The Blind Beggar of Alexandria*, Aegiale asks, 'Ah, my Cleanthes, where art thou become?' (1.8).

neat spruce] Both words meant elegant, or dapper, in this period.

7. *pickèd*] synonymous with 'neat' and 'spruce'. Holofernes of *Love's Labour's Lost* believes Don Armado to be 'too picked, too spruce, too affected' (5.1.13–14).

8. *in print*] in the height of fashion. 'In print' was a common phrase applicable to many situations, indicating that something was done in a precise and perfect way.

9–10.] Decorative pins were a popular fashion accessory; points were pieces of ribbon or lace used for attaching hose to a doublet.

10. *tie*] knot (*OED* n. 1).

14. *tires*] attire, apparel, often written in the plural (*OED* tire n.¹ 2).

16. *Rialto*] the mercantile district of Venice, where Shylock plies his trade. This has the appearance of a 'howler' in a play supposedly set in Florence, but by Chapman's time 'Rialto' had become a generic term for any business centre. In William Rowley's

SC. 2]   ALL FOOLS   169

    One pair of gloves pretty or well perfumed,
    And from a pair of gloves of half a crown
    To twenty crowns, will to a very scute   20
    Smell out the price. And for these womanly parts
    He is esteemed a witty gentleman.
                             Enter DARIOTTO

Fortunio. See, where he comes.
Dariotto.   God save you, lovely ladies.
Valerio. Ay, well said, lovely Paris. Your wall-eye
    Must ever first be gloating on men's wives.   25
    You think to come upon us, being half drunk,
    And so to part the freshest man among us.
    But you shall overtake us, I'll be sworn.
Dariotto. Tush, man, where are your dice? Let's fall to them.
Claudio. We have been at 'em.—Drawer, call for more.   30
Valerio. First let's have wine. Dice have no perfect edge
    Without the liquid whetstone of the syrup.
Fortunio. True, and to welcome Dariotto's lateness,
    He shall unpledged carouse one crownèd cup
    To all these ladies' health.
Dariotto.   I am well pleased.   35
Valerio. Come on, let us vary our sweet time
    With sundry exercises. Boy, tobacco!
    And, drawer, you must get us music too.

---

prose tale, *A Search for Money* (1609), the narrator and his friend search an unnamed city in search of Money, personified as a wandering knight. After stops at such places as a barber's, a tavern, a brothel, and a usurer's house, they 'were come to the Rialto', where they heard 'the news from many lands', but alas, no tidings of the 'lost traveller' (p. 22).

    20. *scute*] *scudo*, an Italian coin, of different value in different states (Collier).
    21. *parts*] qualities (*OED* n. 15).
    24. *Paris*] As Menelaus is the father of all cuckolds (2.1.281n.), Paris is the father of all cuckolders.
    wall-eye] a name given to various afflictions, one of which is having one eye appear to have a divergent squint, or 'gloat' (cf. following n.).
    25. *gloating*] looking with a furtive or sidelong glance (*OED* gloat v. 1).
    26. *half drunk*] One assumes that this means Dariotto has already been drinking heavily, but Valerio is saying that he has only had half as much as the others.
    27. *part ... us*] depart the soberest man here.
    31–2. *Dice ... syrup*] A dice game is no fun without drinking.
    34.] A crowned cup is one filled to the brim, and Dariotto must drink it 'unpledged', without the formality of the others joining him as a gesture of good will. This way he will catch up with everyone else more quickly.

170 ALL FOOLS [ACT 5

  Call's in a cleanly noise. The slaves grow lousy.
Drawer. You shall have such as we can get you, sir. *Exit.* 40
Dariotto. Let's have some dice, I pray thee. [*Dariotto inspects the dice
  given him.*] They are cleanly.
Valerio. Page, let me see that leaf!
Page.   It is not leaf, sir.
  'Tis pudding-cane tobacco.
Valerio.   But I mean
  Your linstock, sir. What leaf is that, I pray?
Page. I pray you see, sir, for I cannot read. 45
Valerio. 'Sfoot, a rank, stinking satire. This had been
  Enough to have poisoned every man of us.
Dariotto. And now you speak of that, my boy once lighted
  A pipe of cane tobacco with a piece
  Of a vile ballad, and I'll swear I had 50
  A singing in my head a whole week after.
Valerio. Well, th' old verse is, *A potibus incipe io-c-um.*

41. SD.] *This ed.; not in Q.* 50. vile] *Reed;* vild *Q.*

 39. *cleanly noise*] good musicians. Valerio means 'cleanly' in the sense of skilled, or artful (*OED* adj. 5a); 'noise' can be either music, or, as here, the musicians who play it (*OED* n. 3). The best-known musical ensemble in Elizabethan drama would be 'Sneak's noise' of *2 Henry IV* (2.4.11).
 41 *cleanly*] here, not 'loaded' or otherwise adulterated (*OED* clean adj. 13 a). Gilbert Walker's *Manifest Detection of Dice Play* (1532) lists no less than fourteen varieties of loaded dice (pp. 154–5, 350).
 43.] Normally, a scullery-page would be addressed as 'boy', as he is at l. 37. He is 'page' here so that Valerio can pun on 'leaf'. As Parrott notes, Chapman makes the same verbal play in *Sir Giles Goosecap*, when Will, one of Eugenia's two pages, describes himself and his colleague Jack to their mistress as 'your two little pages, which are less by half than two leaves' (2.1.238–9).
 43. *pudding-cane tobacco*] tobacco compressed and made into rolls, resembling a pudding, or sausage. In his *Gull's Horn-Book*, Dekker advises the fashionable gallant, 'be able to discourse whether your cane or your pudding be sweetest, and which pipe has the best bore, and which burns black, which breaks in the burning' (2: 265).
 44. *linstock*] a staff about three feet long, having a forked head to hold a lighted match (usually made from cotton soaked in saltpetre and dipped into melted sulphur), for igniting the priming powder in a cannon (cf. Edelman, *Military*, p. 208). A smoker's linstock could be any burning piece of paper. Here it is a page from a 'stinking satire' (l. 46).
 48–51.] Dariotto's story of a man who lit his pipe with a piece of paper that had an old ballad printed on it is identical to the joke Ben Jonson shared with Willliam Drummond, as recorded in the *Informations*: 'One who had fired a pipe of tobacco with a ballad the next day having a sore head, swore he had a great singing in his head, and he thought it was the ballad' (372–3).
 52. *A potibus incipe io-c-um*] Let the drinks begin the joking (Hudston).

SC. 2]   ALL FOOLS   171

    Enter Drawer, *with wine and a cup.*

Valerio. Drawer, fill out this gentleman's carouse,
 And harden him for our society.
Dariotto. Well, ladies, here is to your honoured healths. 55
Fortunio. What, Dariotto, without hat or knee?
Valerio. Well said, Fortunio. [*To Dariotto*] O you're a rare courtier.
 Your knee, good signor, I beseech your knee.
Dariotto. Nay, pray you, let's take it by degrees,
 Valerio, on our feet first, for this 60
 Will bring's too soon upon our knees.
Valerio.   Sir, there
 Are no degrees of order in a tavern.
 Here you must, I charge ye, run all ahead.
 'Slight, courtier, down!
 I hope you are no elephant. You have joints? 65
Dariotto. Well, sir, here's to the ladies, on my knees.
Valerio. I'll be their pledge.

    Enter GOSTANZO *and* RINALDO [*behind*].

Fortunio.   Not yet, Valerio.

---

57. SD.] *This ed.; not in* Q. 63. charge] *Shepherd;* chargd Q.
67. SD. behind] *Parrott¹; not in* Q.

---

53. *fill this gentleman's carouse*] The drawer is told to fill Dariotto's cup to the brim (*OED* carouse n. 2).

56. *without hat or knee*] When offering a toast to a lady, the custom was to remove one's hat and bend the knee, as Seagull does in *Eastward Ho*: 'Whatsoever she be, here's to her health, noble colonel, both with cap and knee' (3.3.73–4).

59–61. *Nay ... knees*] This is printed as two lines of prose in Q. Parrott's verse lineation is followed here.

59. *let's take it by degrees*] let us take things step by step (*OED* degree n. 2b).

60–1. *on our feet ... upon our knees*] Dariotto wants to remain standing, for if he makes a formal toast, the others will have to join in, rendering everyone 'legless'.

62.] Valerio puns on Dariotto's use of 'degree' (l. 59) by saying that everyone is equal in a tavern. The situation is different at Dunsinane, as Macbeth invites the Scottish lords to take their places at the banquet table: 'You know your own degrees, sit down' (3.4.1).

63. *all ahead*] headlong (Parrott).

64. *down!*] Kneel, and offer a toast!

65.] A popular myth was that an elephant has no joints in its legs and can neither kneel nor run. In a major scientific breakthrough, researchers at Stanford University discovered in 2003 that not only can an elephant do both these things, but it runs with its knees bent at all times, just like Groucho Marx ('Researchers Say Elephants Run Like Groucho Marx', *Los Angeles Times*, 5 April 2003).

67. *I'll be their pledge*] Valerio will join Dariotto in drinking to the ladies.

172　　　　　　　　ALL FOOLS　　　　　　　　[ACT 5

  This he must drink unpledged.
Valerio. He shall not. I will give him this advantage. [*Dariotto and*
  Valerio kneel and drink.]
Gostanzo. [*Aside to Rinaldo*] How now, what's here? Are these the
  officers?　　　　　　　　　　　　　　　　　　　　　　　　　70
Rinaldo. [*To himself*] 'Slight, I would all were well.

     Enter CORNELIO [*behind*].

Valerio.　　　　　　　　　　　　　　　　　Here is his pledge.
  Here's to our common friend Cornelio's health.
Dariotto. Health to Gazetta, poison to her husband!　　*He kneels.*
Cornelio. [*Aside*] Excellent guests! These are my daily guests!
Valerio. Drawer, make even th'impartial scales of justice.　　　75
  Give it to Claudio, and from him fill round.
  Come, Dariotto, set me. Let the rest
  Come in when they have done the ladies right.
Gostanzo. [*Aside*] Set me! Do you know what belongs to setting?
Rinaldo. [*Aside*] What a dull slave was I to be thus gulled!　　80
Cornelio. [*Aside to Rinaldo*] Why, Rinald, what meant you to entrap
  your friend
  And bring his father to this spectacle?

---

69. SD.] *This ed.; not in* Q.　　70. SD.] *Parrott¹* (*subst.*); *not in* Q.
71. SD.] *This ed.; Aside Parrott¹; not in* Q.　　71.1. SD. behind] *Parrott¹; not in* Q.
73. SP.] *Parrott¹; Clau.* Q.　　74. SD.] *Parrott¹; not in* Q.
77. the] *Parrott¹;* mee Q.　　79. SD.] *Parrott¹; not in* Q.
80. SD.] *Parrott¹; not in* Q.　　81. SD.] *Parrott¹; not in* Q.

---

 69. *give ... advantage*] award him this point, as in tennis. As we know from the description of a match in John Florio's English–Italian phrase book, *Second Fruits* (p. 25), tennis was scored exactly as it is today. Sometimes points were 'given' to make things more even; Valerio, by drinking along with Dariotto, is willing to let him have the 'advantage' of remaining not quite as drunk by comparison.
 71. *I would all were well*] Rinaldo, for the first and only time, expresses some self-doubt, as he realises that Cornelio has tricked him into bringing Gostanzo to the tavern, where he will discover what his son is really like.
 77. *set me*] make a bet with me.
 77–8. *Let the rest ... right*] Valerio and Dariotto are ready to start gambling, and the others may join in once they have drunk their pledge to the ladies. 'Do me right' was a challenge to match someone drink for drink. In *2 Henry IV*, Justice Silence gets drunk with Falstaff and starts singing an English version of a French song, 'Do me right / and dub me knight / Samingo' (5.3.73–5).
 79.] 'Do you know how to place bets?' Gostanzo cannot believe what he sees.

SC. 2]   ALL FOOLS   173

   You are a friend indeed.
Rinaldo. [*Aside to Cornelio*] 'Tis very good, sir.
   Perhaps my friend, or I, before we part.
   May make even with you.
Fortunio.   Come, let's set him round.   85
Valerio. Do so, at all! [*He casts the dice.*] A plague upon these dice.
   Another health! 'Sfoot, I shall have no luck
   Till I be drunk. Come on, here's to the comfort
   The cavalier, my father, should take in me
   If he now saw me, and would do me right.   90
Fortunio. I'll pledge it, and his health, Valerio.   [*They drink.*]
Gostanzo. [*Aside*] Here's a good husband!
Rinaldo. [*Aside to Gostanzo*]   I pray you, have patience,
   sir.
Valerio. Now have at all, an 'twere a thousand pound.
Gostanzo. [*Coming forward*] Hold, sir! I bar the dice!
Valerio.   What, sir, are
   you there?
   [*To Drawer*] Fill's a fresh pottle—By this light, Sir Knight, 95
   You shall do right.

             Enter MARC ANTONIO.

Gostanzo.   O thou ungracious villain!
Valerio. Come, come, we shall have you now thunder forth

---

83. SD.] *This ed.; not in* Q.   86. SD.] *This ed.; not in* Q.
91. SD.] *This ed.; not in* Q.   92. SD.] *Parrott¹; not in* Q.
92.1. SD.] *Parrott¹; not in* Q.
94. SD. *Coming forward*] *Manley; advancing Parrott¹; not in* Q.
95. SD.] *This ed.; not in* Q.   97. SP. *Valerio*] *Shepherd; no new speaker* Q.

83–5.] Rinaldo seems to recover his composure, and quietly responds to Cornelio's gloating by assuring him that the game is not over.

84. *my friend*] Valerio.

85–6. *set him round ... at all*] To 'set him round' is for everyone to lay their wager against Valerio. 'At all', like 'come-you-seven' (2.2.42n.), is a customary cry of the player as he throws the dice. In *Sir John Oldcastle, Part 1*, Huntington has the first throw in a dice game with Suffolk and King Henry, and says 'Set round, then. So, at all!' (11.40).

87–93.] The split focus of this scene would work very well on the wide Rose stage, with Valerio on one side getting drunker and drunker, and Gostanzo, on the other, becoming increasingly agitated, while Rinaldo nervously approaches him in an attempt to somehow sort out the mess.

89. *cavalier*] knight.

95. *pottle*] a pot containing two quarts (*OED* n.¹).

Some of your thrifty sentences, as gravely:
'For as much, Valerius, as everything has time, and a pudding has
two, yet ought not satisfaction to swerve so much from defalca- 100
tion of well-disposed people, as that indemnity should prejudice
what security doth insinuate.' At all, yet once again!
Marc Antonio. Here's a good sight. [*To Gostanzo*] Y'are well
encountered, sir.
Did not I tell you you'd o'ershoot yourself
With too much wisdom? 105
Valerio. [*To Marc Antonio*] Sir, your wisest do so.
[*To Drawer*] Fill the old man some wine.
Gostanzo. Here's a good infant!
Marc Antonio. [*To Gostanzo*] Why, sir? Alas, I'll wager with your
wisdom
His consorts drew him to it, for of himself
He is both virtuous, bashful, innocent, 110
Comes not at city, knows no city art,
But plies your husbandry, dares not view a wench.
Valerio. Father, he comes upon you.
Gostanzo. Here's a son!

102. at all] *Parrott² (conj. Daniel)*; a tryall *Q*.
103. SD.] *This ed.; not in Q*.   106. SD.] *This ed.; not in Q*,
107. SD.] *This ed.; not in Q*.   108. SD.] *This ed.; not in Q*.

98. *sentences*] maxims (*OED* n. 4a).

99–102.] The gobbledegook that Valerio delivers in mockery of his father does not ring true, since Gostanzo never expresses himself this way.

99–100. *everything ... pudding has two*] This is, literally, doubletalk, for Valerio is combining two sayings. First, there is the familiar verse from Ecclesiastes, which reads, in the Geneva Bible, 'To all things there is an appointed time, and a time to every purpose under the heaven' (3.1). We also have the wisdom about puddings (sausages), offered by Humphrey in *The Knight of the Burning Pestle*, 'as writers say, all things have end, / And that we call a pudding hath his two' (1.1.84–5; cf. Dent E121).

100–1. *defalcation*] diminution, abatement (*OED* n. 1).

102. *At all*] *Q*'s 'a tryall' is not without sense, but since Valerio was about to throw the dice when Gostanzo interrupted him, P. A. Daniel's suggestion of 'at all', cited by Parrott, is persuasive (cf. 5.2.85–6n.).

107. *Fill ... wine*] Valerio happily welcomes Marc Antonio to the party by buying him a drink.

infant] Gostanzo ironically refers to his son as a youth of noble birth (*OED* n. 3).

108–9. *I'll wager ... to it*] I'd bet that according to you, with your superior knowledge, Valerio's friends are to blame. Marc Antonio's sense of triumph is palatable, as he throws Gostanzo's delusions back at him.

113. *he comes upon you*] 'Marc Antonio is having a go at you', an understatement, given the circumstances. The literal meaning of 'come upon' in this context is 'attack', as Gloucester says to Henry V at Agincourt, 'I hope they will not come upon us now' (3.6.168).

SC. 2]   ALL FOOLS   175

Marc Antonio. Whose wife is Gratiana now, I pray?
Gostanzo. Sing your old song no more. Your brain's too short   115
   To reach into these policies.
Marc Antonio.   'Tis true,
   Mine eye's soon blinded, and yourself would say so,
   If you knew all. Where lodged your son last night?
   Do you know that with all your policy?
Gostanzo. You'll say he lodged with you. And did not I   120
   Foretell you all this must for colour sake
   Be brought about, only to blind your eyes?
Marc Antonio. By heaven, I chanced this morn, I know not why,
   To pass by Gratiana's bedchamber,
   And whom saw I fast by her naked side   125
   But your Valerio.
Gostanzo.   Had you not warning given?
   Did not I bid you watch my courtier well,
   Or he would set a crest a your son's head?
Marc Antonio. That was not all, for by them on a stool
   My son sat laughing to see you so gulled.   130
Gostanzo. 'Tis too, too plain.
Marc Antonio.   Why, sir, do you suspect it
   The more for that?
Gostanzo.   Suspect it? Is there any
   So gross a wittol as, if 'twere his wife,
   Would sit by her so tamely?
Marc Antonio.   Why not, sir.

115–16. *Your brain's too short ... policies*] Gostanzo says exactly the same thing about Marc Antonio at 3.1.95–7. The delightful description of a brain being 'too short' is also found in Francis Marbury's interlude *The Marriage between Wit and Wisdom*, where Idleness admits, 'I could have told you even now what a short brained villain am I' (ll. 305–7).

117. *yourself would say so*] You would say the same thing about yourself.

121. *for colour sake*] for the sake of the pretence (Parrott).

126. *given*] given to you.

127. *my courtier*] Valerio.

128.] or he would cuckold your son. The crest is a heraldic ornament on a coat of arms; horns would be appropriate for a cuckold. In *As You Like It*, the Lord sings: 'Take thou no scorn / To wear the horn / It was a crest ere thou wast born. / Thy father's father wore it / And thy father bore it' (4.2.13–16).

131. *'Tis too, too plain*] At this moment, Gostanzo finally realises he is the one who has been tricked. His frank admission, and his promise that the deed shall not go unpunished, is based on Chremes's reaction in *The Self-Tormentor* (907–18).

131–2. *Why, sir ... that*] Marc Antonio does not yet realise that Gostanzo is admitting he was wrong. Perhaps this is understandable; it could be the first time in his life Gostanzo has done so.

    To blind my eyes?
Gostanzo.   Well, sir, I was deceived,   135
    But I shall make it prove a dear deceit
    To the deceiver.
Rinaldo.   Nay, sir, let's not have
    A new infliction set on an old fault.
    He did confess his fault upon his knees.
    You pardoned it, and swore 'twas from your heart.   140
Gostanzo. Swore! a great piece of work! The wretch shall know
    I have a daughter here to give my land to.
    I'll give my daughter all. The prodigal
    Shall not have one poor house to hide his head in.
Fortunio. I humbly thank you, sir, and vow all duty   145
    My life can yield you.
Gostanzo.   Why are you so thankful?
Fortunio. For giving to your daughter all your lands,
    Who is my wife, and so you gave them me.
Gostanzo. Better and better!
Fortunio.   Pray, sir, be not moved.
    You drew me kindly to your house, and gave me   150
    Access to woo your daughter, whom I loved,
    And since, by honoured marriage, made my wife.
Gostanzo. Now all my choler fly out in your wits.
    Good tricks of youth, i'faith, no indecorum.
    Knight's son, knight's daughter! Marc Antonio,   155
    Give me your hand, there is no remedy.
    Marriage is ever made by destiny.
Rinaldo. Silence, my masters! Now here all are pleased,
    Only but Cornelio, who lacks but persuasion
    To reconcile himself to his fair wife.   160
    Good sir, will you, of all men our best speaker,
    Persuade him to receive her into grace?

---

    142. *a daughter here*] Bellanora. The fact that the women have been silently watching everything is discussed in the Introduction (pp. 45–7).

    143–4. *The prodigal ... hide his head in*] Gostanzo is the opposite of the father who welcomes home his prodigal son in Luke's parable (15.11–32),

    147–8.] As Bellanora's husband, Fortunio automatically assumes ownership of all her property.

    153. *fly out ... wits*] disappear, in recognition of your cleverness. The actor might take a long pause before saying this line, since Gostanzo's change of heart seems too sudden to be credible (cf. Introduction, pp. 46–7).

    154–5. *no indecorum ... knight's daughter*] There has been no impropriety, as Bellanora and Fortunio are both of the same social rank.

    157.] proverbial (Dent M682).

    158. *Silence, my masters*] Everyone would be applauding Gostanzo's speech.

Gostanzo. That I will gladly, and he shall be ruled.
  Good Cornelio, I have heard of your wayward jealousy, and I must
    tell you plain as a friend, you're an ass. You must pardon me, I   165
    knew your father—
Rinaldo. Then you must pardon him indeed, sir.
Gostanzo. Understand me: put case Dariotto loved your wife, whereby
    you would seem to refuse her. Would you desire to have such a
    wife as no man could love but yourself?   170
Marc Antonio. Answer but that, Cornelio.
Gostanzo. Understand me: say Dariotto hath kissed your wife, or per-
    formed other offices of that nature, whereby they did converse
    together at bed and at board, as friends may seem to do.
Marc Antonio. Mark but the 'now understand me'.   175
Gostanzo. Yet if there come no proofs but that her actions were cleanly,
    or indiscreet, private, why, 'twas a sign of modesty. And will you
    blow the horn yourself, when you may keep it to yourself? Go
    to, you are a fool, understand me!
Valerio. Do understand him, Cornelio.   180
Gostanzo. Nay, Cornelio, I tell you again, I knew your father. He was
    a wise gentleman, and so was your mother. Methinks I see her
    yet, a lusty stout woman, bore great children. You were the very
    scoundrel of 'em all; but let that pass. As for your mother, she
    was wise. A most flippant tongue she had, and could set out her   185

---

  164. *ruled*] guided, counselled (*OED* rule v. 1 b). Gostanzo is back to his old self, giving advice to everyone (cf. Introduction, pp. 42–3).
  164. *wayward*] self-willed, perverse (*OED* adj. 1)
  168. *put case*] suppose that, used when presenting a hypothesis.
  175.] Marc Antonio happily encourages Cornelio to listen carefully to Gostanzo's speech. Valerio does the same thing five lines later.
  176–7. *cleanly ... private*] 'Cleanly' is now to be taken as morally pure, or innocent, the original meaning (*OED* adj. 1; cf. 5.2.39n., 41n.). Evans notes that 'indiscreet' may be read as 'if indiscreet'—either Gazetta committed no indiscretion, or if she did, it was in private, so the offence is lessened (Evans, p. 309).
  178. *blow the horn yourself*] proclaim that you are a cuckold (cf. 4.1.237n.).
  183. *stout*] magnificent, splendid (*OED* adj. 1b).
  185. *flippant*] fluent, sparkling (1st cit. *OED* adj.).
  185–6. *set out her tale*] tell a story, make conversation. Q has 'Taile', and previous modern spelling editions 'tail', which is consistent with the sexual innuendo of Petruchio's 'What, with my tongue in your tail?' (*Shrew* 2.1.218). The immediate topic, however, is Cornelio's mother's 'flippant tongue', and to set out one's tale, a common expression, fits this context. In *Westward Ho*, Mistress Honeysuckle is looking for 'some wise ass' who will cover for her with an alibi while she is up to no good: 'one that could set out his tale with audacity' (2.3.86, 88–9). Gostanzo praises Valerio's ability to 'tell his tale' at 1.1.193.

tale with as good grace as any she in Florence, come cut and
long-tail, and she was honest enough too. But yet, by your leave,
she would tickle Dob now and then, as well as the best on 'em.
By Jove, it's true, Cornelio, I speak it not to flatter you. Your
father knew it well enough, and would he do as you do, think   190
you? Set rascals to undermine her, or look to her water, as they
say? No, when he saw 'twas but her humour, for his own quietness' sake he made a back-door to his house for convenience,
got a bell to his fore-door, and had an odd fashion in ringing,
by which she and her maid knew him, and would stand talking   195
to his next neighbour to prolong time, that all things might be
rid cleanly out o' the way before he came, for the credit of his
wife. This was wisdom now for a man's own quiet.
Marc Antonio. Here was a man, Cornelio.
Gostanzo. What, I say! Young men think old men are fools, but old   200
men know young men are fools.

186. tale] *This ed.;* Taile *Q.*

---

186. *in Florence*] the second of two times the ostensible locale is explicit (cf. 4.1.297).

186–7. *come cut and long-tail*] proverbial for 'under all circumstances' (Dent C938).
The literal sense is 'come all dogs [or horses], whether with docked or long tails'.
Slender, in *Merry Wives*, promises to maintain Anne Page like a gentlewoman 'come
cut and long-tail, under the degree of a squire' (3.4.46).

188. *Dob*] a nickname for Robin or Robert, and another contribution to the mighty
compendium of names that men have given their penis. Florio's Italian–English dictionary, *A World of Words* (1598), defines *Robinetto* as 'a pillicock, or dildo' (p. 332; cf.
Williams, p. 1163).

on 'em] of 'em (Abbott 181).

191. *look to her water*] literally, analyse her urine. Chapman may be alluding to
Herodotus's story of Pheros, an Egyptian pharaoh who was struck blind, and received
a prophecy that his affliction would be cured if he bathed his eyes in the urine of a
woman who had never been unfaithful to her husband. He tried his wife, who failed
the test, and many other women, with the same result, until at last he found a woman
who was able to restore his sight. 'Then he collected within the walls of a town, now
called Red Clod, all the women except the one whose urine had proved efficacious,
set the place on fire, and burnt them to death, town and all' (p. 124). Beyond this
specific sense, the phrase was also used figuratively, as 'follow her every move'.

193–8. *back-door ... own quiet*] Juvenal sees a husband enabling his wife's adultery
as emblematic of the Rome he lives in. He dismisses a suggestion that epic or heroic
verse can be worth doing, since Rome, hopelessly corrupt, provides so much subject
material for satire. After scornfully rejecting such hackneyed topics as the labours of
Hercules, he asks, 'Will these suffice in an age when each pimp of a husband / Takes
gifts from his own wife's lover—if she is barred in law / From inheriting legacies—and,
while they paw each other, / Tactfully stares at the ceiling, or snores, wide awake, in
his wine?' (*Satires* 6.54–9).

200–1.] proverbial (Dent M610). William Camden attributes the saying to Nicholas
Metcalfe (1475–1539), Archdeacon of Rochester and Master of St John's College,
Cambridge (*Remains*, p. 228).

Cornelio. Why, hark you, you two knights. Do you think I will forsake Gazetta?
Gostanzo. And will you not?
Cornelio. Why, there's your wisdom. Why did I make show of divorce, think you? 205
Marc Antonio. Pray you why, sir?
Cornelio. Only to bridle her stout stomach. And how did I draw on the colour for my divorce? I did train the woodcock Dariotto into the net, drew him to my house, gave him opportunity with my 210 wife—as you say my father dealt with his wife's friends—only to train him in, let him alone with my wife in her bedchamber, and sometimes found him abed with her, and went my way back again softly, only to draw him into the pit.
Gostanzo. This was well handled indeed, Cornelio. 215
Marc Antonio. Ay, marry, sir, now I commend your wisdom.
Cornelio. Why, if I had been so minded as you think, I could have flung his pantofle down the stairs, or done him some other disgrace. But I winked at it, and drew on the good fool more and more, only to bring him within my compass. 220
Gostanzo. Why, this was policy in grain.
Cornelio. And now shall the world see I am as wise as my father.
Valerio. Is't come to this? Then will I make a speech in praise of this reconcilement, including therein the praise and honour of the most fashionable and authentical horn! Stand close, gentles, and 225 be silent. *He gets into a chair.*
Gostanzo. Come on, let's hear his wit in this potable humour.
Valerio. The course of the world, like the life of man, is said to be divided into several ages. As we into infancy, childhood, youth,

---

205. *there's your wisdom*] For Cornelio to say, ironically, 'don't you people know anything?', is a wonderful comic moment.

208. *stout stomach*] high spirits. Cornelio now claims he threatened a divorce only to frighten Gazetta out of her wayward behaviour.

208-9. *draw on the colour*] establish the pretext.

209. *woodcock*] The woodcock was proverbially known to be stupid and easy to snare, as Fabian says of Malvolio, 'Now is the woodcock near the gin' (2.5.81).

212. *train*] lure (*OED* v.^{2}).

218. *pantofle*] slipper (*OED* n.).

220. *compass*] reach, as in Sonnet 116, 'Love's not Time's fool, though rosy lips and cheeks / Within his bending sickle's compass come' (9-10).

221. *in grain*] through and through, from the expression 'dyed in grain' (*OED* grain n.^{1} 10).

227. *potable*] drinkable, here reminding everyone that Valerio has already had more than a few drinks.

and so forward to old age, so the world into the golden age, the 230
silver, the brass, the iron, the leaden, the wooden, and now into
this present age, which we term the horned age. Not that but
former ages have enjoyed this benefit as well as our times, but
that in ours it is more common, and nevertheless precious. It is
said that in the golden age of the world the use of gold was not 235
then known: an argument of the simplicity of that age. Lest
therefore succeeding ages should hereafter impute the same fault
to us which we lay upon the first age, that we, living in the
horned age of the world, should not understand the use, the
virtue, the honour, and the very royalty of the horn, I will in 240
brief sound the praises thereof, that they who are already in
possession of it may bear their heads aloft as being proud of
such lofty accoutrements, and they that are but in possibility
may be ravished with a desire to be in possession.

A trophy so honourable and unmatchably powerful that it is 245
able to raise any man from a beggar to an emperor's fellow, a
duke's fellow, a nobleman's fellow, alderman's fellow, so glorious that it deserves to be worn—by most opinions—in the most
conspicuous place about a man. For what worthier crest can you
bear than the horn, which if it might be seen with our mortal 250
eyes, what a wonderful spectacle would there be, and how highly

---

238–311.] Long prose speeches in dramatic texts are not usually divided into paragraphs, but I agree with the quarto's compositor and all previous editors that it is necessary here.

230–2. *golden age ... horned age*] Chapman draws directly on Juvenal, who begins the sixth *Satire* with a description of ages past, when men and women lived happier lives. 'Thereafter, by slow degrees, / Justice withdrew to heaven, and Chastity went with her. / Two sisters together, beating a common retreat. / To bounce your neighbour's bed, my friend, to outrage / Matrimonial sanctity is now an ancient and long / Established tradition' (6.19–24). The earliest known source of the Ages of Man legend is Hesiod's *Works and Days*. Hesiod describes five: golden, silver, bronze, heroic, and iron. Valerio seems to follow Ovid in reducing the number to four by not including the heroic age, and then invents three of his own: leaden, wooden, and the current 'horned age' (Hesiod, ll. 109–201; Ovid, *Metam*. 1.89–150).

235–6. *the use ... known*] This point is not explicit in Hesiod, although the people of the golden age had no need for gold itself, since the land offered abundant supply of everyone's needs: 'the fruitful earth unforced bare them fruit abundantly and without stint. They dwelt in ease and peace upon their lands with many good things, rich in flocks and loved by the blessed gods' (ll. 118–20).

246. *fellow*] companion, equal in dignity (*OED* n. 1).

249. *crest*] as at l. 128, a pun on the heraldic symbol.

they would ravish the beholders? But their substance is incorporal, not falling under sense, nor mixed of the gross concretion of elements, but a quintessence beyond them, a spiritual essence, invisible and everlasting. 255
And this hath been the cause that many men have called their being in question, whether there be such a thing in *rerum natura*, or not, because they are not to be seen, as though nothing were that were not to be seen. Who ever saw the wind? Yet what wonderful effects are seen of it! It drives the clouds, yet no man 260 sees it. It rocks the house, bears down trees, castles, steeples, yet who sees it? In like sort does your horn: it swells the forehead, yet none sees it. It rocks the cradle, yet none sees it. So that you plainly perceive, sense is no judge of essence. The moon to any man's sense seems to be horned, yet who knows not the 265 moon to be ever perfectly round? So likewise your heads seem ever to be round, when indeed they are oftentimes horned. For their original, it is unsearchable. Natural they are not; for where is beast born with horns more than with teeth? Created they were not, for *ex nihilo nihil fit*. Then will you ask me, how came 270 they into the world? I know not, but I am sure women brought them into this part of the world; howsoever, some doctors are of opinion that they came in with the devil. And not unlike, for as the devil brought sin into the world, but the woman brought

---

268. where is] *Collier (conj.)*; there is *Q*.

252–3. *incorporal*] having no material substance (*OED* adj.).
253. *concretion*] coalescence (*OED* n. 1).
254–5. *a quintessence ... everlasting*] At 1.1.44–5, Rinaldo describes beauty in almost exactly the same way as Valerio describes a cuckold's horns here.
257. rerum natura] the nature of things, alluding to *De Rerum Natura*, the great philosophical poem by Lucretius.
267–8. *For ... unsearchable*] The true origins of the horn will never be known.
268–9. *where is beast born*] *Q* has 'there is beast born', while the sense demands either a negative statement or a rhetorical question. Parrott emends to 'there is no beast born', but Collier's suggestion of 'where is beast born' is more attractive, as it does not require an extra word.
270. ex nihilo nihil fit] a paraphrase, rather than an exact quote, from *De Rerum Natura*, which reads *nil posse creari de nilo*, 'nothing can be created from nothing' (1.155–6). It is part of Lucretius's explication of atomist theory, which originated in the works of Democritus and Epicurus. They believed that the universe is comprised of invisible and indivisible atoms—the 'something', rather than 'nothing', from which all matter is constituted.
272. *doctors*] learned men.
273. *not unlike*] not unlikely, probably so.

it to the man, so it may very well be that the devil brought horns
into the world, but the woman brought them to the man.

For their power, it is general over the world. No nation so
barbarous, no country so proud, but doth equal homage to the
horn. Europa, when she was carried through the sea by the
Saturnian bull, was said, for fear of falling, to have held by the
horn. And what is this but a plain showing to us, that all Europe,
which took name from that Europa, should likewise hold by the
horn. So that I say it is universal over the face of the world,
general over the face of Europe, and common over the face of
this country. What city, what town, what village, what street,
nay, what house, can quit itself of this prerogative? I have read
that the lion once made a proclamation through all the forest
that all horned beasts should depart forthwith upon pain of
death. If this proclamation should be made through our forest,
Lord, what pressing, what running, what flying would there be,
even from all the parts of it? He that had but a bunch of flesh

---

281. Europe] *Reed;* Europa *Q.*

279–80. *Europa ... bull*] When Jupiter saw Europa walking along the shore of the Mediterranean at Sidon, he changed himself into a handsome white bull in order to woo her. Charmed by the bull's gentleness, Europa climbed on to its back, whereupon it swam out to sea, heading towards Crete. As Ovid tells the story, Europa rode 'with right hand clutching one horn, and her left / on his back for support, while her fluttering dress swelled out in the sea breeze' (*Metam.* 2.874–5). Richard Armour offers a slightly different verson in *It All Started with Europa*: 'the fact that Jupiter was actually not a bull ... gives us some indication of the uncertainty of those days. All Europa knew was that it was transportation' (p. 11).

280. *Saturnian bull*] Jupiter. The Romans identified Cronus, the father of Jupiter, with Saturn.

281. *showing*] demonstration.

282. *hold by*] be faithful to (*OED* hold v.17), with a pun on Europa's holding on to the bull's horns as it swam across the sea.

287–9. *the lion ... death*] The lion's order that all horned beasts must leave the forest is only incidental to the main point of the popular story in which it appears. As told in *Pasquil's Jests* (1609), a fox, having a large load of geese, rabbits, and chickens he had killed to carry, met an ass along the road. The fox warned the ass about the lion's proclamation, but the ass answered 'that it nothing touched him, for that he had no horns. Oh, but (quoth the fox) take heed, thou hast long ears and if the lion will say that they be horns, then they are as ill as horns. But if thou wilt help me to carry a little poultry that I have taken here for the court, I will warrant thee to go and come safe'. The ass agreed to carry the fox's burden, but soon they met a wolf, and the terrified ass ran away, the moral being 'let never ass follow a fox, lest he meet with a wolf at his journey's end' (sig. D4r–v).

290. *pressing*] pushing forward (*OED* press v^1 8a).

291. *bunch*] protuberance, the original meaning of the word (*OED* n.^{1} 1).

in his head would away, and some, foolishly fearful, would
imagine the shadow of his ears to be horns. Alas, how desert
would this forest be left?
  To conclude, for their force is inevitable. For were they not   295
inevitable, then might either properness of person secure a man,
or wisdom prevent 'em, or greatness exempt, or riches redeem
them. But present experience hath taught us that in this case all
these stand in no stead. For we see the properest men take part
of them, the best wits cannot avoid them—for then should poets   300
be no cuckolds. Nor can money redeem them, for then would
rich men fine for their horns, as they do for offices. But this is
held for a maxim: that there are more rich cuckolds than poor.
Lastly, for continuance of the horn, it is undeterminable till
death. Neither do they determine with the wife's death, howso-   305
ever ignorant writers hold opinion they do, for as when a knight
dies, his lady still retains the title of lady. When a company is
cast, yet the captain still retains the title of captain. So though
the wife die, by whom this title came to her husband, yet, by
the courtesy of the city, he shall be a cuckold during life, let all   310
ignorant asses prate what they list.
Gostanzo. [*To Valerio*] Notable wag! Come, sir, shake hands with him
In whose high honour you have made this speech.

295, 296. inevitable] *Brereton (conj. cited Parrott¹);* irrevitable *Q;* irrenitable *Parrott¹*.
312. SD.] *This ed.; not in Q.*

---

293. *desert*] an archaic word for barren, or abandoned (*OED* adj.). *OED*'s earliest citation for 'deserted' is 1629.

295, 296. inevitable] *Q* has 'irrevitable' in both instances. Brereton's suggestion that the compositor read 'rr' for the orthographically similar 'n' is persuasive (Brereton, cit. Parrott, p. 730).

296. *properness*] elegance, handsomeness (*OED* n. 1).

302. *fine*] pay a fine. It was common to buy oneself out of having to serve as a civic official. In *The Alchemist*, Subtle says that Abel Drugger will soon be made a sheriff, 'But he'll be wise, preserve his youth, and fine for't' (1.3.40).

304. *undeterminable*] unending (cit. *OED* adj. 1).

305. *determine*] come to an end, chiefly a legal term (*OED* v. 2).

306–7. *for as when ... lady*] Valerio is perfectly correct, although a knighthood cannot be inherited.

308. *cast*] cashiered, dismissed (*OED* adj.² 3).

309–10. *by the courtesy of the city*] If Chapman had actually set his play in London, rather than a London-like Florence, Valerio would say 'by courtesy of England'. Under this law, according to Cowell's *Interpreter*, if a wife is in possession by inheritance of certain kinds of property, upon her death the husband shall 'keep the land during his life, and is called tenant *per legen Angliae*, or by the courtesy of England' (sig. V2v).

311. *what they list*]. what they like (*OED* list v.¹ 2a).

Marc Antonio. [*To Cornelio*] And you, sir, come, join hands, you're one
   amongst them.
                                            [*Valerio and Cornelio shake hands.*]
Gostanzo. Very well done. Now take your several wives,   315
   And spread like wild geese, though you now grow tame.
   Live merrily together and agree.
   Horns cannot be kept off with jealousy.
                                                              [*Exeunt.*]

---

314. SD.] *Manley; not in Q.*   314.1. SD.] *This ed.; not in Q.*
318.1. SD.] *This ed.; FINIS Q.*

---

316. *spread*] extend over a larger area by increase or by separation, disperse (cit.
OED v. 15a).

Epilogue

Since all our labours are as you can like,
We all submit to you, nor dare presume
To think there's any real worth in them.
Sometimes feasts please the cooks and not the guests,
Sometimes the guests, and curious cooks contemn them.　　　5
Our dishes we entirely dedicate
To our kind guests. But since ye differ so,
Some to like only mirth without taxations,
Some to count such works trifles, and such like,
We can but bring you meat, and set you stools,　　　10
And to our best cheer say, you all are welcome.

---

11. are welcome] *Q(u)*, are ( ) welcome *Q(c)*.

---

5. *curious*] painstaking, diligent (*OED* adj. 1).
contemn] disdain, scorn (*OED* v. 1).
8. *taxations*] reproofs (*OED* n.), probably meant in the sense of personal attacks. In *As You Like It*, Celia warns Touchstone, 'you'll be whipped for taxation one of these days' (1.2.84–5).
9. *trifles*] Chapman continues the culinary metaphor. Along with being something of little value, a trifle was (and is) a popular sweet dish. In *A World of Words* (1598), Florio describes the Italian dish *mantiglia* 'as a kind of clotted cream called a fool or a trifle in English' (p. 216).
11. *all are welcome*] Obviously, the audience expects 'all are fools'. *Q*, in its uncorrected state, sets these words out as given here, but corrected sheets show 'all are ( ) welcome', making the joke all too obvious. Subsequent editors either retain the empty parentheses or substitute a long dash. I prefer the original version, leaving it up to the actor, who might decide that a quick delivery, with no pause, is actually more effective.

To my long lou'd and Honourable friend Sir Thomas Walsingham Knight.

SHould I expose to euery common eye,
    The least allow'd birth of my shaken braine;
  And not entitle it perticulerly
     To your acceptance, I were wurse then vaine.
And though I am most loth to passe your sight
  with any such light marke of vanitie,
Being markt with Age for Aimes of greater weight,
  and drownd in darke Death-vshering melancholy,
Yet least by others stealth it be imprest,
  without my pasport, patcht with others wit,
Of two enforst ills I elect the least;
  and so desire your loue will censure it;
    Though my old fortune keepe me still obscure,
    The light shall still bewray my ould loue sure.

Appendix
The Walsingham Sonnet

John Payne Collier's 1825 edition of *All Fools* contains this dedicatory sonnet, shown here in his spelling and punctuation:

TO

My long lov'd and honourable Friend,
   Sir Thomas Walsingham, Knight.
Should I expose to every common eye
The least allow'd birth of my shaken brain,
And not entitle it particularly
To your acceptance, I were worse than vain.
And though I am most loth to pass your sight
With any such light mark of vanity,
Being mark'd with age for aims of greater weight,
And drown'd in dark death-ushering melanch'ly;
Yet least by others stealth it be imprest
Without my passport, patch'd with other's wit.
Of two enforc'd ills I elect the least,
And so desire your love will censure it:
Though my old fortune keep me still obscure
The light shall still bewray my old love sure.

Collier notes that the sonnet

> is now for the first time inserted, the copies of *All Fools* seen and used by Mr Reed[1] being without it. Whether it was inserted in a few impressions in 1605, and afterwards cancelled, does not appear, though it seems probable that it was so, because in the dedication of his *Byron's Conspiracy and Tragedy*, 1608, to the same distinguished individual Chapman apologises for previous neglect, and apparent ingratitude to his patron, 'in dispensing with his right in his other impressions'. It was found in a copy in the possession of Mr. Rodd, of Great Newport Street.[2]

Years later, in 1839, Collier had several copies printed in modern type. He sent one to Alexander Dyce, who also owned a quarto of *All Fools*, Collier's letter noting 'it will make a very rare play of your's [*sic*] still rarer, by supplying only one other copy that I know of has—the dedication'.[3]

Because 'forgery' has been spelled 'C-o-l-l-i-e-r' for over one hundred and fifty years, the authenticity and provenance of this dedication has always been open to serious doubt. Before proceeding to that question, let us examine it on its own terms.

As noted by Virgil B. Heltzel, printed texts of plays written for the public stage almost never had a dedication addressed to a patron—the first unambiguous example is the one Collier mentions—Chapman's dedication of *The Conspiracy and Tragedy of Charles, Duke of Byron* (printed 1608) to the same Sir Thomas Walsingham.[4] However, the *All Fools* sonnet is not, strictly speaking, a dedication, but a specially printed page to be inserted in one copy of the text and sent as a private gift to the recipient. Jonson had two such leaves printed for *Cynthia's Revels* (1601): one extant quarto has a Latin tribute to his old schoolmaster William Camden, from *Benjamin Jonsonius, alumnus olim, aeturnum amicus*, another has a poem honouring Lucy Russell, Countess of Bedford:[5]

> *Author ad Librum*
> Go, little book, go, little fable,
> Unto the bright and amiable
> Lucy of Bedford; she that bounty
> Appropriates still unto that county.
> Tell her, his muse did invent thee,
> To Cynthia's fairest nymph, hath sent thee,
> And sworn that he will quite discard thee
> In any way she do reward thee
> But with a kiss—if thou canst dare it—
> Of her white hand if she can spare it.

Chapman's sonnet, like Jonson's poem, has no name or initials attached, and the sentiments are equally conventional. He denigrates the work as trivial, saying it would hardly be worth printing if not for the possibility that someone else would produce a false copy under his name. Phyllis Bartlett, editor of *The Poems of George Chapman* (1941), acknowledges the bibliographical problems, but includes the sonnet in her edition

> for the perhaps over-simple reason that it sounds so very much like Chapman. Constant reading of his verse over an extended period of time makes it sound more and more authentic rather than anything cooked up out of his customary diction.[6]

Bartlett adds that 'the printing of extra leaves of dedicatory sonnets is not without precedent in Chapman's career'; a few surviving copies of the *Iliads* (1611) have sonnets addressed to William Cecil, son of the Earl of Salisbury, Robert Carr (see 2.1.173n.), and Sir Edward Phillips, Prince Henry's Chancellor, printed on two inserted leaves.[7]

If a special presentation copy of *All Fools* was made, no one could be a more likely recipient than Sir Thomas Walsingham (1561–1630), second cousin of Sir Francis Walsingham, powerful courtier and patron of poets, including Christopher Marlowe. In 1598, five years after Marlowe's death, Edward Blunt published his edition of *Hero and Leander* and dedicated it to Sir Thomas, 'knowing that in his [Marlowe's] lifetime', Walsingham 'bestowed many kind favours' to him. Chapman's continuation of the poem (Sestiads 3–6), is preceded by his own dedication to Audrey Shelton, Lady Walsingham, then mistress of Queen Elizabeth's bedchamber, and later keeper of Queen Anne's wardrobe. Chapman's conceit is that his work marries the two parts of *Hero and Leander* just as the two dedicatees are married:

> This poor dedication (in figure of the other unity betwixt Sir Thomas and yourself) hath rejoined you with him, my honoured best friend, whose continuance of ancient kindness to my still-obscured estate, though it cannot increase my love to him, which hath ever been entirely circular, yet shall it encourage my deserts to their utmost requital, and make my hearty gratitude speak; to which the unhappiness of my life hath hitherto been uncomfortable and painful dumbness.[8]

As A. R. Braunmuller notes, 'the evidence suggests that the two poet-acquaintances (probably poet-friends) were also joint sharers in the Walsinghams' patronage', and that Chapman continued to enjoy their support, hence the dedication of *Byron* to 'my honourable and constant friend, Sir Thomas Walsingham'.[9] The 'epistle' begins,

> Sir, Though I know you ever stood little affected to these unprofitable rites of dedication (which disposition in you hath made me hitherto dispense with your right in my other impressions), yet, lest the world may repute it a neglect in me of so ancient and worthy a friend (having heard your approbation of these in their presentment) I could not but prescribe them with your name; and that my affection may attend to your posterity, I have entitled to it, herein, your hope and comfort in your generous son.[10]
> (1–12)

The style provides another example of what Stanley Wells calls the 'typically cloudy effusion', for which Chapman is famous.[11] The gist is that Walsingham and his eight-year-old son, who is 'generous' in the latinate sense of high-born, attended a performance of *Byron* at Blackfriars, gave their 'approbration' to the 'presentment' of the play, and this sonnet is Chapman's way of thanking them both.

The first sentence has caused the most trouble: Walsingham, according to Chapman, did not like having books dedicated to him; hence Chapman has never done so before, a statement at odds with the prior existence of the *All Fools* sonnet. As Bartlett comments, 'he would scarcely have made this remark if he had already dedicated *All Fools* to Walsingham'. Collier, as quoted above, offers one possible explanation, that the dedication was cancelled for some reason after only a few copies were printed. Parrott suggested another possibility to Bartlett: that the sonnet is Chapman's, but written for either *May-Day* or *The Widow's Tears* (both printed after *Byron*), and later was wrongly bound into *All Fools*.[12]

We then have two separate problems: the *Byron* dedication, and Collier's reputation. The former is a herring coloured bright crimson, and should be discounted. *All Fools* was never 'dedicated' to Walsingham, any more than *Cynthia's Revels* was dedicated to William Camden or the Countess of Bedford. Chapman's sonnet was to be read only by Sir Thomas and, presumably, Lady Walsingham, while the *Byron* dedication, as G. Blakemore Evans observes, is 'a public declaration to be seen by all, "lest the world may repute it a neglect in me"'.[13]

R. H. Shepherd included the sonnet without comment in his edition of 1874, published before the extent of Collier's forgeries was widely known, but soon thereafter the fact that no one except Collier had ever seen the original had some bibliographers asking where it might be.[14] Parrott, while working on his first edition of *All Fools*, wondered in a *Notes and Queries* article if this was yet one more 'of the "mystifications" of that ingenious scholar'. He also wrote to the distinguished bibliographer and collector Thomas J. Wise, asking if he had recently acquired any copies of *All Fools*, and, if he had, 'whether it possesses the dedicatory sonnet ... None of the copies I have seen possesses it, and so far no one I have spoken or written to has ever seen it'.[15] Neither the readers of *Notes and Queries* nor Wise were able to offer any enlightenment; having failed to locate the original, Parrott relegated the sonnet to an appendix, noting,

> In itself the dedication, which has been generally received since Collier printed it as a genuine poem by Chapman, is not suspicious. Its phrasing and turn of thought seem to me rather like what Chapman might have written, and I do not wish to be considered as peremptorily stigmatising it as a forgery. But Collier was at least as skilful as he was conscienceless in his extraordinary inventions, and the evidence for the authenticity of the dedication rests at present wholly upon Collier's word ... If Collier's copy of *All Fools* should ever come to light the question would, I suppose, be settled positively.[16]

Only a short time after these words had gone to press, Parrott got his wish, but instead of settling the question 'positively', it made things more complicated and confusing than ever.

APPENDIX 191

ENTER THOMAS J. WISE

Thomas James Wise (1859–1937) was an employee and eventually a partner in Herman Rubeck & Co., a very successful manufacturer and dealer of oils for perfumes and food flavourings. His comfortable income was put to collecting first editions of the Victorians: Arnold, the Brownings, Dickens, George Eliot, Kipling, Rosetti, Ruskin, Swinburne, Tennyson, Wordsworth, and others.[17] Many were in the form of pamphlets, shorter works privately printed for the author, before inclusion in a volume for public sale.[18] Wise also had a strong interest in early modern texts, buying as many as he could find at auctions and from other antiquarian book specialists. His collection, the Ashley Library (so named because Wise lived on Ashley Street, London), became England's finest private library of poetry and drama, and Wise was widely respected as a bibliographer.

Wise also earned a good income as a private dealer in rare books, especially for American collectors, at a time when early editions of Shakespeare and his contemporaries were keenly sought. He would either buy books for them directly, earning a commission, or sell spare Ashley copies. Wise's most enthusastic client was the Chicago financier John Henry Wrenn; from the early 1890s until his death in 1911, relying almost exclusively on Wise, Wrenn built a mighty collection, now the Wrenn Library at the University of Texas.

On 20 October 1907, Wise informed Wrenn that he had found and bought the Collier copy of *All Fools*:

> You may guess what surprise and pleasure I felt when I opened the book that afternoon, at the Waverly Hotel. I saw at once that it had the reputed 'Dedication' about which Prof. Parrott had so much to say, and which I told him I believed was a Payne Collier forgery. A moment's inspection satisfied me that the leaf was a forgery. I am convinced that this is the actual copy of the book formerly belonging to Payne Collier; and that this Dedication is the identical forgery fabricated by him.[19]

He also wrote to Parrott with a detailed description, which Parrott quotes extensively in an article published in *The Athenaeum* on 27 June 1908:

> The Dedication it contains is beyond all doubt a palpable forgery. The method employed by Payne Collier when producing this forgery is now perfectly apparent, and it is quite possible to follow his proceedings step by step. He first of all composed the fourteen lines of verse. Having prepared his verses, Payne Collier's next step was to provide himself with a printed copy of them, to the end that when he announced his newest 'discovery' to the literary world, his statement might be promptly and sufficiently supported by optical proof.

Wise goes on to explain how Collier would have had the sonnet printed in period type on a leaf of old paper, and then inserted it in his copy of the quarto:

> But the copy of 'All Fooles' Collier took in hand was a large and fine one, and he evidently found it impracticable to obtain a blank leaf of the same dimensions; or, possibly, he did not regard it as essential that the leaf should be of full size, thinking it unlikely that the fact of the leaf having been mended would occasion any objectionable comment ... the blank leaf he did acquire is considerably smaller than the remaining leaves of which the book is composed, and to bring it up to the level of its fellows the margins have been 'extended' to the required size. This remargining has been beautifully and skilfully executed, but is yet perfectly apparent to a practised eye. To myself the mending was perfectly clear immediately I opened the book.

After also observing that the sonnet leaf is in poor condition, while the two leaves surrounding it 'are large and fresh and clean', Wise concludes,

> I fear you will consider my remarks as being phrased in a somewhat definite (and possibly somewhat assertive) manner. I can only say that the opinion I have formed regarding the leaf is a very definite one indeed.[20]

Although Wise's description of the quarto, which he sold to Wrenn, is accurate in every respect, it does not convict Collier—in fact, it does much to exonerate him. First, the quality and size of the leaf do not mean a great deal. As Evans argues, it 'would presumably have been "sized" in some way before insertion (at whatever date) and since this particular copy was intended, one may suppose, for Walsingham himself, an over-trimmed leaf may have been tipped-in to a specially bound presentation copy after sewing or binding'.[21] As for the leaf's poor quality, if Chapman decided to have the sonnet printed afterwards, the paper would not have been from the same batch, even if Eld did the work, and manufacturing standards for paper were hardly uniform at that time.

Much more important than questions concerning the leaf itself is the fact that all of Collier's forgeries were either hand written, such as the 'corrections' to the Perkins Folio that eventually undid him, or material he made up and then 'lost' the source wherein he found it. In their massive study of Collier's life and work, Robert Freeman and Janet Ing Freeman are quite categorical: 'there has never been a shred of evidence that Collier attempted typographic forgery of any kind'.[22] The reason Wise was so 'definite' and 'assertive' about what Collier had done is that he had been doing the same thing himself for years, in a long career as one of the worst literary forgers and thieves England has ever seen.

Consistent with his bibliographical interests, Wise was active in the Shelley Society, and in 1886 he met fellow member Harry Buxton Forman, a distinguished editor who had done important volumes of Shelley and Keats. Together, they worked on the Society's publication of Shelley reprints; why the two decided to embark on a career of forgery is a mystery, but they had known each other for less than a year before they published Shelley's *Poems and Sonnets*, edited by the imaginary 'Charles Alfred Seymour'. The book had a fake Philadelphia imprint, the real printer being Richard Clay of London, who did all of Wise and Forman's work. As J. F. R. Collins notes,

> this was the forerunner of a clandestine publishing programme of some hundred piracies and forgeries, of which some sixty creative forgeries were the most novel. In broad terms, Forman was the editorial director, and Wise the production manager and sales director. This programme falsified the bibliography and thus the publishing history of Swinburne, Morris, Kipling, Lewis Carroll, Rossetti, Tennyson, Wordsworth, George Eliot, Ruskin, Matthew Arnold, Thackeray, Dickens, Meredith, and the Brownings.[23]

Their most audacious forgery was a pamphlet of Elizabeth Barrett Browning's *Sonnets from the Portuguese*, which she was supposed to have had printed in Reading in 1847, for private distribution. This and other fake editions were given credence by being included in the bibliographies Forman and Wise wrote themselves, and by being catalogued by libraries, including the British Museum, that purchased them.

Despite the skill with which the forgeries were produced, questions were soon being asked. In March 1901 an anonymous article appeared in the *Literary Collector*, a trade journal published by the New York book dealer George D. Smith. It recalled that over the past few years, 'rare' pamphlets by Swinburne, Tennyson, and others were appearing with 'distressing frequency', warning, 'they are easy of fabrication, and we believe they have been fabricated'.[24] Then, in the early 1930s, two young London booksellers, John Carter and Graham Pollard, grew suspicious of Browning's Reading *Sonnets*, and managed to have a chemical analysis done of a fragment of paper from a copy (surreptitiously supplied), followed by an inspection of the typeface. Convinced that the edition was a forgery, they inspected other pamphlets that could be traced to Wise, and in 1934 they published *An Enquiry into the Nature of Certain Nineteenth Century Pamphlets*, showing that a huge fraud had taken place. The title was a pointed imitation of Edmond Malone's exposure of William Henry Ireland's Shakespeare forgeries, *An Inquiry into the Authenticity of Certain*

Papers and Instruments Attributed to Shakespeare—clever, but not as succinct as their original idea, *Wise-Cracking*.[25]

Wise died on 13 May 1937. On 11 September, the Trustees of the British Museum proudly announced in *The Times* that they had bought the Ashley collection 'of some 7000 printed books and manuscripts ... a collection which illustrates almost all that is best in English verse and drama (apart from the writings of Shakespeare) from the end of the sixteenth to the beginning of the twentieth century'. They note that Wise

> admitted no book to his shelves unless it was in the best condition available, and therefore even those volumes which are, in a superficial sense, duplicates of editions already in the Museum, really add something of value to the national collection ... Many of the Museum's rarities have been so much handled by generations of readers that they are now scarcely presentable; and the authorities, who have long held in mind that finer copies ought to be procured, have for some years hoped that the Ashley Library might one day be acquired.

The Trustees acknowledge that 'certain Victorian "first editions", to which he had given prominence, were discovered to be forgeries', but that 'does not affect in the slightest the value and importance of the great library he amassed with unrivalled acumen and taste through more than fifty years'.[26]

Some of the volumes in the Ashley and Wrenn collections were 'made up'. If one owned two defective copies of a book, it was deemed appropriate to take the missing or damaged leaves out of one and place them in the other, producing at least one good text where none existed before. Should Wise acquire a text with missing pages, he would keep it until he found another defective one—in some cases he used three bad copies to make two good ones, keeping one and selling the other.[27] There was nothing inherently wrong with this if Wise owned all the copies, but he often chose a different method. As an eminent bibliographer, he had free access to the British Museum's collection, where he would rip out pages from some of its most precious holdings, take them home, and sew them into both his own quartos and into those he sold to Wrenn. Wise did more than steal particular pages required to make up a specific copy; he took whatever he thought he might need in the future—at the time of his death, he still had a packet of eighty separate leaves.[28]

When the British Museum's librarians began cataloguing the early modern plays in the Ashley trove, they noticed that some obviously inserted leaves were the same ones that were missing from their own copies.[29] They began an extensive forensic investigation; once the status of the Ashley collection was clear, the University of Texas sent the relevant books from the Wrenn collection to London, accompanied by Curator Emeritus Fannie E. Ratchford. The result of their investigation, as Thomas J. Gearty summarises in his 1973 article, is:

> About 206 leaves were stolen from forty-four books (thirty-nine different titles) printed from 1600 to 1659. Wrenn obtained fifty to sixty leaves and Wise acquired ninety for himself. Fifteen more leaves are untraced but may be in the Wrenn copies, and of another forty-one untraced, some may have been discarded.[30]

In her correspondence with Evans, Ratchford suggested that Wise, a typographical forger *par excellence*, might have had the sonnet printed and inserted himself, only to denounce it as Collier's handiwork—do we have a forgery of a forgery?[31] I believe this to be extremely unlikely. Wise's forgeries were all Victorian authors printed in modern type and on modern paper; finding early seventeenth century stock and matching type, even if possible, was not the sort of thing he did. Similarly, it is next to impossible that Wise would have made up the Wrenn copy after finding the sonnet in some other book. Discovery of the page elsewhere would have rendered that book much more valuable than an obviously doctored copy of *All Fools*.

My conclusion is perhaps the most unexpected one. Even though the sonnet passed though the hands of not one but two notorious forgers, it is exactly what it purports to be—a poem that Chapman wrote, had printed, and placed in the copy of *All Fools* he sent as a gift to Sir Thomas Walsingham.

NOTES

1 See Editions, References, Abbreviations, p. xiii. This appendix appeared, in slightly different form, as my *Notes and Queries* article, 'John Payne Collier, Thomas J. Wise, and Chapman's *All Fools*', *NQ* 62 (2015): 231–6.
2 Thomas Rodd established one of London's leading antiquarian bookshops, at 2 Great Newport Street, Covent Garden, in 1809. Upon his death in 1822, his son, also named Thomas, took over management of the business.
3 Arthur Freeman and Janet Ing Freeman, *John Payne Collier: Scholarship and Forgery in the Nineteenth Century*, 2 v. sequentially paginated (New Haven: Yale University Press), p. 1076.
4 Virgil B. Heltzel, 'The Dedication of Tudor and Stuart Plays', *Wiener Beiträge zur Englischen Philologie* 65 (1957): 79, 82.
5 Quotations from Eric Rasmussen and Matthew Steggle, ed., *Cynthia' Revels: Quarto Version*, in *The Cambridge Edition of the Works of Ben Jonson*, v. 1 (Cambridge University Press, 2012). The quarto with the Camden inscription is at the Huntington Library; the copy with the Countess of Bedford poem is at the Clark Library, UCLA.
6 Phyllis Bartlett, ed., *The Poems of George Chapman* (Oxford University Press, 1941), p. 470.

7 Bartlett, p. 484.
8 Marlowe, *The Poems*, ed. Millar Maclure (London: Methuen, 1968), pp. 3, 43–4.
9 A. R. Braunmuller, *Natural Fictions: George Chapman's Major Tragedies* (Newark: Delaware University Press, 1992), p. 21.
10 Quotations from John Margeson, ed., *The Conspiracy and Tragedy of Charles, Duke of Byron* (Manchester University Press, 1988).
11 Stanley Wells, *Shakespeare and Co.* (London: Allen Lane, 2006), p. 142. Wells refers to Chapman's commendatory poem to Jonson in the quarto of *Sejanus* (1605).
12 Bartlett, pp. 470, 484.
13 G. Blakemore Evans, ed., *All Fooles*, *The Plays of George Chapman: The Comedies*, gen. ed. Allan Holaday (Urbana: University of Illinois, 1970), p. 232.
14 *NQ* 7th ser. v. 6 (21 July 1888): 47; *NQ* 7th ser. v. 8 (2 March 1889): 177; NQ 7th ser. v. 10 (19 July 1890): 50–1.
15 T. M. Parrott, 'Chapman's "All Fools"', *NQ* 10th ser. v. 5 (5 May 1906): 347; Fannie E. Ratchford, *Letters of Thomas J. Wise to John Henry Wrenn: A Further Inquiry into the Guilt of Certain Nineteenth-Century Forgers* (New York: Knopf, 1944), p. 429.
16 Parrott, ed., *All Fooles and The Gentleman* Usher (Boston: D. C. Heath, 1907), p. 142.
17 Ratchford, p. 37.
18 John Carter, *Books and Book-Collectors* (London: Hart-Davis, 1956, p. 130; D. F. Foxon, 'Forger and Thief: New Chapter in Cautionary Tale of Thomas J. Wise', *The Times* (18 October 1956): 11.
19 Ratchford, p. 486.
20 Parrott, 'Chapman's 'All Fooles' and J. P. Collier' (*Athenaeum*, 27 June 1908): 789.
21 Evans, p. 230.
22 Freeman, p. 212.
23 J. F. R. Collins, 'Harry Buxton Forman', *DNB*.
24 Ratchford, p. 45.
25 John Collins, *The Two Forgers: A Biography of Harry Buxton Forman and Thomas James Wise* (Aldershot: Ashgate, 1992), p. 251.
26 'A Great Library', *The Times* (11 September 1937): 11.
27 Thomas J. Gearty Jr, 'Thomas J. Wise: A Brief Survey of his Literary Forgeries', *Courier* 11 (1973): 51.
28 Collins, *Two Forgers*, p. 181.
29 Foxon, 11. The complete story of the investigation is told in Foxon's book *Thomas J. Wise and the Pre-Restoration Drama: A Study in Theft and Sophistication* (London: Bibliographical Society, 1959).
30 Gearty, p. 51.
31 Evans, p. 231.

Index

a potibus incipe io-c-um 5.2.52
abodement 4.1.338–9
acceptation 5.1.9
Acocella, Joan p. 23
acrostic 2.1.172
adhorns 2.1.240
adultery pp. 21, 23; penalties for 4.1.246, 4.1.249; *see also* cuckold, cuckoldry
advant 2.1.158
advantage 4.1.4, 5.2.69
Aesop 1.1.92–3
affection 1.1.207
affiances 4.1.317
alabaster 1.1.83
Aldrovandri, Ulisse pp. 44–5
Alleyn, Edward p. 1
ambuscado 2.1.308
Andrelini, Fausto 2.1.91 SD
Andrews, Richard p. 22
Apollodorus p. 6
applausive 2.1.336
apprehension 2.1.32
Arcaeus, Franciscus 3.1.388–9, 3.1.389
Archer, William p. 15
Arden of Faversham p. 21
Argus eyes 1.2.70–1
Aristophanes Prol.14, Prol.14–15
Aristotle p. 33; *Magna Moralia* 2.1.91, *Problems* 2.1.345–6, 3.1.184–5
Armour, Richard 5.2.279–80
Arnott, W. Geoffrey p. 41
aspired 1.1.6
assayed 3.1.134
at all 5.2.85–6, 5.2.102
atonement 1.1.241
Augustine of Hippo p. 8
Augustus, Emperor pp. 26, 27
authentical 4.1.290
avoid 4.1.329

badge 3.1.343
bailie 1.1.138
Bancroft, Richard 3.1.335–8
barley-break 1.2.65–7

barren 2.1.162
Bartlett, Phyllis pp. 188, 189, 190
basted 3.1.302
battery 1.1.22
bear a brain 4.1.204
Beaumont, Francis *Knight of the Burning Pestle* 5.2.99–100; *Woman Hater* 1.1.68–9
bed and board 4.1.310–11
bedfellow 1.1.27
Bedford, Countess of pp. 188, 190
Bedingfeld, Thomas 2.1.344
beffa pp. 22, 31–2, 36
bel-regard 2.1.158
bench-whistlers 2.1.177
besides their books 2.1.334
Bevington, David p. 33
Bibbiena, Bernardo Dovizio da p. 31, 2.1.396–7
black ball 3.1.123
Blackfriars Theatre pp. 4–5, 28, 48, 189, Prol.0, Prol.1–4
blank 2.1.181
blaze 1.1.63
blowze 4.1.97
Blunt, Edward p. 189
board 2.1.224
Boccaccio, Giovanni pp. 21–2, 23
Boorde, Andrew 3.1.218–19
bootless 5.1.22
bourd 5.1.24
brack 3.1.198
Braden, Gordon p. 40
Braun, Susanna Morton p. 19
Braunmüller, A. R. p. 189
brisk 3.1.261
brittle 1.1.50
broad 2.1.338
Brown, Peter 3.1.289
buckler 3.1.163–4
buckram bag 2.1.342–3
Bugbears 3.1.343
Bullen, A. H. p. 15
bunch 5.2.291
Burbage Richard p. 4

INDEX

Burghley, Lord pp. 33–4
Burton, Robert 1.2.53
Butiro et Caseo 4.1.293

Camden, William pp. 188, 190, 1.1.16, 5.2.200–1
capon pp. 44–5, 3.1.207; *see also* cuckold
Captain Thomas Stukeley 3.1.93
care's the less 3.1.73
Carr, Robert p. 188, 2.1.173
Carroll, William C. p. 32
carriage 2.1.220
Carter, John p. 193
cast 5.2.308
Castiglione, Baldassare pp. 30–1, 1.1.12, 1.1.107–10, 1.1.117–18, 2.1.344, 2.1.377–8, 2.1.396–7, 3.1.361–2
cavalier 5.2.89
censure Prol.26
Chaeremon 1.2.123–4
Chapman, George at Blackfriars Theatre p. 4; at Rose Theatre pp. 1–3; *Achilles' Shield* p. 1, 2.1.228; *Andromeda Liberata* 1.2.173; *Blind Beggar of Alexandria* pp. 1, 23, 49, 5.1.5; *Conspiracy and Tragedy of Charles, Duke of Byron* pp. 187, 188, 189, 190, 1.1.35, 2.1.356–7; *Divine Poem* 1.1.99; *Eastward Ho* pp. 48–9, 3.1.374–5, 5.2.56; *Iliads of Homer* p. 188, 3.1.243, 3.1.305; *Homer's Odysseys* 3.1.14–15, 3.1.268–9, 4.1.233; *Humorous Day's Mirth* pp. 1, 6, 12, 21, 23–4, 42, 46, 49, 1.1.33, 1.1.123–32, 2.1.23, 5.1.7, 5.1.64; *May Day* p. 22; *Monsieur D'Olive* 1.1.3; *Ovid's Banquet of Sense* p. 15, 1.1.43, 1.1.47; *Seven Books of the Iliad* p. 1; *Shadow of Night* 1.1.43; *Sir Giles Goosecap* 5.2.43; *Widow's Tears* 2.1.140, 3.1.61, 5.1.7
charge 1.1.125
chattel 4.1.254
Chaucer, Geoffrey pp. 22, 23, 1.1.39, 3.1.243–4
chimera 3.1.243
chopping logic 1.2.51
Cicero p. 17, 1.1.324, 1.2.123–4
Cinthio *see* Giraldi
Clay, Richard p. 193
cleanly 5.2.41
close, closely 1.1.130, 2.1.257, 3.1.362, 5.1.45
Clowes, William p. 36, 3.1.368, 3.1.372
clownery 2.1.85
cloyed 1.2.4
cockatrice 3.1.323
cockerel-drone 4.1.268
Coleridge, Samuel Taylor p. 15
Collier, John Payne pp. 187, 188, 190, 191, 192, 195
Collins, J. F. R. 193
columbine 2.1.234
come cut and long-tail 5.2.186–7
come-you-seven 2.1.42
Commedia dell'Arte pp. 16, 22, 37–8, 3.1.119–20
compass 5.2.220
competency, competent 1.1.278, 1.1.292
concretion 5.2.253
confess 1.1.294
congé 2.1.156
consumption 1.1.286
contemn Epil.5
contests 2.1.61
Cooke, John 3.1.315
copesmate 2.1.229, 4.1.243–4
counterbuff 4.1.363
courtesy of the city 5.2.309–10
Cowell, John 3.1.398
coxcomb 3.1.282
Cratinus Prol.14
crest 5.2.128, 5.2.249
cross-capers 2.21.346
crowned 5.2.34
cuckold, cuckoldry pp. 22–3, 28–30, 44–5, 1.2.57, 2.1.365–6, 3.1.106, 3.1.207, 3.1.243–4, 3.1.343, 4.1.345–6, 5.2.128
cuckoo pp. 22–3, 2.1.365–6, 3.1.106, 3.1.218–19, 4.1.345–6
cullion 2.1.145
curious Epil.5
Curtain Theatre p. 24

dance in nets 2.1.252
daughter 4.1.193
Davies, Sir John 1.1.207, 1.2.79, 2.1.335–8
deceived by breath 2.1.63
declaration 2.1.329–30
defalcation 5.2.100–1
defeasances 4.1.319
defraud 3.1.10
degrees 5.2.62
Dekker, Thomas pp. 2, 24; *2 Honest Whore* 3.1.152; *Gull's Horn-Book*

Prol.26, Prol.30–1, 5.2.43; *If This Be Not a Good Play* 2.1.342–3; *News from Hell* 2.1.346; *Northward Ho* 4.1.284; *Satiro-mastix* Prol.19; *Sun's Darling* 2.1.346; *Westward Ho* 5.2.185–6
desert 1.1.25, 1.1.94, 3.1.274, 5.2.293
deserve 1.1.234
determine 5.2.305
disfurnished 2.1.55
disgrace 3.1.58
dislocated 3.1.382
disparagement 1.1.266
distempers 5.1.72
divorce pp. 36–9, 4.1.230, 4.1.310–11
Dob 5.2.188
Dodoens, Rembert 2.1.223
Donne, John p. 9, 1.1.116
dooms Prol.25
Doran, Madeleine p. 17
dormer 4.1.314
Downton, Thomas p. 2
drinking 2.1.163
Drummond, William p. 48, 5.2.48–51
Dryden, John p. 7
Dyce, Alexander p. 187

easement's chamber 4.1.314
effects Prol.3–4
eftsoon, eftsoons 2.1.391, 4.1.309
egress 4.1.283
Eld, George p. 48
elephant 5.2.65
Elizabeth, Queen pp. 24, 34
eloign 4.1.310
endear 2.1.60
entertainment 2.1.126
epigrams 2.1.173
epithalamions 2.1.173
Erasmus pp. 8, 33, 1.1.78, 2.1.91 SD, 3.1.65, 3.1.218
Essex, Earl of pp. 33–4, 48, 3.1.169–70, 3.1.330–1
Estienne, Henri 4.1.26
Ethiope 1.1.60
Eupolis Prol.14
Europa 5.2.279–80
Evans, G. Blakemore pp. 190, 192, 195
Evans, Henry p. 4
evening crowns the day 2.1.208
everted 4.1.107
ex nihilo nihil fit 5.2.270
exorbitant 3.1.382

exordium 2.1.172
expenseful 2.1.189
experient 1.1.206
explications 4.1.320
exploded Prol.16

fabliaux pp. 21, 22
Family of Love 4.1.274
fanes 1.1.88
far gone 4.1.205
feminine 2.1.175
fence and dancing schools 2.1.185
Fenton, Geoffrey 3.1.372
Ficino, Marsilio p. 15, 1.1.8, 1.1.43, 1.1.112–15
fine 5.2.302
firk 3.1.252
Fitzgeoffrey, Charles p. 6
Fitzherbert, John 1.1.143, 4.1.268
Fleetwood, William 3.1.376
flippant 5.2.185
Florio, John p. 31, 3.1.207, 5.2.69, 5.2.188, Epil.9
foeffments 4.1.319
fond 2.1.79
forma juris 4.1.284
Forman, Harry Buxton p. 193
Foxe, John 3.1.413
freehold 3.1.21
Freeman, Robert and Janet Ing p. 192
frivol 2.1.68
Frye, Northrop p. 19
fury 1.1.90

Gale, Thomas 3.1.382
Galen 1.1.8, 3.1.400
gear 3.1.23
Gearty, Thomas J. p. 195
Gerard, John 2.1.234
Giles, Nathaniel p. 4
Giraldi, Giambattista p. 7
gloating 5.2.25
glory 4.1.356
good hearing 2.1.250
Grahame, Simion Prol.23
grate 2.1.53
Greene, Robert *Mamillia* 4.1.212; *Pandosto* 2.1.252
groom 1.1.160
ground 1.1.49
gudgeon 3.1.93
Guicciardini, Francesco 3.1.372
Guilpin, Everard 2.1.335–8, 5.1.20–1

INDEX

Half Moon 5.1.55
Hall, Joseph 2.1.335–8
happy 1.2.1
Harrison, William 3.1.147–8
Harvey, Gabriel 5.1.24
haughty 1.1.109
have at 3.1.255
hazard 3.1.386
head rung noon 3.1.405–6
heavy case 3.1.177
Heltzel, Virgil P. p. 188
Heminge, William 5.1.14
Henslowe, Philip pp. 1–2, 3, 4
Heresbach 1.1.128–9, 3.1.119
Herodotus 5.2.191
Herrick, Robert 3.1.138
Hesiod p. 33, 3.1.183–4, 5.2.230–2, 5.2.235–6
Heywood, Thomas 3.1.405–6
high set 3.1.189
Hippocrates 3.1.400
Hoby, Sir Thomas *see* Castiglione
hoised 1.1.291
Holbein, Hans 1.1.47
Holland, Philemon 1.2.5
Horace Prol.14–15
horn, horns *see* cuckold
Howard, Frances 1.2.173
howlet 4.1.345–6
humane 2.1.82
humorous, humour, humours 1.1.33, 1.1.137, 1.2.53, 3.1.178
husbandry 1.1.127

iam sumus ergo pares 5.1.75
imbriered 4.1.367
impeach 3.1.219
incorporal 5.2.252–3
infant 5.2.107
informs 1.1.104
Ingram, Martin p. 45
instrument 4.1.277
Isidore of Seville 3.1.354–5

jackdaw 3.1.354–5
James, King pp. 48, 49
jogs and wrings 2.1.255
Jonson, Ben pp. 2, 6, 8, 48, Prol.14–15, Prol.19, 5.2.48–51; *Alchemist* 1.2.101, 4.1.329, 5.2.302; *The Case is Altered* p. 6; *Eastward Ho see* Chapman; *Epicene* p. 46, 1.1.368, 3.1.262–4, 4.1.92; *Every Man in His Humour* pp. 6, 12, 16, 21, 24–5, 42, 44, 46, 2.1.271–95, 2.1.305–6, 3.1.153–4, 3.1.378–9, 4.1.335–6; *Every Man Out of His Humour* p. 42, Prol.29–30, 2.1.135–6, 2.1.145; 2.1.355–6, 3.1.353, 5.1.64; *Informations* 5.2.48–51; *Magnetic Lady* p. 7; *Ode in Celebration* 2.1.393; *Poetaster* p. 26; *Sejanus* 2.1.139, *Volpone* p. 16, 1.1.133–4
Journal of the Siege of Rouen p. 33
Joyce, James p. 21
judgements Prol.2
Juvenal p. 15, 1.1.65, 1.1.69–72, 1.1.73–4, 1.1.75–6, 3.1.145, 5.2.193–8, 5.2.230–2

keeper's fee 3.1.147–8
kite 3.1.356
Knutson, Roslyn Lander p. 3
Kyd, Thomas *Spanish Tragedy* 2.1.208, 4.1.118

La Primaudaye, Pierre de 1.1.43
last day 3.1.27
leeful 4.1.308–9
leger-de-heel 3.1.152
lenity 2.1.1
Levenson, Jill p. 32
linstock 5.2.44
liripoop 4.1.161
living 4.1.83
Loane, George G. 4.1.366
lodestar 1.1.201
lodestone 4.1.32
logic 1.2.101
look to her water 5.2.191
love-sports 1.2.5
Lucian 1.1.80–91
Luckyj, Christina p. 46
Lucretius, 5.2.257, 5.2.270
Lyly, John pp. 33, 34; *Endymion* p. 33; *Euphues* p. 34, 1.1.77, 3.1.198–9; *Mother Bombie* 3.1.51–2, 4.1.85–92, 4.1.161; *Pap with an Hatchet* 4.1.161; *Sappho and Phao* p. 33, 4.1.161

Machiavelli, Niccolò p. 21, 1.1.148, 2.1.344
main chance 2.1.294–5
Malone, Edmond p. 193
mankind 4.1.235
Manley, Frank p. 40

Manners, George 1.2.39
Manningham, John pp. 4–5, 3.1.223–5, 3.1.376
Marbury, Francis 5.2.115–16
mark, marker 3.1.305, 4.1.300
Marlowe, Christopher p. 189; *Dido, Queen of Carthage* 1.1.111; *Elegies* p. 26; *Hero and Leander* pp. 1, 15, 1.1.88, 3.1.184–5
Marston, John p. 48, Prol.14–15, 2.1.335–8; *Antonio and Mellida* 2.1.335–8, 5.1.69; *Antonio's Revenge* 2.1.335–8, 3.1.184–5; *Eastward Ho* see Chapman; *Malcontent* 2.1.342–3; *Scourge of Villainy* Prol.6–9, 2.1.173, 2.1.335–8
Martial *Epigrams* 5.1.75
Marx, Groucho 5.2.65
masculine 2.1.175
mazer 3.1.268
Melchiori, Giorgio p. 22
Menander pp. 6–7, 9, 10, 11, 12
mercer 1.2.73
Mercurio 3.1.174
mere 2.1.371
mess of broth 4.1.115–16
metamorphosed 3.1.44
Middleton, Thomas *Ant and the Nightingale* 1.1.66; *Chaste Maid in Cheapside* 2.1.365–6, *Roaring Girl* 3.1.384–5; *Wit at Several Weapons* 2.1.244; *Your Five Gallants* 2.1.63–4, 2.1.270
minions 1.1.34
Molière p. 9
Morley, Thomas 4.1.366
Morpheus 3.1.14–15
Munday, Anthony 2.1.334
Murray, Sir James p. 48
Murray, Sir John p. 48
Musaeus, Grammaticus 1.1.99
mystery Prol.27

Nashe, Thomas *Anatomy of Absurdity* 1.1.80–91; *Lenten Stuff* p. 6
nature 1.1.345
nature's debt 1.2.77–8
neighbourhood 2.1.20
new-turned 2.1.215
nice 5.1.50
no time past 2.1.270
Norman, Marc p. 28
notary pp. 21, 37–8, 4.1.230

obsequies 1.2.19
obtains 1.1.35
odds 2.1.39
one piece 5.1.14
ordinaries 1.1.156
organs 2.1.109
oversight 2.1.122
Ovid pp. 25–8; *Amores* pp. 25, 26–9, 43, 2.1.255, 2.1.256, 3.1.273, 3.1.284–8, 3.1.411, 4.1.273; *Art of Love* pp. 26–9, 1.2.57, 3.1.268–9, 3.1.275; *Metamorphoses* pp. 25–6, Prol.35, 1.1.90, 1.2.70–1, 2.1.193, 3.1.14–15, 5.2.230–2, 5.2.279–80; *On Facial Treatment for Ladies* 1.1.57–8; *Tristia* p. 26
Owl and the Nightingale 1.2.33–5

page p. 32
panegyric Prol.24
pansy 2.1.223
pantofle 5.2.218
Parrott, Thomas Marc pp. 14, 16, 47, 190, 191
partial 1.1.16
Pasquil's Jests 5.2.287–9
Peele, George *Battle of Alcazar* 1.1.27, 2.1.122; *Edward I* 3.1.73
pennyworths 2.1.301
perfect 4.1.362
pericranion 3.1.382
Perne, Andrew 5.1.24
Persius Prol.35
petition 2.1.329–30
petticoat 2.1.166
picked 5.2.7
pigeon 2.1.345–6
pike 1.1.358
pills 5.1.20–1
Plato *Symposium* 1.1.8, 1.1.43, 1.1.112–15; *Timaeus* 1.1.99
Plautus pp. 5–6, 8, 12, 17, 19, 25; *Amphitryon* p. 6; *Captives* pp. 6, 12; *Comedy of Asses* 1.1.199–200, 4.1.98–101; *Epidicus* 1.1.199–200; *Ghost* 1.2.82–3; *Plot of Gold* 1.1.284–6; *Two Menaechmuses* p. 6
playest the stallion 3.1.262–4
Plutarch 1.2.5, 1.2.123–4, 3.1.123
politic, politician 1.1.401, 2.1.202
poll deeds 4.1.318
Pollard, Graham p. 193

post to pillar 3.1.178
potable 5.2.227
pottle 5.2.95
pox 3.1.368, 3.1.372
presumptions 4.1.265
properness 5.2.296
Prynne, William p. 8
pudding cane 5.2.43
pure dames Prol.23
put case 5.2.168

qualify 2.1.106
quatorzanies 2.1.174
quick Prol.20
quintessence 1.1.44, 5.2.254–5

rack and manger 1.2.118
Radice, Betty 3.1.289
railing 2.1.335–8
Ratchford, Fannie E. p. 195
rattle, rattling 2.1.328, 3.1.65
ravish, ravished Prol.21, 2.1.329
receipt 3.1.47
recognisance 5.1.31
red lattice 5.1.69
reflected, reflecting 1.1.105, 1.1.331
regress 4.1.283
rejoinder 2.1.329–30, 4.1.320–1
remanences 4.1.313
repair 2.1.12, 4.1.218
replication 2.1.329–30
rerum natura 5.2.257
respective 1.1.36
reverence 1.2.86
Rialto 5.2.16
Rich, Barnabe 1.1.156
ridicules 3.1.413
Rose Theatre pp. 1–3, 28, Prol.0
Rowley, William *Search for Money* 5.2.16; *Wit at Several Weapons see* Middleton
Runyon, Damon p. 19
rusticity 2.1.85

Salingar, Leo Prol.1–4
satires 2.1.173, 2.1.335–8
Saturnian bull 5.2.280
Saviolo, Vincentio 3.1.332
schooled 3.1.60
scute 5.2.20
sdrucciola 2.1.176
seal 3.1.184–5

seld 1.2.9
senate 2.1.344
sensual 5.1.9
sentences 5.2.98
sequester 4.1.310
sergeant 1.2.81
serpent noddle 4.1.263
set face 3.1.315
set him round 5.2.85–6
set out her tale 5.2.185–6
setting on 3.1.51–2
Shakespeare, William *All's Well that Ends Well* p. 22, 2.1.46; *As You Like It* 1.1.135–40, 3.1.119–20, 5.1.48, 5.2.128, Epil.8; *Comedy of Errors* p. 6; *Hamlet* p. 4, 1.1.44, 1.1.67, 1.2.37, 1.2.81, 2.1.162, 2.1.285, 2.1.338, 2.1.345–6, 3.1.396–8, 4.1.205; *1 Henry IV* 2.1.202, 3.1.261; *2 Henry IV* 1.1.287, 3.1.319, 5.2.39, 5.2.77–8; *Henry V* 1.1.358, 3.1.311, 3.1.372, 5.2.113; *2–3 Henry VI* p. 21; *3 Henry VI* 4.1.338–9; *Love's Labour's Lost* pp. 23, 32, 1.1.207, 2.1.38, 2.1.49, 2.1.63, 5.1.7; *Macbeth* 5.2.62; *Merry Wives of Windsor* pp. 20, 21, 22, 5.2.186–7; *Midsummer Night's Dream* p. 20, 2.1.79, 2.1.366, 3.1.35, 4.1.124; *Much Ado About Nothing* 1.1.267, 3.1.163–4; *Othello* pp. 7, 21, 24, 1.1.83, 2.1.84; *Richard III* 1.1.406–7, 1.2.85, 3.1.323, 3.1.347; *Romeo and Juliet* 1.1.1, 1.2.51, 2.1.308, 3.1.339–42, 4.1.204; *Sonnets* 1.2.174, 1.2.175, 5.2.220; *Taming of the Shrew* p. 37, 1.1.316, 2.1.250, 4.1.216, 4.1.277, 5.2.185–6; *Tempest* 3.1.274; *Titus Andronicus* 3.1.177; *Troilus and Cressida* 3.1.378–9; *Twelfth Night* pp. 4, 22, 1.1.281, 2.1.224, 3.1.118, 5.2.209; *Venus and Adonis* 1.1.22, 4.1.4; *Winter's Tale* 4.1.185–6
Shapiro, Michael Prol.1–4
sheep's head 2.1.128
Shelton, Audrey, Lady Walsingham pp. 189, 190
Shepherd, R. H. p. 190
short 3.1.35, 5.2.115–16
shrewd 5.1.48
shuttlecock 1.1.66
Sidney, Sir Philip 1.2.69, 2.1.176
Sir John Oldcastle Part 1 5.2.85–6

INDEX

siren 4.1.233
sister 3.1.35
Smith, Sir Thomas 2.1.215
smock-faces 5.1.7
sollar 4.1.314
sonnets in dozens 2.1.174
soothes 1.1.207
sort 2.1.307
spark 2.1.46
spending 2.1.49
Spenser, Edmund *Amoretti* 1.1.10, 1.1.253–7; *Faerie Queene* 1.1.81, 2.1.105, 2.1.422; *Shepherd's Calendar* 1.1.63
Spewack, Bella and Samuel p. 19
spial 1.2.69
spleen Prol.16, Prol.24, 2.1.105, 2.1.345–6
sponged 1.1.74
spread 5.2.316
spruce 5.2.5
Stone, Lawrence p. 48
Stoppard, Tom p. 28
stout 5.2.183, 5.2.208
strains 1.1.3
strait 1.1.24
Stubbes, Philip 3.1.207
subjects 1.1.1
substance 5.1.51
Suckling, John 1.2.68
sunt 4.1.287
superannated 3.1.235
supple 2.1.186
suppuration 3.1.400
surgeon 3.1.367, 3.1.368
surrejoinders 4.1.320–1
suspect 1.1.177
swaggering 2.1.228
Swan, John 4.1.345–6
Swinburne, Algernon Charles p. 41
Swinburne, Henry 3.1.7
sworn of a book 4.1.274

taxations Epil.8
tenure piece 3.1.249
Terence pp. 5–20, 25; in education pp. 7–9; influence on later comedy pp. 6–7; love and marriage in pp. 19, 25; role of luck in p. 17; Roman society in pp. 12–13; *Brothers* pp. 6, 8, 10–11, 13, 14, 15, 16, 17, 19, 41–2, 1.1.140–1, 1.1.206–9, 1.2.82–3; *Eunuch* pp. 5, 7, 8, 9, 2.1.205–8,
3.1.289, 4.1.261; *Mother-in-Law* p. 9; *Phormio* p. 9, *Self-Tormentor* pp. 6, 9–10, 11, 13, 15, 19, 20, 41, 1.1.178–83, 1.1.192, 1.1.240–2, 1.1.274–6, 1.1.284–6, 1.1.306, 1.1.329, 1.2.140, 2.1.150–79, 3.1.27, 3.1.86, 3.1.108–10, 3.1.289, 4.1.26, 5.2.131
Theophrastus 1.2.123–4
theorbo 2.1.392
thing you wot on 2.1.244
Thorpe, Thomas p. 48
thrifty 1.1.195, 1.1.339. 3.1.6
tires 5.1.14
tittle 2.1.256
toys Prol.18, 2.1.382, 3.1.77–8
treads o'th' toe 2.1.255
trifles Epil.9
trull 4.1.97
trump 3.1.361–2
turn thee loose 2.1.63–4
turtle 1.1.3
two parts in one 4.1.366
Tydeman, William p. 8

Udall, Nicolas 3.1.65
undeterminable 5.2.304
undressed 1.1.73
unnourishing 1.1.185

vapours 1.1.8
vaulting houses 1.1.157
Vega, Lope de pp. 5–6
venerian Prol.20
visnomy 2.1.159
vowed 3.1.7
Vulcan's snare 3.1.268–9

wall-eye 5.2.24
Walsingham, Sir Thomas pp. 187, 188–91, 195
watches 1.1.30
Watson, Thomas 1.2.174
wayward 5.2.164
Webster, John *Duchess of Malfi* 4.1.336; *Northward Ho*, *Westward Ho see* Dekker
wedlock 1.2.118, 3.1.234, 4.1.222
Wells, Stanley p. 189
whirligig 1.1.281
white son 4.1.29
Whitgift, John 2.1.335–8
Wiggins, Martin p. 21

Wilcockson, Colin p. 21
Wilde, Oscar p. 36
Wise, Thomas J. pp. 190, 191–5
wits Prol.5
wittol, wittolry pp. 30, 43, 45, 2.1.287
Wolfall, John p. 1
woodcock 5.2.209
wreath 2.1.193

Wrenn, John Henry pp. 191, 192, 194, 195
writ of error 3.1.398

Yamada, Akihiro p. 49
yellow fury 3.1.138
Youngman, Henny p. 44
your second self 2.1.91

EU authorised representative for GPSR:
Easy Access System Europe, Mustamäe tee 50,
10621 Tallinn, Estonia
gpsr.requests@easproject.com